350 best salads & dressings

350 best
salads
& dressings

George Geary

Robert
ROSE

350 Best Salads and Dressings
Text copyright © 2010 George Geary
Color photographs © 2010 Robert Rose Inc.
Cover and text design copyright © 2010 Robert Rose Inc.

Some of the recipes in this book were previously published in *500 Best Sauces, Salad Dressings, Marinades & More* published in 2009 by Robert Rose.

For complete cataloguing information, see page 285.

Disclaimer

The recipes in this book have been carefully tested by our kitchen and our tasters. To the best of our knowledge, they are safe and nutritious for ordinary use and users. For those people with food or other allergies, or who have special food requirements or health issues, please read the suggested contents of each recipe carefully and determine whether or not they may create a problem for you. All recipes are used at the risk of the consumer.

We cannot be responsible for any hazards, loss or damage that may occur as a result of any recipe use.

For those with special needs, allergies, requirements or health problems, in the event of any doubt, please contact your medical adviser prior to the use of any recipe.

Editor: Carol Sherman
Recipe Editor: Jennifer MacKenzie
Copy Editor: Jo Calvert
Indexer: Gillian Watts
Design and Production: Kevin Cockburn/PageWave Graphics Inc.
Color Photography: Colin Erricson
Food Styling: Kathryn Robertson
Prop Styling: Charlene Erricson

Black and White Photography
Pages 7, 10: © iStockphoto.com/Olga Lyubkina
Pages 13, 18, 30: © iStockphoto.com/Anna Sedneva
Page 22: © iStockphoto.com/Wando Studios
Page 26: © iStockphoto.com/Klaudia Steiner

Cover image: Spinach and Avocado Salad (page 125)

We acknowledge the financial support of the Government of Canada through the Book Publishing Industry Development Program (BPIDP) for our publishing activities.

Published by Robert Rose Inc.
120 Eglinton Avenue East, Suite 800, Toronto, Ontario, Canada M4P 1E2
Tel: (416) 322-6552 Fax: (416) 322-6936

Printed and bound in Canada.

1 2 3 4 5 6 7 8 9 TCP 18 17 16 15 14 13 12 11 10

Mixed Sources
Product group from well-managed forests, controlled sources and recycled wood or fibre
www.fsc.org Cert no. SW-COC-000952
© 1996 Forest Stewardship Council

Contents

To Monica and Pattie,
My two sisters.
You're the best.

Acknowledgments

I could never have created this book without "my team" of family and friends, and I thank you all from the bottom of my heart: My parents, who are always ready to help at a moment's notice and are always saying how proud you are of me — I am the proudest of you. My sisters, Monica and Pattie, my two roses, for always putting up with this thorn. Neil, always ready to step in when someone does not show up, to clean my dishes at the eleventh hour, to take me to the airport before the sun comes up and to pick me up hours after it goes down — thank you for being you. Jonathan, for all the years of friendship. Sean and Chris at Sephno Systems, for keeping my media going. The entire staff at Corona Tuscany Starbucks, for always having my drink ready, and asking about my latest project. My two main gals at United (ONT) Airlines, Robin and Reena, for always smiling at 4 a.m. when I am flying off to who knows where (I am glad you know where I am going) — you both make traveling so much easier.

My recipe testers, friends and colleagues: Teri, for being my longest-running student and always laughing, even in France. Carol Ann, for support and ideas. The "craft group" that often gathers at the house for recipe testing, cooking and crafts — Buzz, Chris, Don, Eilena, Jack, Jeff, Sean and Ted. Nancie McDermott, Phillis Carey, Denise Vivaldo, Cathy Thomas and Tim Haskell, for being the best colleagues. Annette, Josephine and Lauren at the Los Angeles County Fair. It was a great 29 years. The

Yorba Linda Danish Cultural Center for bringing in this "Non-Dan" into your group, and every one of my students at the center. Placenta, La Mirada and Anaheim parks and recreation groups, for giving this teacher a chance. My second hand in the kitchen, Adrianna Hyman, for knowing exactly how to make everything look great, even under pressure. Erika and Sara at Holland America Line for believing in me, putting me on your "Dam" ships, and letting me share my love of food around the world. Karen Tripson, my personal copy editor, for being a friend and a colleague for years — I cherish your friendship and direction. Lisa Ekus-Saffer, for being a great friend for so long and now my literary agent — I wish we weren't 3,000 miles apart. Bob Dees, my publisher and friend, for putting up with all of my jokes, rants and raves for seven books now — thank you for trusting and investing in me. Carol Sherman, for making me laugh and keeping my voice for six books now. Jennifer MacKenzie, for testing and editing recipes and giving her guidance. Jo Calvert, for careful copy editing and asking all the right questions. The entire staff at PageWave Graphics, including Kevin Cockburn, Andrew Smith, Joseph Gisini and Daniella Zanchetta, for making this book a piece of art. Photographer Colin Erricson, food stylist Kathryn Robertson and prop stylist Charlene Erricson. And, finally, all of my students, and the cooking schools and directors across the globe, for welcoming me into their kitchens.

Introduction

Great starters for any meal, salads also shine as complementary side dishes or complete meals on their own. And — since the 1970s when salad bars became *de rigueur* in even the smallest North American restaurants — we've all embraced fresh and easy salads as an everyday addition to our diets. To satisfy this healthy craving, I've created an array of appealing recipes to help you expand your repertoire. From light, cooling combinations to serve on hot summer days through to substantial, heartwarming salads that combat winter's chill, there's something here to suit every taste and time of year. You'll find some familiar favorites and classic mixes, but I've also included exotic flavors and exciting salads that I've sampled on my travels around the world.

Dressing adds the distinctive finishing touch and flavoring to any salad — and the fresher the dressing, the better. That's why you'll also find my collection of simple and delicious dressings, mayos and vinaigrettes to choose and make fresh for each salad.

Start by stocking up on a few pantry staples (see Common Ingredients, page 14), then shop fresh for the other ingredients. After that, it's all fun and fast in the kitchen — and fabulous, seasonal salads on the table.

Tools and Equipment

Many of the tools you'll need will have other uses in your kitchen and will last a long time, so it's worth purchasing quality equipment the first time.

Balloon whisk
To achieve perfectly beaten egg whites or whipped cream, use a sturdy whisk. They come in many sizes for different jobs. If you buy only one whisk, select a medium-size one.

Dry measuring cups
The most accurate way to measure dry ingredients is with nesting metal measuring cups. They usually come in sets of four to six cups, in sizes ranging from $\frac{1}{4}$ cup (60 mL) to 1 cup (250 mL). Spoon the dry ingredient into the appropriate cup, then level it off by sliding the flat end of a knife or spatula across the top of the cup. Brown sugar and shortening need to be packed firmly into the cup for correct measurement.

Food processor
Select a sturdy processor that is large enough to handle the volume of ingredients in the recipes you use most often. My 11-cup (2.75 L) Cuisinart has worked well for me over many years.

Garlic press
A garlic press is the fastest way to turn a clove of garlic into small bits. When you use a garlic press, your crushed garlic will have a stronger flavor, because of the release of oils, than garlic minced with a knife.

Liquid measuring cups
The most accurate way to measure liquid ingredients is with a glass or Pyrex measuring cup with a pouring spout. They are widely available in sizes ranging from 1 cup (250 mL) to 8 cups (2 L). Place the measure on a flat surface and add the liquid until it reaches the desired level. When checking for accuracy, bend over so that your eye is level with the measure. (Angled liquid measures are now available that allow you to measure ingredients without bending — the markings are inside the cup for easy viewing.) Pyrex cups can also be used in the microwave to melt butter and heat water.

Mandoline

Mandolines are hand-powered slicers that cut fruits and vegetables quickly, in consistent sizes and shapes. Some dice, as well. Although there are many expensive models, I find that my OXO Good Grips does the job at a reasonable price, and I can put its parts into the top of my dishwasher for easy cleaning.

Measuring spoons

The most accurate measuring spoons are metal. You'll need a set of sturdy spoons ranging from $\frac{1}{8}$ tsp (0.5 mL) to 1 tbsp (15 mL) to measure small amounts of both liquid and dry ingredients.

Microplane zester/grater

A Microplane zester/grater with a handle is the best tool for quickly removing zest from lemons and other citrus fruits. To use it, rub the Microplane over the skin until you can see the zest. Do not zest any of the white pith, as it has a bitter taste. The Microplane is also good for grating hard cheeses and chocolate.

Mixing bowls

A nested set of small, medium and large mixing bowls will be used countless times. Having the right size bowl for the job, whether it's beating an egg white or whipping a quart (1 L) of cream, helps the cooking process. Ceramic, glass and stainless-steel bowls all have their merits, but I think stainless steel is the most versatile.

Rubber spatulas

A rubber spatula is the perfect tool for scraping a bowl clean. It also allows for the most thorough mixing of ingredients, the least waste when turning ingredients into the baking pan and an easy cleanup. The new silicone spatulas, which are heatproof to 800°F (427°C), are ultra-efficient because they can go from the mixing bowl to the stovetop. Commercial-quality spatulas are more flexible and durable than grocery-store brands.

Salad (herb) spinner

I was skeptical when these came on the market a few years back. Now I use them every time I make salad. Place your salad greens in the "colander" part of the spinner. Wash your salad greens, and shake off excess water. Place the colander into the bowl of the spinner, place the lid on and, depending on the model, pump or crank the top. The spinner, using centrifugal force, forces the water into the bottom of the spinner bowl. There are smaller versions available for fresh herbs.

Common Ingredients

Oils

I use a variety of oils, some to add flavor and some to balance the acidity in foods that I'm preparing. If you don't have the oil that's called for in any recipe, use another type. You may create a new sauce or dressing.

Canola oil

Produced in Canada, canola oil is low in saturated fatty acids, and is the healthiest of all commonly used cooking oils. It is pressed from canola seeds grown mainly in Canada and the northern States. You can use canola oil in any recipe calling for soybean or vegetable oil.

Corn oil

There is little to no taste in this oil. I use it when I am relying on flavor from other ingredients in my recipe.

Hot chile oil

This is a neutral-flavored oil infused with chile peppers.

Olive oils

I try to keep only a few bottles of oil on hand, so it keeps fresh. When you're choosing oil, always check the expiration date on the bottle — the fresher the better. The U.S. Department of Agriculture and the International Olive Oil Council use different designations and descriptions for basic olive oil types but here's a general description of the types available:

Extra virgin olive oil: From the cold first pressing of the olives, this oil has no more than 0.8% acidity.

Extra light virgin olive oil: This is "light" in flavor not in calories.

Virgin olive oil: Smooth in taste, this oil has no more than 2% acidity.

100% pure olive oil: This is the lowest grade of olive oil.

Herbed olive oil: This describes olive oil that has been infused with fresh herbs for a few weeks.

Nut oils

These oils exhibit a slight taste and aroma of the nuts from which they were extracted.

Sesame oil

Cold-pressing the seeds for this oil results in a light cooking oil. When the oil is pressed from toasted sesame seeds, it has a stronger flavor and darker color, and is often used for garnishing.

Soybean oil

A byproduct of processing soybean meal, this oil has a flavor that's light and delicate. Soybean oil can be substituted for the canola or vegetable oil called for in recipes.

Vegetable oil

Most oils labeled "vegetable" are soybean or canola oil, or a blend of different oils. Corn and olive oil blends may also contain vegetable oil.

Vinegars

For the recipes in this book, I call for an array of vinegars. You may interchange them and create a different, but likely successful, result. The word "vinegar" derives from the Old French *vin aigre*, which means "sour wine."

Apple cider vinegar

Also labeled as cider vinegar, this is made from apple cider.

Balsamic vinegar

Traditionally manufactured in Modena, Italy, from concentrated grape juice, this is a very dark brown. The finest examples have been aged in successive casks made of various types of woods. True balsamic vinegars are aged 4 to 12 years; some are aged up to 100 years, and will be priced as a rare antique. It is said that every winemaker should start a cask of balsamic vinegar upon the birth of each daughter, to be part of her dowry in 18 years and the gift of a lifetime of balsamic vinegar for the new family.

Fruit vinegars

These vinegars are made from fruit wines, and the vinegars are more commonly produced in Canada, Europe and Asia than in America.

Herb vinegars

These are flavored with a fresh herb such as tarragon, thyme or oregano. You can make your own by infusing a light, mild tasting vinegar, such as white wine vinegar, with a fresh herb for a few weeks.

Malt vinegar

Made from aged, malted barley, this light brown vinegar is used in chutneys.

Rice vinegar

A popular ingredient in Asian cuisines, rice vinegar is found in an array of shades, from white and colorless to red to black. I prefer the white, which is available natural or seasoned. The natural is light in color and mild in taste, while seasoned rice vinegar contains sake, salt and sugar.

Wine vinegars

Made from wine, these have a smoother flavor than apple cider vinegar. Their varying prices reflect the quality of the wines used, but all are valued for the delicate flavors they impart. They include red wine vinegar, Cabernet Sauvignon vinegar, Champagne vinegar, white wine vinegar and sherry wine vinegar.

Other Ingredients

Capers
Pickled buds from the plant of the same name, which grows wild throughout the Mediterranean, capers are prized for their salty flavor.

Chili sauce
You can find so many types of chili sauce. Any thick, flavorful version will add body in a recipe, but the best is the one you make yourself (see Bold Chili Sauce, page 115).

Dill pickles
I like using crunchy dill pickles when I cook, but you can replace them with pickle relish to save time chopping.

Hoisin sauce
This sweet and spicy Chinese dipping sauce is found in the "international" section of the supermarket. Traditional hoisin sauce is made with sweet potatoes, but today's varieties are made with fermented soybeans with sweet potatoes added for texture.

Horseradish
Part of the mustard and wasabi family, horseradish is available prepared in jars and as a fresh root that you can grate and mix with vinegar or cream.

Hot pepper sauce
I like to use a plain hot pepper sauce, such as Tabasco, that's available in small bottles and keeps for a long time.

Ketchup
Make a batch of ketchup when you have a garden filled with too many tomatoes — you will never use the bottled varieties again (see pages 106 to 110). In a pinch, of course, store-bought ketchup is fine to cook with.

Mayonnaise
I have a number of recipes for homemade mayonnaise (see pages 100 to 105). You can always save time by using a manufactured brand, but if you make mayonnaise from scratch, you will never go back. I guarantee it.

Mustards

You can find many varieties of mustards on store shelves. It's so easy, I tend to make my own versions (see pages 111 to 114). All are interchangeable, but sometimes you want the special zest of whole grains or flavored mustard.

Pimentos

These roasted red peppers are commonly found in jars and stuffed into the centers of some Spanish green olives.

Plum jam

Thickened plums, this jam is sometimes sweetened. You can substitute a berry jam.

Soy sauce

This is made with fermented soybeans. I like to use the reduced-sodium variety as typical soy sauce adds too much salt to the dish. Check the label to make sure the sauce is made from soybeans and not just additives and colorings.

Teriyaki sauce

This sweet sauce contains soy sauce, mirin and a sweetener. I like the common bottled varieties found in the "international" sections of major supermarkets.

Tomatoes, fresh and canned

The juiciest, tastiest tomatoes are the ones you grow yourself. The second best come from a nearby farmers' market. Third in line are the Roma (plum) tomatoes from your local grocery store or canned. If a recipe calls for either canned tomatoes or fresh, and you don't have the specified type, you can substitute one for the other by weighing your tomatoes using a scale.

To substitute fresh for canned or vice versa, here is a quick chart:

$2\frac{1}{2}$ lbs (1.25 kg) fresh Roma (plum) tomatoes produce 3 cups (750 mL) tomato purée — halve and seed uncooked tomatoes, then pass them through the fine plate of a food mill.

$1\frac{1}{2}$ lbs (750 g) diced fresh Roma (plum) tomatoes are equivalent to a 28-oz (796 mL) can diced tomatoes — dice the tomatoes or crush them to the thickness you need.

2 lbs (1 kg) cooked fresh Roma (plum) tomatoes are equivalent to a 28-oz (796 mL) can stewed tomatoes.

Tomato paste

You can find paste in small cans and in tubes. If your recipe calls for an entire can, use that. I use the tube paste when I only need a little bit for a recipe, then seal it up and keep it refrigerated and ready for the next use.

White miso

This soybean product is available in paste or powder form in Asian markets. Use it to make a beverage or soup, or to add flavor.

Worcestershire sauce

Originally made in Worcester, England, by two chemists, John Lea and William Perrins, this sauce is a fermented liquid condiment with sweet overtones. It's mainly used in sauces and on steaks.

Sugars

Brown sugar
When measuring brown sugar, lightly pack it into a measuring cup. Unless a recipe is specific, you can interchange dark or light brown sugar.

Granulated sugar
Granular (white) sugar is the most common form. Choose pure sugarcane sugar, rather than sugar made from beets. I find the crystals of the cane sugar work better because they dissolve more easily in recipes.

Liquid sugars
Liquid sugars come in a variety of flavors, and can be used to add sweetness to vinaigrettes. Store in a cool, dry place for the longest shelf life.

Corn syrup
Corn syrup is made from cornstarch and is available in light (white) and dark (golden) varieties. Use the dark version when its color isn't a problem and the caramel flavor is an asset to the recipe. Both types are used as table syrups and in frosting, candy and jam.

Liquid honey
Made by bees from flower nectar, honey is a natural sugar. That doesn't mean it has fewer calories, though; it actually has more. Because it is sweeter than other liquid sweeteners, use less honey when substituting it for them.

Molasses
Made from sugarcane or sugar-beet syrup, molasses is available in three grades: light (fancy), dark (cooking) and blackstrap. Light molasses is typically used as table syrup, while dark molasses provides the distinctive, sweet flavor of gingerbread and Boston baked beans. Blackstrap molasses is slightly more nutritious than the other versions, and is not commonly used in baking.

Pure maple syrup
This is made by boiling sap collected from maple trees in the spring. I use only pure maple syrup. I find that the imitation syrups, which are a mixture of corn syrup and maple extracts, have a strange aftertaste.

Dairy Products

Cheese

Hard/semihard cheese

Buy chunks of fresh cheese and shred or grate it yourself to ensure the best quality and save the expense of ready-made grated cheese. Varieties used for the recipes in this book include:

- *Asiago cheese* is an Italian cheese with the characteristics of Parmesan and Romano, and can be interchanged for them in recipes.

- *Cheddar* is a firm, ripened cheese that can be mild to sharp in flavor. In color, it ranges from white to orange (which gets its color from annatto, a natural dye). It is popularly served plain with crackers, cooked in casseroles and sauces, or shredded as a garnish.

- *Parmesan* is ripened for 2 or more years to a hard, dry state, which makes it perfect for grating or shaving. The rich, sharp flavor of the premium-aged versions imported from Italy is easily distinguished from that of the grocery-store brands of grated cheese.

- *Romano* is named after Rome, where it's been manufactured for more than 2,000 years. Romano cheese is a dry cheese that needs to be grated. It is made from sheep's milk (pecorino romano) or goat's milk (caprino romano).

Soft cheese

Soft cheese can be used in small chunks, which will melt in hot liquids such as pasta sauce. Varieties used for the recipes in this book include:

- *Cottage cheese* is a fresh cow's milk cheese that comes in small, medium and large curds with various fat contents. The moisture content is high. The creamed style has extra cream added and extra calories as a result. Cottage cheese is drained to become other styles of cheese, of which the driest version is farmer's cheese.

- *Cream cheese* is made from cow's milk. It contains 33% fat and less than 55% moisture. Whipped cream cheese, which is soft because it has air whipped into it, has slightly fewer calories, but is not recommended in these recipes. Nonfat cream cheese, of course, has no calories from fat. Use it on a bagel or sandwich, but not in these recipes.

- *Goat cheese* is derived from goat's milk. Fresh goat cheese is very soft, like cream cheese; aged goat cheese is firmer, and is often labeled chèvre.

- *Mascarpone* is an Italian double- or triple-cream cheese that can be easily spread. The delicate, buttery texture is delicious with fruit, but it is very versatile as a cooking ingredient, and is found in both savory and sweet recipes.

- *Neufchâtel cheese* is a reduced-fat cream cheese. It contains 23% fat, so it has fewer calories. In recipes, it can be substituted for regular cream cheese.

- *Provolone* is an Italian cow's milk cheese made from whole milk, and has a smooth skin. It is aged for up to a year, or even more, to create its mild, smoky flavor. It is good for cooking. The varieties that are aged the longest are firm enough to grate.

Blue cheese

Blue cheese is aptly named for the blue veins running through it — a result of being treated with molds and ripened. This aging process intensifies the flavor of the cheese, which is popular in salads and salad dressings, and with fruit. It is also used in cooking. The texture is firm enough for crumbling. My favorite brands are Maytag from Iowa, and Point Reyes from Northern California. Well-known international blue cheeses include Gorgonzola from Italy, Stilton from England and Roquefort from France. In the European Union, blue cheeses are protected by designation of origin, which means they can only bear the place names if they are manufactured there. All are interchangeable, some are stronger than others.

Butter
I use unsalted butter so I know how much salt is going into any recipe. If I am making an all-butter recipe (such as compound butter), I use one of the higher-fat European or Irish butters found in specialty-food stores.

Buttermilk
Buttermilk is lower in fat than regular milk because the fat has been removed to make butter. It has a thick and sour taste. If you don't have buttermilk, you can add 1 tbsp (15 mL) lemon juice to 1 cup (250 mL) whole milk, and use it instead.

Sour cream
Made from cream, this contains 12 to 16% butterfat. Its tang comes from the lactic acid.

Yogurt
Produced by the bacterial fermentation of milk, yogurt is available in an array of flavors. You can also find soy yogurt, made from soy milk.

Yogurt cheese
To make yogurt cheese: Place 3 cups (750 mL) plain yogurt in a cheesecloth-lined strainer set over a bowl, then let it drain overnight in the refrigerator (discard the liquid). Makes about $1\frac{1}{2}$ to $1\frac{3}{4}$ cups (375 to 425 mL).

Heavy cream
Heavy cream is 36% or more butterfat. It is also known as whipping cream or table cream. If you can find cream that has only been pasteurized and not ultra-pasteurized, you will have a more flavorful product. Freeze any unused cream that is close to its expiry date. It won't make nice whipped cream, but is fine for other purposes.

Butterfat in Milk Products

Percentage of Butterfat	Product
82 to 85%	European butters
80%	U.S. butters
40%	Manufacturing cream
36%	Heavy cream
30 to 35%	Whipping cream
25%	Medium cream
18 to 30%	Light or table cream
10.5 to 18%	Half-and-half cream
3.25%	Whole milk
2%	Reduced, partly-skimmed or 2% milk
1.5 to 1.8%	Semi-skimmed milk
1%	Low-fat or 1% milk
0.0 to 0.5%	Nonfat or skim milk

Eggs

The recipes in this book were tested using large eggs. In some areas you can purchase a pasteurized liquid egg product (this is not liquid egg substitute), which is a great product for making recipes that call for raw eggs if you have food-safety concerns. Please consult your medical professional prior to making or serving dishes with raw eggs if this is a concern for you.

Produce

Whenever I can, I like to shop at my local farmer's market so I can buy in season from the source. If it is not possible, I go to the grocery store, but only purchase enough for a few days. It is assumed all produce with inedible peels and pits are peeled and pitted before using unless otherwise specified.

Fruit

In most of these recipes you can substitute a similar type of fruit if the specified fruit is out of season or hard to find.

Avocado

There are many varieties of avocado. The Hass variety is a large avocado with a slightly bumpy skin. Because the flesh is creamy and flavorful, I prefer Hass avocados.

Berries

At the supermarket, look for firm berries that have been stored in a refrigerator, or buy berries from a local source. Refrigerate them as soon as you get home. For every hour the berries are out of the refrigerator, you will lose 1 day of freshness.

Citrus Fruits

All citrus fruits are interchangeable so, if your region does not have one of the fruits called for in a recipe, by all means substitute another. The amount of zest and juice yielded by a citrus fruit depends on the weight and thickness of the rind. Choose fruits that feel heavy.

- *Citrus zest (orange, lemon or lime):* Use a Microplane (see page 13) to zest the fruits.

- *Clementine:* The clementine season is very short, and in my market you have to buy them by the case. You can substitute tangerines.

- *Dried peel (orange, lemon or lime):* You can find this in spice stores.

- *Lemon juice:* I joke in classes about why lemon juice comes in a green bottle — so you can't see the brown liquid. Real lemon juice should be light in color. Squeeze a fresh lemon, instead, whenever possible.

- *Lime juice:* Fresh limes are best. You do not need to purchase the expensive key lime juice, regular lime juice will do.

- *Orange juice:* If I don't have fresh oranges on hand, I use frozen orange juice concentrate from a can, then dilute it according to the package directions, unless the recipe calls for concentrate. It's the same and less expensive than juice from a carton.

Mangos

Ripe mangos feel firm in your hand, but yield slightly to gentle pressure. For attractive slices: cut the flesh in half along each side of the pit and separate. Invert to slice lengthwise, then cut off the skin.

Pears or apples

Buy whatever is in season. The fruit will be fresher and also less expensive. My favorites are Bosc or Bartlett pears and Rome, Granny Smith or McIntosh apples.

Asian pears

These are crisp like an apple, but not as sweet. They bruise so easily, they are usually wrapped individually with netting.

Tomatillos

These look like unripe tomatoes, each surrounded by a papery husk. Pull off the husks, then wash the stickiness off the tomatillo skins under cool water.

Vegetables

Garlic

Look for a tight bulb. Most U.S. garlic is harvested in the late spring or early summer. In Canada, garlic is harvested from mid- to late-summer. When you buy garlic at any other time of year, it's likely to have been in cold storage or imported from China.

To roast garlic: Preheat oven to 400°F (200°C). Cut off and discard about 1/4 inch (0.5 cm) from the top of the bulb, then drizzle it with 1 tsp (5 mL) oil. Wrap in foil and roast until golden brown and very soft, 30 to 35 minutes. Let it cool, then turn it upside down and press out the cloves.

Gingerroot

Use the edge of a spoon to scrape off the outer layer, then slice, mince or grate on a Microplane (see page 13) or ginger grater.

Mushrooms

Never submerge mushrooms in water — they are like sponges and all of the soil on the surface will be sucked into their pores. Instead, brush the mushrooms with a moistened towel. When selecting button mushrooms, make sure the area between each stem and cap is tight. If they are separating, that's a sign of age.

Root vegetables

These are harvested when they're ready to eat. Look for crisp and firm radishes, leeks and jicama.

Herbs

In recent years, major grocery stores have begun to carry fresh herbs at good prices, a luxury when there's a few feet of snow on the ground. Dried herbs are more intensely flavored than fresh. If you must substitute dried for fresh, use half as much dried as the fresh herb called for. Dried herbs go stale quickly, especially if they're finely ground. Keep dried herbs in airtight containers in a cool, dry, dark place. Once they lose their aroma, be ruthless and discard them.

Here is a list of the herbs used in the recipes and tips on how to chop them. I wash fresh herbs and dry them in a salad spinner (see page 14), then roll them in moist paper towel and put that inside a plastic bag which goes into the refrigerator.

- *Basil:* Use only the leaves. *To chiffonade:* Stack the leaves with the largest on the bottom. Roll them up tightly, jelly-roll fashion, then finely slice across the roll. This prevents the basil from being bruised in the cutting, and prematurely darkening.

- *Chives:* Place the chives in a row, then finely slice across their blades.

- *Cilantro:* Also known as Mexican or Chinese parsley, it is used in salsas and has a distinctive taste. If you want, you can substitute Italian flat-leaf parsley.

- *Dill:* Remove the light feathery leaves, discarding any of the thicker stems, and chop.

- *Mint:* There are many types of mint, but the most commonly available are wintergreen and spearmint. Remove all the leaves, discarding the stems, then chop.

- *Oregano:* Remove the leaves, discarding any flowers and the stems, then chop.

- *Parsley:* Since the parsley with the very curly leaves lacks flavor, I use Italian flat-leaf parsley, instead.
- *Sage:* The soft velvety leaves contain the flavor. Remove them, discarding the stems, then chop.
- *Tarragon:* Hold the top of the stem and strip off the leaves with your other hand; discard the stem and any brown leaves, then chop.
- *Thyme:* Remove the leaves and chop.

Chiles

Chiles are a powerful flavor enhancer for sauces, rubs and salad dressings. In most cases, they're interchangeable. For the best texture in any dish, substitute a fresh chile for another fresh chile, or dried for dried. The names can be confusing and may vary if the chiles are dried, canned and or fresh.

I am asked all the time which chiles are the hottest. In 1912, chemist Wilber Scoville created a scale designating the heat level of different chiles by measuring the capsaicin that makes the chiles hot. Bell peppers are 0 and the hottest, Naga Jolokia, which I do not use, measures more than 1,000,000 heat units. Select chiles that fit your desire for more or less heat.

Chiles	Scoville Heat Scale
Fresh	
Banana	0 to 250
Anaheim	500 to 1,500
New Mexico	500 to 1,500
Poblano	1,250 to 2,500
Jalapeño	5,000 to 10,000
Serrano	10,000 to 25,000
Habanero	100,000 to 500,000
Dried	
Ancho (dried poblano)	1,500 to 2,500
Guajillo	2,000 to 4,500
Chipotle	5,000 to 10,000
Serrano	10,000 to 25,000
Habanero	100,000 to 500,000

Spices and Ground Herbs

Spices go stale all too quickly, especially those that are finely ground. The shelf life of herbs and spices is highly variable. Generally, whole spices may stay flavorful and fragrant for up to 4 years and ground spices for up to 2 years; ground herbs (such as oregano) may stay flavorful and fragrant for up to 6 months to 2 years, with proper storage. If they have lost their intense fragrance, they are probably past their prime.

For the best flavor, purchase whole spices and grind them as you need them. When you're purchasing ground spices, I recommend buying them from one of the sources I list on page 274. They grind their spices daily, and you cannot get any that are fresher. Keep spice containers tightly sealed, and store them in a cool, dry, dark place.

Patty Erd from the Spice House in Chicago suggests that you sprinkle dried-out herbs on the coals of your barbecue to harvest their last bit of flavor while you grill.

- *Adobe seasoning:* This blend of spices has a flavorful, smoked-chile taste, but it's not fiery hot.

- *Bouquet garni (also known as herb bouquet):* It typically includes thyme, oregano, savory and bay leaves that are tied together with string or wrapped in cheesecloth. A bouquet garni allows you to cook herbs in a packet, so you can remove them easily before serving the dish.

- *Chile pequin powder:* You may purchase whole, dried chile de arbol peppers and grind them yourself. You can also buy ready-made powder.

- *Dried onion flakes and minced dried garlic:* I get asked why I use dried instead of fresh. Using dried onion flakes or minced dried garlic produces an intense flavor you cannot achieve by using fresh.

- *Dried red and/or green bell pepper flakes:* Concentrated, finely diced red and/or green bell peppers yield a fresh taste and flavor when soaked in liquid. If dried flakes are not available, replace them with twice as much minced fresh bell pepper.

- *Dry mustard:* It comes in three different heat levels — regular yellow, mild yellow and hot.

- *Mustard seeds:* These come in three different types — brown, regular yellow and hot yellow.
- *Herbes de Provence:* This blend is used in French Provençal cooking. Grown in the region, these herbs include rosemary, thyme, tarragon, basil, savory, fennel, marjoram and lavender.

Seasoning

Seasonings are spices and herbs blended to create a balanced flavor all in one jar.

- *Dried tomato powder:* This is made of the sweetest red tomatoes, dried and ground into a fine powder (see Sources, page 274).
- *Italian seasoning:* This blend includes oregano, basil, marjoram, thyme and rosemary.
- *Paprika:* I like Hungarian the best, but other types — such as Californian, Spanish or North African — are also fine to use. Some are hot and some are sweet.
- *Taco seasoning:* This is a blend of paprika, salt, dried onion flakes, tomato powder, cumin, garlic, oregano, black pepper, cocoa powder and allspice.

- *Tandoori seasoning:* This blend includes coriander, cumin, sweet Hungarian paprika, garlic, ginger, cardamom and saffron.

Spices and Extracts

- *Allspice:* Versatile, this adds flavor in baking, as well as in jerk and some grilling seasonings.
- *Cinnamon:* Currently you can find about five different types of cinnamon on the market. I like the Vietnamese cassia cinnamon for its sweet, strong flavor.
- *Ground ginger:* This powder from China is best finely ground.
- *Vanilla:* Use a pure vanilla extract, and preferably one that has been cold-processed in water and ethyl alcohol, then aged, instead of by cooking and steeping the extract out of the pods. Pure vanilla extract has a distinctive flavor and aroma.

Salt and Pepper

Lately, it seems, there are so many different types of salts and peppers on the market. They have been around for a long time, but recently they've become widely available. To keep it simple, I use only a few types.

- *Kosher salt, coarse and fine:* This refined rock salt is available coarse-grained or finely ground.
- *Sea salt, coarse and fine:* Most sea salt is coarse-grained, but some finely ground varieties are available. There are many kinds of sea salt, each reflecting the unique environment from which it was harvested.
- *Black peppercorns:* I like to grind my pepper fresh each time. I have a number of pepper grinders, set differently for coarse or fine grinds.
- *Szechwan peppercorns:* Not really peppercorns at all, but marketed that way, these dried berries are spicy, fragrant and a must for Asian recipes.
- *White pepper, coarse and fine:* Finely ground white pepper has traditionally been used in Western cooking for white sauces, cream soups, fish dishes and other foods in which specks of black pepper would be unattractive. Coarse white pepper is the size and type of pepper preferred in Southeast Asia where it is generously sprinkled on meat (especially beef and pork) before grilling, broiling or stir-frying.

Wine

Many salad dressings call for wine. If you like the wine to drink, you will like it to cook with. Sometimes I create recipes just to use up a leftover cup of wine.

Liqueurs

I purchase the well-known brands of liqueurs. They are not that much more expensive than the store brands and are better quality.

Nuts and Seeds

Nothing can ruin a recipe more than rancid nuts, so I purchase mine from a specialty store that has a high turnover. You should refrigerate or freeze shelled nuts that won't be used right away. I package the leftovers in vacuum-pack bags and freeze them, then defrost and toast them before use — with great results. Nuts provide nutrition, including a generous serving of "good" monounsaturated fat. Because of the fat content, they have the corresponding calories, too. I only keep nuts for 3 months.

To toast nuts: Preheat oven to 350°F (180°C). Spread in a single layer on a rimmed baking sheet and bake, checking a few times to make sure they don't burn, until fragrant, 6 to 10 minutes (some nuts may require longer baking times). Let cool before chopping.

Different Types of Lettuce

When I was growing up, salad was always iceberg lettuce with a few tomatoes thrown in. Today the variety of lettuce and packaged blends is amazing. Packaged blends are great for one salad or to try new lettuce. If you eat salad a few times a week, though, you can purchase all of the lettuce separately and save a bundle.
Lettuce is divided into four categories by farmers and growers.

1. *Crisphead:* Iceberg is a crisphead. The leaves are thin, light green and very densely packed as they are in a cabbage. Crisphead lettuce is known for its crispy texture and mild flavor, and is grown in cold-weather areas.

2. *Romaine:* This tall lettuce has ridged leaves tightly packed together. The leaves are dark green on the outside and get lighter toward the center. Hearts of romaine are the light leaves, and are sold in packages of two, three or more.

3. *Butterhead:* Small in size, its leaves are not packed. These are tender, with a smooth and light texture; the flavor is "buttery" and mild. Boston and Bibb are common types.

4. *Loose-leaf:* The leaves are loose and attached at the base. Oak leaf is a common type.

Varieties of Lettuce

- *Arugula (also called rocket or roquette):* This has flat leaves with long stems that look like dandelion leaves and has a peppery taste. It's normally paired with other varieties to balance out the taste.

- *Belgian endive (also called French endive):* Related to chicory and escarole, this bullet-shaped lettuce has tightly packed leaves that are yellow or white, crisp and slightly bitter. Keep it tightly wrapped to prevent it from turning green.

- *Chicory (also called curly endive):* This lettuce is slightly bitter, with darker outer leaves and paler or even yellow leaves toward the center. The ragged leaves are on long thin stems.

- *Escarole:* Another member of the chicory family, this lettuce has broad wavy leaves and a milder taste than chicory.

- *Oak leaf:* The varieties are named after their colors — from red to dark green or bronze — and have curly or ruffled leaves.

- *Radicchio:* This variety looks like red cabbage, but it's actually related to chicory. Because of its steep cost, the soft leaves are used only for accents in salads. A small head of radicchio goes a long way.

- *Watercress:* The tender stalks and small dark green leaves have a peppery flavor, reflecting the mustard family they belong to. Use watercress quickly.

Packaged Salads

You will find many different brands and sizes of packaged blends in your grocer's produce department. If you need more lettuce or want to save money, make your own blends. Here's a sampling of blends to make:

- *American:* iceberg, romaine, carrots, cabbage and radishes

- *European:* romaine, iceberg, radicchio, endive and loose-leaf lettuce

- *Field greens:* loose-leaf lettuce, curly endive, radicchio and carrots

- *Italian blend:* romaine and radicchio

- *Mediterranean blend:* escarole, loose-leaf lettuce, radicchio and endive

- *Spring mix:* baby lettuce, endive and mustard greens

- *Baby spinach:* a blend of small spinach leaves

Selection, Storage and Use

Lettuce is a very delicate vegetable so care should be taken when selecting and storing it. When choosing your leaves be sure that they are fresh and crisp, with no signs of wilting or dark spots on the edges.

Lettuce keeps well in plastic bags in the crisper section of the refrigerator. Iceberg lettuce keeps the best, lasting around 2 weeks, while romaine keeps about 10 days, and butterhead types and endives last approximately 4 days. The very delicate greens don't last very long, so it's best to buy only as much as you need at one time and use them immediately. I like to purchase mine at the farmers' market, directly from the growers. Farmers' market greens typically last longer than grocery-store purchases.

Salad greens should not be stored near fruits (such as apples) that produce ethylene gases, as this will increase brown spots on the lettuce leaves and hasten spoilage. Greens that are bought in bunches should be checked for insects. Those leaves that have roots should be placed, root down, in a glass of water with a bag over the leaves, and stored in the refrigerator.

Remove any brown, slimy or wilted leaves. For all lettuce types, you should thoroughly wash and "dry" the leaves to remove any dirt or lingering insects. If you eat lettuce often, it's wise to invest in a salad spinner (see page 14). Simply rinse the leaves, then use the spinner to remove the excess water.

In addition to their most common use in salads, certain lettuce varieties can be braised, steamed, sautéed and even grilled to create wonderful and different taste treats. Try halving a head of radicchio or romaine lengthwise, then brush on some extra virgin olive oil and grill the halves, cut-side down, until they soften and just begin to brown — absolutely delicious.

Salad Dressings

continued on next page

Salad Dressings

Lower-Fat Dressings

Vinaigrettes

Homemade vinaigrette makes fresh greens from a grocery store or farmers' market really pop. They are the simplest dressings to make. You don't need special equipment — a bowl and a whisk are sufficient. In many cases you can put all of the ingredients into a jar, then cover and shake it for a few seconds. The main components of vinaigrette are acid (such as vinegar or lemon juice), flavorings (such as herbs and garlic) and oil. Oil is slowly whisked into the other ingredients until the mixture emulsifies (thickens).

Many ingredients may be in your pantry already. Some oils and vinegars may seem expensive, but they have a long shelf life and can be used in many recipes. Think of them as valuable tools that can create new flavors for your family and make any salad a standout instead of just a side dish.

Most of these dressings work well with lighter lettuce such as butterhead or European blends. Refrigerate any unused portion of vinaigrette in a covered container or bottle for up to 1 week, unless otherwise stated.

Emulsifying

Many of these recipes say to "whisk until emulsified." You've probably noticed that some store-bought vinaigrettes separate and have to be shaken to blend them before use. This is what you are doing when you pour oil into the other ingredients while whisking. You want to whisk vigorously so the dressing becomes thicker and cloudy. The whisking also causes the fat globules to break up into small drops that disperse in the vinegar so the mixture looks blended. Honey, mustard and egg are the classic ingredients in emulsified dressings. I also instruct you to pour in the oil in a steady stream, because you want the other ingredients to incorporate slowly with the oil. If you add all of the oil at once, it just sits on top and won't emulsify. When it sits, it separates; if you refrigerate any leftover dressing, shake it prior to use.

Apple Cider Vinaigrette

This vinaigrette can be served warm. Simply microwave the dressing for 15 seconds and it's perfect for a wilted spinach salad.

Tip

You should take about 45 seconds to incorporate the oil to ensure it gets emulsified with the other ingredients. If you pour too fast it will float on top.

2 tbsp	balsamic vinegar	30 mL
2 tbsp	apple cider vinegar	30 mL
1 tbsp	liquid honey	15 mL
½ tsp	sea salt	2 mL
¾ cup	vegetable or peanut oil	175 mL

1. In a bowl, whisk together balsamic and cider vinegars, honey and salt. While whisking, pour in oil in a thin steady stream until emulsified.

Cabernet Sauvignon Vinaigrette

When I have a few tablespoons of wine left, I use it to create my salad dressing for the next day.

2 tbsp	Cabernet Sauvignon wine	30 mL
2 tbsp	Cabernet Sauvignon vinegar	30 mL
½ tsp	dried oregano	2 mL
½ tsp	dried onion flakes	2 mL
¾ cup	soybean oil	175 mL

1. In a bowl, whisk together wine, vinegar, oregano and onion flakes. Whisk in oil.

Champagne Vinaigrette

Use a dry rosé Champagne for this dressing and you'll have a light pink vinaigrette — perfect for Valentine's Day.

2 tbsp	dry Champagne	30 mL
2 tbsp	Champagne vinegar	30 mL
¼ tsp	garlic salt	1 mL
¼ tsp	onion salt	1 mL
¼ tsp	granulated sugar	1 mL
⅛ tsp	sea salt	0.5 mL
⅛ tsp	ground white pepper	0.5 mL
¾ cup	light extra virgin olive oil	175 mL

1. In a bowl, whisk together Champagne, vinegar, garlic salt, onion salt, sugar, salt and white pepper. Whisk in oil.

Chenin Blanc Vinaigrette

Here's a light sharp vinaigrette to dress any salad.

Tip

Dried red or green bell peppers are concentrated small diced bell peppers that yield a fresh taste and flavor. They are available in bulk food and spice stores. If you can't find them use a double amount of diced fresh bell peppers instead.

2 tbsp	Chenin Blanc wine	30 mL
2 tbsp	white wine vinegar	30 mL
1 tsp	dricd onion flakes	5 mL
1 tsp	dried red bell peppers (see Tip, left)	5 mL
½ tsp	dried basil	2 mL
½ tsp	ground ginger	2 mL
¾ cup	soybean oil	175 mL

1. In a bowl, whisk together wine, vinegar, onion flakes, dried red bell pepper, basil and ginger. Whisk in oil.

Cilantro and Lime Vinaigrette

Makes 1 cup (250 mL)

It's great on salad, but I also like to drizzle this over grilled fish.

½ cup	apple juice	125 mL
¼ cup	extra virgin olive oil	60 mL
¼ cup	white wine vinegar	60 mL
2 tbsp	finely chopped fresh cilantro	30 mL
1 tsp	grated lime zest	5 mL
2 tsp	freshly squeezed lime juice	10 mL
1 tsp	granulated sugar	5 mL
	Salt and freshly ground black pepper	

1. In a bowl, whisk together apple juice, oil, vinegar, cilantro, lime zest and juice and sugar. Season with salt and pepper to taste.

Crushed Blueberry Vinaigrette

Makes 1½ cups (375 mL)

This vinaigrette is sweet and tangy, with a beautiful purple hue from the blueberries.

Tip

The blueberries quickly break down and lose their appeal, so this vinaigrette can only be kept in the refrigerator for up to 2 days.

⅓ cup	white wine vinegar	75 mL
2 tbsp	granulated sugar	30 mL
2 tsp	Dijon Mustard (page 112) or store-bought	10 mL
⅔ cup	soybean oil	150 mL
½ cup	fresh or frozen blueberries, crushed	125 mL

1. In a bowl, whisk together vinegar, sugar and mustard. While whisking, pour in oil in a thin steady stream until emulsified. Toss in crushed blueberries.

Honey Poppy Seed Vinaigrette

Tip

Valued for their color and sweetness, blue poppy seeds aren't always available in stores. If you can't find them, check out online retailers (see Sources, page 274) or use regular poppy seeds.

3 tbsp	white wine vinegar	45 mL
2 tbsp	liquid honey	30 mL
1 tbsp	blue poppy seeds	15 mL
½ cup	peanut oil	125 mL

1. In a bowl, whisk together vinegar, honey and poppy seeds. While whisking, pour in oil in a thin steady stream until emulsified.

Hot Bacon Vinaigrette

¼ cup	white wine vinegar	60 mL
2 tbsp	real bacon bits	30 mL
2 tsp	freshly squeezed lemon juice	10 mL
1 tsp	dried onion flakes	5 mL
1 tsp	dried red bell peppers (see Tip, page 39)	5 mL
¼ cup	corn oil	60 mL
¼ cup	soybean oil	60 mL

1. In a bowl, whisk together vinegar, bacon bits, lemon juice, onion flakes and red bell peppers. Whisk in corn and soybean oils.

2. In a small saucepan, heat vinaigrette over low heat for 2 minutes, or microwave for 3 to 4 seconds, prior to use.

Italian Herb Vinaigrette

**Makes 1 cup
(250 mL)**

*This vinaigrette is a
full-flavor dressing
made with simple
pantry ingredients.*

2 tbsp	white wine vinegar	30 mL
2 tbsp	balsamic vinegar	30 mL
1 tbsp	dried basil	15 mL
1 tbsp	dried rosemary	15 mL
2 tsp	Dijon Mustard (page 112) or store-bought	10 mL
¾ cup	light extra virgin olive oil	175 mL

1. In a bowl, whisk together white wine and balsamic vinegars, basil, rosemary and mustard. While whisking, pour in oil in a thin steady stream until emulsified.

Lemon Dijon Vinaigrette

**Makes 1¼ cups
(300 mL)**

*I like to drizzle
this vinaigrette on
salads made with
fresh shrimp.*

2 tbsp	white wine vinegar	30 mL
2 tbsp	balsamic vinegar	30 mL
1 tsp	grated lemon zest	5 mL
2 tbsp	freshly squeezed lemon juice	30 mL
2 tbsp	granulated sugar	30 mL
2 tbsp	liquid honey	30 mL
2 tsp	Dijon Mustard (page 112) or store-bought	10 mL
⅔ cup	soybean oil	150 mL

1. In a bowl, whisk together white wine and balsamic vinegars, lemon zest and juice, sugar, honey and mustard. While whisking, pour in oil in a thin steady stream until emulsified.

Lemon Mint Cilantro Chile Vinaigrette

Makes 1 cup (250 mL)

Here's a vinaigrette that adds a little heat and spice.

Tip

When seeding and dicing chile peppers, wear rubber gloves.

1 tsp	grated lemon zest	5 mL
3 tbsp	freshly squeezed lemon juice	45 mL
2 tbsp	granulated sugar	30 mL
1 tbsp	finely chopped fresh mint	15 mL
1 tbsp	finely chopped fresh cilantro	15 mL
1	jalapeño pepper, seeded and finely chopped (see Tip, left)	1
½ cup	soybean oil	125 mL

1. In a bowl, whisk together lemon zest and juice, sugar, mint, cilantro and jalapeño. Whisk in oil.

Lucca Vinaigrette

Makes 1 cup (250 mL)

This vinaigrette reminds me of Lucca, a little village in Tuscany where I ate a fantastic salad.

Tip

To toast pine nuts: Place nuts in a single layer on a baking sheet in a preheated 350°F (180°C) oven for 6 to 8 minutes, or until fragrant and golden, stirring once or twice.

2 tbsp	white wine vinegar	30 mL
2 tbsp	balsamic vinegar	30 mL
1 tsp	Dijon Mustard (page 112) or store-bought	5 mL
1 tsp	grated lemon zest	5 mL
⅔ cup	soybean oil	150 mL
2 tbsp	pine nuts, toasted and finely chopped (see Tip, left)	30 mL

1. In a bowl, whisk together white wine and balsamic vinegars, mustard and lemon zest. While whisking, pour in oil in a thin steady stream until emulsified. Toss in pine nuts.

Old Venice Italian Vinaigrette

**Makes 1 cup
(250 mL)**

*When you taste this
dressing, you might
think you're eating
in a small trattoria
beside a Venetian
canal.*

2 tbsp	white wine vinegar	30 mL
2 tbsp	balsamic vinegar	30 mL
2 tsp	Dijon Mustard (page 112) or store-bought	10 mL
2 tsp	minced garlic	10 mL
2 tsp	dried onion flakes	10 mL
1 tsp	hot pepper flakes	5 mL
1 tsp	freshly ground black pepper	5 mL
¼ cup	soybean oil	60 mL
¼ cup	canola oil	60 mL

1. In a bowl, whisk together white wine and balsamic vinegars, mustard, garlic, onion flakes, hot pepper flakes and black pepper. While whisking, pour in soybean and canola oils in a thin steady stream until emulsified.

Orange Blossom Vinaigrette

**Makes 1¼ cups
(300 mL)**

*The aroma of this
vinaigrette reminds
me of orange
blossoms that bloom
not far from my
home in Southern
California.*

2 tbsp	white wine vinegar	30 mL
2 tbsp	orange vinegar (see Tip, left)	30 mL
¼ cup	freshly squeezed orange juice	60 mL
2 tsp	minced dried shallots	10 mL
1 tsp	dried thyme	5 mL
½ tsp	ground white pepper	2 mL
½ tsp	sea salt	2 mL
¾ cup	extra virgin olive oil	175 mL

1. In a bowl, whisk together white wine and orange vinegars, orange juice, shallots, thyme, white pepper and salt. Whisk in oil.

Tip

If you can't find orange
vinegar, add 2 tsp
(10 mL) each white
wine vinegar and
orange juice.

Orange Cinnamon Vinaigrette

Makes 1 cup (250 mL)

Add a spiced citrus zing to your greens.

Tip
Natural rice vinegar, also called unseasoned rice vinegar, has no added sugar or salt and I prefer it over the seasoned variety.

2 tsp	grated orange zest	10 mL
1/2 cup	freshly squeezed orange juice	125 mL
1/4 cup	sunflower oil	60 mL
1/4 cup	natural rice vinegar (see Tip, left)	60 mL
1 tsp	ground cinnamon	5 mL
	Salt and freshly ground black pepper	

1. In a bowl, whisk together orange zest and juice, oil, vinegar and cinnamon. Season with salt and pepper to taste.

Parmesan Vinaigrette

Makes 1 cup (250 mL)

Freshly grate your cheese to create a flavorful dressing.

1/4 cup	sherry wine vinegar	60 mL
1 tsp	minced dried garlic	5 mL
1 tsp	dried oregano	5 mL
1 tsp	dried basil	5 mL
1/4 cup	freshly grated Parmesan cheese	60 mL
1/4 cup	extra virgin olive oil	60 mL
1/4 cup	canola oil	60 mL

1. In a bowl, whisk together vinegar, garlic, oregano, basil and Parmesan. Whisk in olive and canola oils.

Peach Citrus Vinaigrette

Makes 1½ cups (375 mL)

The combination of mint and peach makes this a perfect summertime dressing.

Tip

Since the peach is uncooked, it will eventually brown, so this vinaigrette only keeps for up to 2 days in the refrigerator.

½ cup	sherry wine vinegar	125 mL
1	small ripe peach, puréed	1
1 tsp	dried mint	5 mL
1 tsp	dried cilantro	5 mL
½ tsp	grated lemon zest	2 mL
½ cup	canola oil	125 mL
¼ cup	extra virgin olive oil	60 mL

1. In a bowl, whisk together vinegar, peach purée, mint, cilantro and lemon zest. While whisking, pour in canola and olive oils in a thin steady stream until emulsified.

Pomegranate Vinaigrette

Makes 1¾ cups (425 mL)

This red vinaigrette is perfect for Christmas dinner.

½ cup	sherry wine vinegar	125 mL
½ cup	pomegranate seeds, crushed	125 mL
1 tbsp	liquid honey	15 mL
½ tsp	sea salt	2 mL
½ tsp	ground white pepper	2 mL
¾ cup	soybean oil	175 mL

1. In a bowl, whisk together vinegar, pomegranate seeds, honey, salt and white pepper. While whisking, pour in oil in a thin steady stream until emulsified.

Radda Vinaigrette

Makes 1¼ cups (300 mL)

Radda is the beautiful village in Tuscany that is home to the Chianti wineries.

¼ cup	sherry wine vinegar	60 mL
¼ cup	Chianti wine	60 mL
2 tsp	dried Italian seasoning	10 mL
½ cup	canola oil	125 mL
¼ cup	extra virgin olive oil	60 mL

1. In a bowl, whisk together vinegar, wine and Italian seasoning. Whisk in canola and olive oils.

Raspberry Vinaigrette

Makes 1¾ cups (425 mL)

A spring salad will burst with flavor when dressed with this vinaigrette made with fresh berries.

Tip
Vinaigrette keeps for up to 2 days in the refrigerator.

¼ cup	white balsamic vinegar	60 mL
¼ cup	Chablis wine	60 mL
1 tbsp	granulated sugar	15 mL
2 tsp	sea salt	10 ml
1 tsp	ground white pepper	5 mL
½ cup	soybean oil	125 mL
¼ cup	canola oil	60 mL
½ cup	raspberries, crushed	125 mL

1. In a bowl, whisk together vinegar, wine, sugar, salt and white pepper. Whisk in soybean and canola oils. Toss in raspberries.

Red Balsamic Vinaigrette with Kalamata Olives

I enjoyed a similar dressing on a visit to the Greek island of Santorini. It's such a perfect dressing for Greek salads, I just had to get the recipe for you.

2 tbsp	red wine vinegar	30 mL
2 tbsp	balsamic vinegar	30 mL
1 tsp	Dijon Mustard (page 112) or store-bought	5 mL
1 tsp	chopped fresh thyme	5 mL
1 tsp	chopped fresh oregano	5 mL
¾ cup	soybean oil	175 mL
¼ cup	kalamata olives, pitted and finely chopped	60 mL

1. In a bowl, whisk together red wine and balsamic vinegars, mustard, thyme and oregano. While whisking, pour in oil in a thin steady stream until emulsified. Toss in chopped olives.

Roasted Garlic Vinaigrette

Makes 1½ cups (375 mL)

This dressing makes roasting the garlic worthwhile.

¼ cup	white wine vinegar	60 mL
¼ cup	freshly grated Parmesan cheese	60 mL
1 tsp	dried oregano	5 mL
½ cup	canola oil	125 mL
¼ cup	extra virgin olive oil	60 mL
1	medium head garlic, roasted and puréed (see Tip, left)	1

1. In a bowl, whisk together vinegar, Parmesan and oregano. While whisking, pour in canola and olive oils in a thin steady stream until emulsified. Whisk in roasted garlic. Refrigerate in a bottle with a tight-fitting lid for at least 2 hours to fully infuse the vinaigrette with garlic flavor.

Tip

To roast garlic: Preheat oven to 400°F (200°C). Cut about ¼ inch (0.5 cm) off the top of the bulb and drizzle with 1 tsp (5 mL) olive oil. Wrap in foil and roast until golden brown and very soft, 30 to 35 minutes. Let cool, turn upside down and press cloves out of bulb.

Roasted Red Pepper Vinaigrette

Makes 1¼ cups (300 mL)

This vinaigrette is sweet with flavor and bold with color.

¼ cup	red wine vinegar	60 mL
¼ cup	minced roasted red bell peppers	60 mL
1 tsp	minced dried garlic	5 mL
1 tsp	dried oregano	5 mL
1 tsp	dried basil	5 mL
½ tsp	dried thyme	2 mL
½ tsp	hot pepper flakes	2 mL
½ cup	canola oil	125 mL
¼ cup	extra virgin olive oil	60 mL

1. In a bowl, whisk together vinegar, roasted peppers, garlic, oregano, basil, thyme and hot pepper flakes. While whisking, pour in canola and olive oils in a thin steady stream until emulsified.

Sandwich Dressing

Makes 1 cup (250 mL)

Here's the perfect juicy dressing to accompany subs, torpedoes and hoagies.

¼ cup	red wine vinegar	60 mL
¼ cup	freshly squeezed lemon juice	60 mL
2 tsp	Dijon Mustard (page 112) or store-bought	10 mL
2 tsp	minced dried garlic	10 mL
2 tsp	dried onion flakes	10 mL
¼ cup	soybean oil	60 mL
¼ cup	extra virgin olive oil	60 mL

1. In a bowl, whisk together vinegar, lemon juice, mustard, garlic and onion flakes. While whisking, pour in soybean and olive oils in a thin steady stream until emulsified.

Tip

Refrigerate this dressing in a squirt bottle, so it's easy to squeeze out over sandwich fillings.

Sherry Vinaigrette

**Makes 1 cup
(250 mL)**

*I like to pour this tart
vinaigrette on fresh
garden tomatoes.*

¼ cup	sherry wine vinegar	60 mL
¼ cup	freshly grated Romano cheese	60 mL
1 tbsp	Dijon Mustard (page 112) or store-bought	15 mL
1 tsp	minced dried shallots	5 mL
½ cup	canola oil	125 mL
¼ cup	extra virgin olive oil	60 mL

1. In a bowl, whisk together vinegar, Romano, mustard and shallots. While whisking, pour in canola and olive oils in a thin steady stream until emulsified.

Smoked Chipotle Vinaigrette

**Makes 1½ cups
(375 mL)**

*Here's a smoky,
spicy dressing that's
perfect for a Mexican
salad.*

¼ cup	red wine vinegar	60 mL
1	chipotle pepper in adobo sauce, drained, seeded and minced	1
2 tsp	Dijon Mustard (page 112) or store-bought	10 mL
2 tsp	minced dried garlic	10 mL
1 tsp	sea salt	5 mL
1 tsp	freshly ground black pepper	5 mL
½ tsp	hot pepper flakes	2 mL
¾ cup	soybean oil	175 mL

1. In a bowl, whisk together vinegar, chipotle, mustard, garlic, salt, pepper and hot pepper flakes. While whisking, pour in oil in a thin steady stream until emulsified.

Stilton Vinaigrette

¼ cup	white wine vinegar	60 mL
2 tsp	Dijon Mustard (page 112) or store-bought	10 mL
2 tsp	dried onion flakes	10 mL
1 tsp	freshly ground black pepper	5 mL
¾ cup	soybean oil	175 mL
¼ cup	Stilton blue cheese, crumbled	60 mL

1. In a bowl, whisk together vinegar, mustard, onion flakes and pepper. While whisking, pour in oil in a thin steady stream until emulsified. Toss in blue cheese.

White Balsamic Vinaigrette

2 tbsp	white balsamic vinegar	30 mL
2 tbsp	white wine vinegar	30 mL
2 tsp	Dijon Mustard (page 112) or store-bought	10 mL
2 tsp	minced garlic	10 mL
1 tsp	grated orange zest	5 mL
1 tsp	star anise powder (see Tip, left)	5 mL
¼ cup	soybean oil	60 mL
¼ cup	canola oil	60 mL
1 tbsp	extra virgin olive oil	15 mL

1. In a bowl, whisk together balsamic and white wine vinegars, mustard, garlic, orange zest and star anise powder. While whisking, pour in soybean, canola and olive oils in a thin steady stream until emulsified.

International Dressings

If you are looking for a dressing with international flair then you've come to the right place. This chapter includes everything from Asian to German to Russian dressings with ingredients that are readily available and you don't even have to travel abroad to get them.

Asian All-Purpose Dressing

Makes ¾ cup (175 mL)

This light summer salad dressing perfectly suits a combination of grated Asian cabbage and carrots.

Tip

Natural rice vinegar, also called unseasoned rice vinegar, has no added sugar or salt, and I prefer it over the seasoned variety.

2 tbsp	natural rice vinegar (see Tip, left)	30 mL
1½ tbsp	soy sauce	22 mL
1 tbsp	granulated sugar	15 mL
½ tsp	freshly grated gingerroot	2 mL
1 tbsp	coarsely chopped fresh cilantro	15 mL
½ cup	canola oil	125 mL
1½ tsp	sesame oil	7 mL
3	drops hot chili oil	3

1. In a bowl, whisk together vinegar, soy sauce, sugar, ginger and cilantro. While whisking, pour in canola, sesame oil and hot chili oils in a steady stream until emulsified for 1 minute.

Caesar Dressing

Makes ½ cup (125 mL)

This dressing was made famous by Caesar Cardini at his restaurant in Tijuana, Mexico, in the 1940s. Today his restaurant is gone, but the salad is still served at the same spot by Caesar's Sports Bar and Grill. Romaine lettuce is a good choice for the base.

Tips

This recipe contains raw egg yolks. If you are concerned about the safety of using raw eggs, use pasteurized eggs in the shell or pasteurized liquid whole eggs, instead.

Because of the egg yolk, this dressing does not store well. Make it fresh and use it right away.

1	egg yolk, at room temperature, or 2 tbsp (30 mL) pasteurized eggs (liquid or in the shell) (see Tips, left)	1
1 tbsp	freshly squeezed lemon juice	15 mL
½ tsp	sea salt	2 mL
6 tbsp	olive oil, divided	90 mL
1	clove garlic, minced	1
½ tsp	Worcestershire sauce	2 mL
½ tsp	Dijon Mustard (page 112) or store-bought	2 mL
½ tsp	apple cider vinegar	2 mL
	Freshly ground black pepper	
3 tbsp	freshly grated Parmesan cheese	45 mL

1. In a bowl, whisk together egg yolk, lemon juice, salt and 1 tbsp (15 mL) of the oil. Whisk in garlic, Worcestershire sauce, mustard and vinegar. While vigorously whisking, pour in remainder of oil in a thin steady stream until emulsified. Add pepper and Parmesan.

Chasen's French Dressing

Makes 2 cups (500 mL)

This is adapted from a dressing served at Chasen's Restaurant, the famed star-studded Los Angeles establishment that closed its doors in 1995. The restaurant is now a grocery store, which has a few of the original booths preserved, so you can sit where the famous once sat.

¾ cup	red wine vinegar	175 mL
¼ cup	Country Ketchup (page 107) or store-bought	60 mL
1	clove garlic, minced	1
1 tsp	granulated sugar	5 mL
1 tsp	sea salt	5 mL
1 tsp	freshly squeezed lemon juice	5 mL
½ tsp	Worcestershire sauce	2 mL
¼ tsp	freshly ground black pepper	1 mL
¼ tsp	dry mustard	1 mL
¼ tsp	hot pepper sauce	1 mL
¼ tsp	ground white pepper	1 mL
½ cup	soybean oil	125 mL
½ cup	extra virgin olive oil	125 mL

1. In a bowl, whisk together vinegar, ketchup, garlic, sugar, salt, lemon juice, Worcestershire sauce, black pepper, dry mustard, hot pepper sauce and white pepper. While whisking, pour in soybean and olive oils in a thin steady stream until emulsified.

English Stilton Dressing

• **Food processor**

4 oz	cream cheese, softened	125 g
4 oz	small-curd cottage cheese	125 g
1/2 cup	sour cream	125 mL
1/4 cup	Traditional Mayonnaise (page 100) or store-bought	60 mL
1 tbsp	freshly squeezed lemon juice	15 mL
1 1/2 tsp	fresh dill	7 mL
1/2 tsp	dried onion flakes	2 mL
1/2 tsp	whole black peppercorns	2 mL
1/4 tsp	garlic powder	1 mL
2 oz	Stilton blue cheese, crumbled	60 g

1. In a food processor fitted with a metal blade, process cream cheese, cottage cheese, sour cream, mayonnaise, lemon juice, dill, onion flakes, peppercorns and garlic powder until smooth, for 45 seconds. Place in a bowl. Fold in crumbled blue cheese.

Fresh Spicy Ginger Dressing

3 tbsp	white wine vinegar	45 mL
2 tbsp	reduced-sodium soy sauce	30 mL
1 tbsp	granulated sugar	15 mL
1 tbsp	freshly grated gingerroot	15 mL
1/2	jalapeño pepper, seeded and finely minced	1/2
1/4 tsp	cayenne pepper	1 mL
2/3 cup	canola oil	150 mL
2 tsp	sesame oil	10 mL

1. In a bowl, whisk together vinegar, soy sauce, sugar, ginger, jalapeño and cayenne for 1 minute. While vigorously whisking, pour in canola and sesame oils in a thin steady stream until emulsified.

German Dressing

**Makes 1 cup
(250 mL)**

*Light and full of
flavor, this dressing
is delicious with
cooked small red
potatoes, so it's
perfect for German
potato salad. Use
about 3 pounds
(1.5 kg) of potatoes
with this amount
of dressing.*

¼ cup	tarragon vinegar	60 mL
1 tsp	granulated sugar	5 mL
1 tsp	paprika	5 mL
½ tsp	sea salt	2 mL
½ tsp	dry mustard	2 mL
½ tsp	celery seeds	2 mL
¼ tsp	freshly ground black pepper	1 mL
¾ cup	olive oil	175 mL

1. In a bowl, whisk together vinegar, sugar, paprika, salt, dry mustard, celery seeds and pepper. While vigorously whisking, pour in oil in a thin steady stream until emulsified.

Island Salad Dressing

**Makes ½ cup
(125 mL)**

*When you're
visiting any tropical
island, you'll find
the hotel buffets
feature a dressing
used as "sauce"
on pineapples or
lettuce. Try this
dressing on fresh
tropical fruits such as
pineapple, papaya,
mangos and kiwis
and sprinkle with
toasted shredded
coconut.*

2 tbsp	freshly squeezed lemon juice	30 mL
2 tbsp	freshly squeezed lime juice	30 mL
2 tbsp	granulated sugar	30 mL
1 tbsp	dark rum	15 mL
¼ cup	coarsely chopped fresh mint	60 mL

1. In a bowl, whisk together lemon juice, lime juice, sugar, rum and mint.

Japanese Dressing

Makes ¼ cup (60 mL)

I like to marinate Japanese cucumbers in this dressing, but other vegetables — such as carrots, snow peas and radishes or any combination of these — work just as well.

1 tbsp	natural rice vinegar (see Tip, page 52)	15 mL
1 tsp	reduced-sodium soy sauce	5 mL
2 tbsp	canola oil	30 mL
1 tsp	sesame oil	5 mL
Pinch	ground white pepper	Pinch
Pinch	sea salt	Pinch

1. In a bowl, whisk together vinegar, soy sauce, canola oil, sesame oil, salt and white pepper.

Malaysian Dressing

Makes ¾ cup (175 mL)

Toss this dressing with bell peppers, pineapple, golden raisins, bean sprouts and bamboo shoots.

Tip

To toast sesame seeds: Place seeds on a baking sheet and toast in a preheated 350°F (180°C) oven for 5 to 7 minutes, or until fragrant and golden, stirring once or twice.

¼ cup	natural rice vinegar (see Tip, page 52)	60 mL
¼ cup	unsweetened pineapple juice	60 mL
3 tbsp	reduced-sodium soy sauce	45 mL
1 tbsp	freshly grated gingerroot	15 mL
	Zest and juice of 1 orange	
1	clove garlic, minced	1
1 tsp	sesame seeds, toasted (see Tip, left)	5 mL

1. In a bowl, whisk together rice vinegar, pineapple juice, soy sauce, ginger, orange zest and juice, garlic and sesame seeds.

Russian Dressing

Makes 1¾ cups (425 mL)

This dressing enhances an array of firm lettuce leaves, such as romaine, or any type of cabbage.

1 cup	Traditional Mayonnaise (page 100) or store-bought	250 mL
½ cup	Country Ketchup (page 107)	125 mL
1 tbsp	finely chopped Italian flat-leaf parsley	15 mL
1½ tsp	dried onion flakes	7 mL
¼ tsp	dry mustard	1 mL
¼ tsp	Worcestershire sauce	1 mL
4	drops hot pepper sauce	4

1. In a bowl, blend mayonnaise, ketchup, parsley, onion flakes, dry mustard, Worcestershire sauce and hot pepper sauce.

South-of-the-Border Dressing

Makes 1½ cups (375 mL)

This hot, spicy dressing is a good match for a Mexican dinner, and is perfect on a taco salad.

Tip

Make sure your avocado is ripe for the best flavor and texture. *To determine if your avocado is ripe:* Hold it in the palm of your hand and press. The avocado should feel like a tomato that has a little "give."

- **Food processor**

4 oz	cream cheese, softened	125 g
½ cup	buttermilk	125 mL
½ cup	Traditional Mayonnaise (page 100) or store-bought	125 mL
1	ripe avocado (see Tip, left)	1
2 tsp	fresh dill	10 mL
1 tsp	freshly squeezed lemon juice	5 mL
2	chipotle peppers in adobo sauce, drained	2

1. In a food processor fitted with a metal blade, process cream cheese, buttermilk, mayonnaise, avocado, dill, lemon juice and chipotle peppers until smooth, about 45 seconds.

Sweet-and-Sour Dressing

**Makes about
1/4 cup (60 mL)**

*This simple warm
dressing is designed
for spinach leaves.*

5	thick slices bacon	5
3 tbsp	apple cider vinegar	45 mL
1 tsp	granulated sugar	5 mL
1/2 tsp	paprika	2 mL
1/4 tsp	freshly ground black pepper	1 mL
1/4 tsp	dry mustard	1 mL

1. In a skillet over medium heat, fry bacon until crisp, about
   7 minutes. Transfer bacon to a paper towel to drain. Add
   1/3 cup (75 mL) water, vinegar, sugar, paprika, pepper
   and dry mustard to pan. Simmer, stirring, until sugar is
   dissolved, about 5 minutes. Chop bacon and return to pan,
   stirring to combine with other ingredients. Serve hot.

Thai Peanut Dressing

**Makes 2 cups
(500 mL)**

*I like to use this
dressing as a
marinade for Thai
chicken or with
napa cabbage.*

1/2 cup	smooth peanut butter	125 mL
1/2 cup	peanut oil	125 mL
1/4 cup	white wine vinegar	60 mL
1/4 cup	reduced-sodium soy sauce	60 mL
1/4 cup	freshly squeezed lemon juice	60 mL
4	cloves garlic, minced	4
2 tsp	cayenne pepper	10 mL
1 tsp	freshly grated gingerroot	5 mL

1. In a bowl, whisk together peanut butter, peanut oil,
   vinegar, soy sauce, lemon juice, garlic, cayenne and ginger.

Wafu Dressing

**Makes 1 cup
(250 mL)**

*A popular vinaigrette
in Japan, this
dressing tastes great
with napa cabbage.*

Tip

I like to use the
reduced-sodium soy
sauce because typical
soy sauce adds too
much salt to the dish.
Check the label to
make sure the sauce is
made from soybeans
and not just additives
and colorings.

½ cup	Traditional Mayonnaise (page 100) or store-bought	125 mL
2 tbsp	reduced-sodium soy sauce (see Tip, left)	30 mL
1	clove garlic, minced	1
Pinch	ground ginger	Pinch
2 tbsp	natural rice vinegar (see Tip, page 52)	30 mL
2 tbsp	sesame oil	30 mL
2 tbsp	whole milk	30 mL

1. In a bowl, combine mayonnaise, soy sauce, garlic and
ginger. Whisk in vinegar, sesame oil and milk.

Creamy Dressings

Many people think that creamy dressings tend to be higher in fat. Not true. You can create dressings using lower-fat ingredients, such as buttermilk or yogurt. Creamy dressings tend to work better on heartier leaf lettuces such as romaine and iceberg.

Avocado Dressing

**Makes about
2 cups (500 mL)**

*Here's a dressing
with a light green
color that's perfect
for St. Patrick's Day.*

● **Food processor**

4 oz	cream cheese, softened	125 g
1/2 cup	buttermilk	125 mL
1/2 cup	Traditional Mayonnaise (page 100) or store-bought	125 mL
1	ripe avocado (see Tip, page 58)	1
2 tsp	chopped fresh dill	10 mL
1 tsp	freshly squeezed lemon juice	5 mL

1. In a food processor fitted with a metal blade, process cream cheese, buttermilk, mayonnaise, avocado, dill and lemon juice until smooth, about 2 minutes.

Baja Dressing

**Makes 1 1/2 cups
(375 mL)**

*Use this spicy, zippy
dressing on salad
or as a dip for celery
and carrot sticks.*

● **Food processor**

4 oz	cream cheese, softened	125 g
1/2 cup	buttermilk	125 mL
1/2 cup	Traditional Mayonnaise (page 100) or store-bought	125 mL
1 tsp	freshly ground black pepper	5 mL
1 tsp	taco seasoning	5 mL
1	chipotle pepper in adobo sauce, drained	1
1 tsp	freshly squeezed lemon juice	5 mL

1. In a food processor with a metal blade, process cream cheese, buttermilk, mayonnaise, black pepper, taco seasoning, chipotle pepper and lemon juice until smooth, about 2 minutes.

Blue Cheese Dressing

Makes 1½ cups (375 mL)

Here's a rich and fresh creamy dressing with chunks of blue cheese.

Tip

If you process the blue cheese in the food processor instead of folding it into the dressing, it will be become an unattractive gray/blue color.

● **Food processor**

4 oz	plain yogurt (see Tip, page 70)	125 g
½ cup	buttermilk	125 mL
¼ cup	Traditional Mayonnaise (page 100) or store-bought	60 mL
¼ cup	sour cream	60 mL
1 tsp	dried onion flakes	5 mL
½ tsp	garlic salt	2 mL
2 oz	blue cheese, crumbled (see Tip, left)	60 g

1. In a food processor fitted with a metal blade, process yogurt, buttermilk, mayonnaise, sour cream, onion flakes and garlic salt until smooth, about 2 minutes. Transfer to a small bowl and fold in blue cheese.

Buffalo Blue Cheese Dressing

Makes 1½ cups (375 mL)

As well as a classic salad dressing, it's a dandy dipping sauce for Buffalo wings.

● **Food processor**

4 oz	cream cheese, softened	125 g
½ cup	buttermilk	125 mL
¼ cup	Traditional Mayonnaise (page 100) or store-bought	60 mL
1 tsp	dried onion flakes	5 mL
½ tsp	garlic salt	2 mL
½ tsp	hot pepper sauce	2 mL
¼ tsp	hot pepper flakes	1 mL
2 oz	blue cheese, crumbled (see Tip, above)	60 g

1. In a food processor fitted with a metal blade, process cream cheese, buttermilk, mayonnaise, onion flakes, garlic salt, hot pepper sauce and hot pepper flakes until smooth, about 2 minutes. Transfer to a small bowl and fold in blue cheese.

Cajun Spice Dressing

Makes 1 cup (250 mL)

I had a similar dressing in New Orleans one spring day.

- **Food processor**

4 oz	cream cheese, softened	125 g
½ cup	Traditional Mayonnaise (page 100) or store-bought	125 mL
¼ cup	buttermilk	60 mL
½ tsp	hot pepper flakes	2 mL
½ tsp	dried onion flakes	2 mL
½ tsp	paprika	2 mL
½ tsp	garlic salt	2 mL
¼ tsp	caraway seeds	1 mL
3	drops hot pepper sauce	3

1. In a food processor fitted with a metal blade, process cream cheese, mayonnaise, buttermilk, hot pepper flakes, onion flakes, paprika, garlic salt, caraway seeds and hot pepper sauce until smooth, about 2 minutes.

Catalina Dressing

Makes 1½ cups (375 mL)

There are many Catalina dressings on the market but this homemade version has much more fresh flavor.

¼ cup	granulated sugar	60 mL
½ cup	canola oil	125 mL
⅓ cup	Country Ketchup (page 107) or store-bought	75 mL
¼ cup	diced onion	60 mL
¼ cup	cider vinegar	60 mL
1½ tsp	sea salt	7 mL
½ tsp	chili powder	2 mL
½ tsp	celery seeds	2 mL
¼ tsp	dry mustard	1 mL
⅛ tsp	paprika	0.5 mL

1. In a bowl whisk together, sugar, oil, ketchup, onion, vinegar, salt, chili powder, celery seeds, dry mustard and paprika.

Celery Seed Dressing

**Makes 2 cups
(500 mL)**

*Try this dressing as a
sauce for crab cakes.*

● **Food processor**

4 oz	cream cheese, softened	125 g
¼ cup	granulated sugar	60 mL
½ cup	canola oil	125 mL
⅓ cup	County Ketchup (page 107) or store-bought	75 mL
¼ cup	white wine vinegar	60 mL
1 tsp	sea salt	5 mL
½ tsp	dried onion flakes	2 mL
¼ tsp	celery seeds	1 mL
⅛ tsp	paprika	0.5 mL

1. In a food processor fitted with a metal blade, process cream cheese, sugar, oil, ketchup, vinegar, salt, onion flakes, celery seeds and paprika until smooth, about 2 minutes.

Cracked Black Peppercorn Dressing

**Makes 1½ cups
(375 mL)**

*This peppery
dressing livens up
salad served with a
steak dinner.*

● **Food processor**

4 oz	cream cheese, softened	125 g
½ cup	buttermilk	125 mL
½ cup	Traditional Mayonnaise (page 100) or store-bought	125 mL
1 tsp	whole black peppercorns	5 mL
1 tsp	sea salt	5 mL
1 tsp	freshly squeezed lemon juice	5 mL
½ tsp	Hungarian paprika	2 mL

1. In a food processor fitted with a metal blade, process cream cheese, buttermilk, mayonnaise, black peppercorns, salt, lemon juice and paprika until smooth, about 2 minutes.

Cracked Peppercorn and Parmesan Dressing

Makes 1½ cups (375 mL)

Szechwan peppercorns add a punch to this dressing.

Tip
You can replace the Szechwan peppercorns with whole black peppercorns.

● **Food processor**

4 oz	cream cheese, softened	125 g
¼ cup	buttermilk	60 mL
¼ cup	Bold Chili Sauce (page 115) or store-bought	60 mL
¼ cup	Traditional Mayonnaise (page 100) or store-bought	60 mL
1 tsp	Szechwan peppercorns	5 mL
½ tsp	dried onion flakes	2 mL
¼ cup	freshly grated Parmesan cheese	60 mL

1. In a food processor fitted with a metal blade, process cream cheese, buttermilk, chili sauce, mayonnaise, peppercorns, onion flakes and Parmesan until smooth, about 2 minutes.

Creamy Asiago Dressing

Makes 1 cup (250 mL)

Asiago cheese is an Italian cheese with a flavor that's similar to Cheddar and Romano combined.

● **Food processor**

3 oz	cream cheese, softened	90 g
½ cup	Traditional Mayonnaise (page 100) or store-bought	125 mL
¼ cup	half-and-half (10%) cream	60 mL
1 tbsp	County Ketchup (page 107) or store-bought	15 mL
½ tsp	dried dill	2 mL
½ tsp	garlic powder	2 mL
½ cup	shredded Asiago cheese	125 mL

1. In a food processor fitted with a metal blade, process cream cheese, mayonnaise, cream, ketchup, dill and garlic powder until smooth, about 2 minutes. Transfer to a bowl and fold in Asiago.

Creamy California Dressing

Makes 1 cup (250 mL)

I developed this avocado dressing using the Hass variety that was first cultivated in Southern California.

Tip

To determine if your avocado is ripe: Hold it in the palm of your hand and press. The avocado should feel like a tomato that has a little "give."

• **Food processor**

3 oz	cream cheese, softened	90 g
$\frac{1}{2}$ cup	Traditional Mayonnaise (page 100) or store-bought	125 mL
$\frac{1}{2}$	ripe avocado (see Tip, left)	$\frac{1}{2}$
2 tsp	olive oil	10 mL
1 tsp	sea salt	5 mL
$\frac{1}{2}$ tsp	hot pepper flakes	2 mL

1. In a food processor fitted with a metal blade, process cream cheese, mayonnaise, avocado, oil, salt and hot pepper flakes until smooth, about 2 minutes.

Creamy Curried Dressing

Makes 1$\frac{1}{4}$ cups (300 mL)

When serving an Asian dinner, try this dressing on cabbage.

1 cup	Traditional Mayonnaise (page 100) or store-bought	250 mL
$\frac{1}{4}$ cup	buttermilk	60 mL
1 tbsp	freshly squeezed lemon juice	15 mL
1 tsp	mild curry powder	5 mL
$\frac{1}{2}$ tsp	dried onion flakes	2 mL
$\frac{1}{4}$ tsp	freshly ground black pepper	1 mL
$\frac{1}{4}$ tsp	sea salt	1 mL

1. In a bowl, whisk together mayonnaise, buttermilk, lemon juice, curry powder, onion flakes, pepper and salt.

Creamy Dill Dressing

**Makes 1 cup
(250 mL)**

*Try this dressing on
fried fish pieces.*

- **Food processor**

4 oz	cream cheese, softened	125 g
¼ cup	small-curd cottage cheese	60 mL
¼ cup	buttermilk	60 mL
1 tsp	fresh dill	5 mL
½ tsp	dried onion flakes	2 mL
¼ tsp	freshly ground black pepper	1 mL
¼ tsp	sea salt	1 mL

1. In a food processor fitted with a metal blade, process cream cheese, cottage cheese, buttermilk, dill, onion flakes, pepper and salt until smooth, about 2 minutes.

Creamy French Honey Dressing

**Makes 1 cup
(250 mL)**

*I devoured a
dressing similar
to this in Cannes,
France, one spring.*

½ cup	Traditional Mayonnaise (page 100) or store-bought	125 mL
¼ cup	olive oil	60 mL
1 tbsp	liquid honey	15 mL
1 tbsp	freshly squeezed lemon juice	15 mL
2 tsp	prepared horseradish	10 mL
2 tsp	Bold Chili Sauce (page 115) or store-bought	10 mL
2	cloves garlic, minced	2
1 tsp	sea salt	5 mL
½ tsp	dry mustard	2 mL
½ tsp	paprika	2 mL
¼ tsp	freshly ground black pepper	1 mL
⅛ tsp	cayenne pepper	0.5 mL

1. In a bowl, whisk together mayonnaise, oil, honey, lemon juice, horseradish, chili sauce, garlic, salt, dry mustard, paprika, pepper and cayenne.

Creamy Ginger Spice Dressing

Makes 1½ cups (375 mL)

Fresh ginger heightens the flavor of this dressing.

● **Food processor**

8 oz	cream cheese, softened	250 g
¼ cup	buttermilk	60 mL
¼ cup	small-curd cottage cheese	60 mL
1 tbsp	freshly grated gingerroot	15 mL
½ tsp	tandoori seasoning	2 mL
¼ tsp	sea salt	1 mL

1. In a food processor fitted with a metal blade, process cream cheese, buttermilk, cottage cheese, ginger, tandoori seasoning and salt until smooth, about 2 minutes.

Creamy Italian Dressing

Makes 1 cup (250 mL)

Here's a dressing that can be made quickly with pantry items you most likely have on hand.

½ cup	Traditional Mayonnaise (page 100) or store-bought	125 mL
¼ cup	balsamic vinegar	60 mL
¼ cup	light olive oil	60 mL
1 tbsp	dried basil	15 mL
2 tsp	Dijon Mustard (page 112) or store-bought	10 mL
1 tsp	dried rosemary	5 mL

1. In a bowl, whisk together mayonnaise, vinegar, oil, basil, mustard and rosemary.

Creamy Poppy Seed Dressing

**Makes 1 cup
(250 mL)**

*This is a hearty
dressing to keep
on hand.*

Tip
Valued for their color
and sweetness, blue
poppy seeds aren't
always available in
stores. If you can't find
them, check out online
retailers (see Sources,
page 274) or use
regular poppy seeds.

● **Food processor**

4 oz	cream cheese, softened	125 g
1/4 cup	Traditional Mayonnaise (page 100) or store-bought	60 mL
3 tbsp	white wine vinegar	45 mL
2 tbsp	peanut oil	30 mL
2 tbsp	liquid honey	30 mL
1 tbsp	blue poppy seeds (see Tip, left)	15 mL

1. In a food processor fitted with a metal blade, process cream cheese, mayonnaise, vinegar, peanut oil, honey and poppy seeds until smooth, about 2 minutes.

Creamy Roma Dressing

**Makes 1 1/2 cups
(375 mL)**

*Here's a dressing
that's light red with a
burst of flavor.*

● **Food processor**

4 oz	cream cheese, softened	125 g
1/2 cup	Traditional Mayonnaise (page 100) or store-bought	125 mL
1/4 cup	buttermilk	60 mL
1 tbsp	freshly squeezed lemon juice	15 mL
1/2 tsp	hot pepper flakes	2 mL
1/2 tsp	dried onion flakes	2 mL
1/4 cup	diced, seeded Roma (plum) tomatoes	60 mL

1. In a food processor fitted with a metal blade, process cream cheese, mayonnaise, buttermilk, lemon juice, hot pepper flakes and onion flakes until smooth, about 2 minutes. Transfer to a bowl and fold in tomatoes.

Creamy Two-Cheese Italian Dressing

Makes 1¼ cups (300 mL)

This dressing blends two of my favorite Italian cheeses — Parmesan and Romano.

- **Food processor**

4 oz	cream cheese, softened	125 g
¼ cup	Traditional Mayonnaise (page 100) or store-bought	60 mL
1 tbsp	balsamic vinegar	15 mL
1 tbsp	light olive oil	15 mL
1 tbsp	dried basil	15 mL
2 tsp	Dijon Mustard (page 112) or store-bought	10 mL
1 tsp	dried rosemary	5 mL
¼ cup	freshly grated Parmesan cheese	60 mL
¼ cup	freshly grated Romano cheese	60 mL

1. In a food processor fitted with a metal blade, process cream cheese, mayonnaise, vinegar, oil, basil, mustard and rosemary until smooth, about 2 minutes. Transfer to a bowl and fold in Parmesan and Romano cheeses.

Creamy Zesty Chipotle Dressing

Makes 1 cup (250 mL)

Be forewarned — this is a red-hot dressing. I like to use it for a bold flavor.

Tip

Depending on the brand, you may need to drain the yogurt to avoid a watery dressing.

- **Food processor**

4 oz	cream cheese, softened	125 g
½ cup	Traditional Mayonnaise (page 100) or store-bought	125 mL
¼ cup	plain yogurt (see Tip, left)	60 mL
½ tsp	hot pepper flakes	2 mL
½ tsp	dried onion flakes	2 mL
2	chipotle peppers in adobo sauce, drained	2
⅛ tsp	sea salt	0.5 mL
⅛ tsp	freshly ground black pepper	0.5 mL

1. In a food processor fitted with a metal blade, process cream cheese, mayonnaise, yogurt, hot pepper flakes, onion flakes, chipotle peppers, salt and black pepper until smooth, about 2 minutes.

Crushed Pecan Blue Cheese Dressing

Makes about 2 cups (500 mL)

Pecans are the perfect nuts to go with the blue cheese in this dressing.

Tip

If you process the blue cheese in the food processor instead of folding it into the dressing, it will be become an unattractive gray/blue color.

To toast pecans: Place nuts in a single layer on a baking sheet in a preheated 350°F (180°C) oven for 10 to 12 minutes for halves, 8 to 10 minutes for chopped, or until fragrant and golden, stirring once or twice.

- **Food processor**

4 oz	cream cheese, softened	125 g
½ cup	buttermilk	125 mL
¼ cup	Traditional Mayonnaise (page 100) or store-bought	60 mL
¼ cup	small-curd cottage cheese	60 mL
1 tsp	dried onion flakes	5 mL
½ tsp	garlic salt	2 mL
½ tsp	hot pepper sauce	2 mL
2 oz	blue cheese, crumbled (see Tips, left)	60 g
¼ cup	pecans, toasted and crushed (see Tips, left)	60 mL

1. In a food processor fitted with a metal blade, process cream cheese, buttermilk, mayonnaise, cottage cheese, onion flakes, garlic salt and hot pepper sauce until smooth, about 2 minutes. Transfer to a bowl and fold in blue cheese and pecans.

Cucumber Garlic Creamy Dressing

Makes 2 cups (500 mL)

Use this creamy dressing as a dip for radishes or any root vegetables.

• **Food processor**

1	cucumber, peeled, seeded and cut into 4 pieces	1
4 oz	cream cheese, softened	125 g
1/2 cup	canola oil	125 mL
1/2 cup	red wine vinegar	125 mL
1/3 cup	County Ketchup (page 107) or store-bought	75 mL
1/3 cup	granulated sugar	75 mL
2	cloves garlic, coarsely chopped	2
1 tsp	sea salt	5 mL
1/2 tsp	dried onion flakes	2 mL
1/4 tsp	celery seeds	1 mL
1/8 tsp	Hungarian paprika	0.5 mL

1. In a food processor fitted with a metal blade, process cucumber and cream cheese until smooth, about 2 minutes.

2. Add oil, vinegar, ketchup, sugar, garlic, salt, onion flakes, celery seeds and paprika and process until smooth, about 45 seconds.

Feta Cheese Dressing

Makes 1 1/2 cups (375 mL)

This fast and easy dressing has a zip of feta.

• **Food processor**

4 oz	cream cheese, softened	125 g
1/4 cup	balsamic vinegar	60 mL
1/4 cup	light olive oil	60 mL
2 tsp	Dijon Mustard (page 112) or store-bought	10 mL
1 tsp	dried rosemary	5 mL
4 oz	feta cheese, crumbled	125 g

1. In a food processor fitted with a metal blade, process cream cheese, vinegar, oil, mustard and rosemary until smooth, about 2 minutes. Transfer to a bowl and fold in feta.

French Honey Dressing

**Makes about
1¾ cups (425 mL)**

*Lavender makes this
dressing très French.*

• **Food processor**

¾ cup	extra virgin olive oil	175 mL
4 oz	cream cheese, softened	125 g
¼ cup	freshly squeezed lemon juice	60 mL
2 tbsp	Traditional Mayonnaise (page 100) or store-bought	30 mL
2 tbsp	liquid honey	30 mL
2	cloves garlic, coarsely chopped	2
2 tsp	Bold Chili Sauce (page 115) or store-bought	10 mL
1 tsp	sea salt	5 mL
½ tsp	dry mustard	2 mL
½ tsp	Hungarian paprika	2 mL
¼ tsp	freshly ground black pepper	1 mL
¼ tsp	dried lavender	1 mL
⅛ tsp	cayenne pepper	0.5 mL

1. In a food processor fitted with a metal blade, process oil, cream cheese, lemon juice, mayonnaise, honey, garlic, chili sauce, salt, dry mustard, paprika, pepper, lavender and cayenne until smooth, about 2 minutes.

Fresh Orange French Dressing

**Makes 1¾ cups
(425 mL)**

*This dressing will
make your taste
buds pop!*

¾ cup	olive oil	175 mL
½ cup	Traditional Mayonnaise (page 100) or store-bought	125 mL
¼ cup	freshly squeezed orange juice	60 mL
¼ cup	liquid honey	60 mL
3	cloves garlic minced	3
1 tsp	sea salt	5 mL
1 tsp	Hungarian paprika	5 mL
1 tsp	Bold or Spicy Chili Sauce (pages 115 and 117) or store-bought	5 mL
½ tsp	dry mustard	2 mL
¼ tsp	ground white pepper	1 mL

1. In a bowl, whisk together oil, mayonnaise, orange juice, honey, garlic, salt, paprika, chili sauce, dry mustard and white pepper.

Golden Honey Mustard Dressing

Makes 1¼ cups (300 mL)

So rich, this dressing is surprisingly quick and easy to make.

1 cup	Traditional Mayonnaise (page 100) or store-bought	250 mL
¼ cup	buttermilk	60 mL
2 tbsp	liquid honey	30 mL
1 tbsp	Honey Stone-Ground Mustard (page 113) or store-bought	15 mL
1 tsp	sea salt	5 mL

1. In a bowl, whisk together mayonnaise, buttermilk, honey, mustard and salt.

Green Goddess Dressing

Makes 2¼ cups (550 mL)

I've updated this dressing, which was all the rage in the 1960s.

2 cups	Traditional Mayonnaise (page 100) or store-bought	500 mL
4	anchovy fillets, minced	4
1	green onion, chopped	1
1 tbsp	chopped Italian flat-leaf parsley	15 mL
1 tbsp	tarragon vinegar	15 mL
2 tsp	chopped fresh chives	10 mL
1 tsp	chopped fresh tarragon	5 mL

1. In a bowl, blend together mayonnaise, anchovies, green onion, parsley, vinegar, chives and tarragon.

Lime Cilantro Cream Dressing

Makes 1¼ cups (300 mL)

This zippy lime dressing has a touch of cilantro.

- Food processor

4 oz	cream cheese, softened	125 g
¼ cup	buttermilk	60 mL
¼ cup	Traditional Mayonnaise (page 100) or store-bought	60 mL
¼ cup	plain yogurt (see Tip, page 70)	60 mL
½ tsp	grated lime zest	2 mL
¼ cup	freshly squeezed lime juice	60 mL
1 tsp	dried cilantro	5 mL
½ tsp	dried onion flakes	2 mL

1. In a food processor fitted with a metal blade, process cream cheese, buttermilk, mayonnaise, yogurt, lime zest and juice, cilantro, and onion flakes until smooth, about 2 minutes.

Louis Dressing

Makes ¾ cup (175 mL)

Since this dressing is so good as a dipping sauce for cooked shrimp, I've named it after Louis sauce, a traditional seafood sauce.

½ cup	Traditional Mayonnaise (page 100) or store-bought	125 mL
¼ cup	Bold Chili Sauce (page 115) or store-bought	60 mL
2	green onions, chopped	2
1	green chile pepper, minced	1

1. In a bowl, combine mayonnaise, chili sauce, green onions and chile pepper.

Louisiana French Dressing

Makes 2 cups
(500 mL)

Louisiana has strong French roots as you can taste in the flavors of many of its recipes, including this one.

- Food processor

1 cup	Traditional Mayonnaise (page 100) or store-bought	250 mL
¾ cup	extra virgin olive oil	175 mL
¼ cup	freshly squeezed lemon juice	60 mL
2	cloves garlic, coarsely chopped	2
2 tsp	Bold Chili Sauce (page 115) or store-bought	10 mL
1 tsp	sea salt	5 mL
1 tsp	Hungarian paprika	5 mL
½ tsp	dry mustard	2 mL
½ tsp	cayenne pepper	2 mL
¼ tsp	freshly ground black pepper	1 mL

1. In a food processor fitted with a metal blade, process mayonnaise, oil, lemon juice, garlic, chili sauce, salt, paprika, dry mustard, cayenne and black pepper until smooth, about 2 minutes.

Maple Balsamic Dressing

Makes 1 cup
(250 mL)

Maple syrup is a wonderful natural sweetener in dressings.

- Food processor

4 oz	cream cheese, softened	125 mL
¼ cup	balsamic vinegar	60 mL
¼ cup	light olive oil	60 mL
2 tbsp	pure maple syrup	30 mL
1 tbsp	dried basil	15 mL
1 tsp	dried rosemary	5 mL

1. In a food processor fitted with a metal blade, process cream cheese, vinegar, oil, maple syrup, basil and rosemary until smooth, about 2 minutes.

Marriott's Creamy Peppercorn Dressing

Makes 4 cups (1 L)

One of my first jobs was in the banquet kitchen of the Anaheim Marriott Hotel in California, where I learned so much about quality and production. This was my favorite dressing, which I enjoyed every day on my lunch salad. When I asked, the company was happy to share the recipe with you.

Tips

To make onion juice: In a food processor fitted with metal blade, process 1 sweet onion until puréed, about 2 minutes. Press the juice through a fine-mesh strainer, discarding the solids.

This dressing keeps well, covered and refrigerated, for up to 3 weeks.

Variation

Add 4 oz (125 g) blue cheese instead of the Parmesan cheese.

● **Food processor**

4 cups	Traditional Mayonnaise (page 100) or store-bought	1 L
¼ cup	onion juice (see Tips, left)	60 mL
1½ tbsp	apple cider vinegar	22 mL
1½ tbsp	whole black peppercorns	22 mL
1½ tsp	Worcestershire sauce	7 mL
1½ tsp	freshly squeezed lemon juice	7 mL
1 tsp	hot pepper sauce	5 mL
1	clove garlic, coarsely chopped	1
⅓ cup	freshly grated Parmesan cheese	75 mL

1. In a food processor fitted with a metal blade, process mayonnaise, onion juice, vinegar, peppercorns, Worcestershire sauce, lemon juice, hot pepper sauce and garlic until peppercorns are ground, for 45 seconds. Transfer to a bowl. Fold in Parmesan.

Oahu Dressing

**Makes about
1½ cups (375 mL)**

*I first had this
dressing in Oahu,
Hawaii on my first
visit to the islands.
Here it is for you.*

Tip

*To toast macadamia
nuts:* Place nuts in a
single layer on a baking
sheet in a preheated
350°F (180°C) oven for
10 to 12 minutes for
halves, 8 to 10 minutes
for chopped, or until
fragrant and golden,
stirring once or twice.

- **Food processor**

4 oz	cream cheese, softened	125 g
½ cup	plain yogurt (see Tip, page 70)	125 mL
2 tbsp	unsweetened pineapple juice	30 mL
2 tbsp	liquid honey	30 mL
½ cup	chopped macadamia nuts, toasted (see Tip, left)	125 mL
¼ cup	flaked sweetened coconut	60 mL

1. In a food processor fitted with a metal blade, process cream cheese, yogurt, pineapple juice and honey until smooth, about 2 minutes. Transfer to a bowl and fold in macadamia nuts and coconut.

Pecan Pesto Dressing

**Makes 1¾ cups
(425 mL)**

*Basil and pecans
come together to
make a very flavorful
dressing.*

- **Food processor**

½ cup	packed fresh basil	125 mL
2 tbsp	extra virgin olive oil	30 mL
4 oz	cream cheese, softened	125 g
½ cup	buttermilk	125 mL
¼ cup	Traditional Mayonnaise (page 100) or store-bought	60 mL
1 tsp	dried onion flakes	5 mL
½ tsp	garlic salt	2 mL
¼ cup	finely chopped pecans, toasted	60 mL

1. In a food processor fitted with a metal blade, pulse basil and oil about 10 times. Add cream cheese, buttermilk, mayonnaise, onion flakes and garlic salt and process until smooth, about 2 minutes. Transfer to a bowl and fold in pecans.

Ranch Dressing

Makes 1 cup (250 mL)

This is the best all-purpose creamy herb dressing to use with vegetables, chicken, and salads.

½ cup	buttermilk	125 mL
½ cup	sour cream	125 mL
1 tbsp	granulated sugar	15 mL
1½ tsp	dried bell peppers (see Tip, page 39)	7 mL
1 tsp	sea salt	5 mL
1 tsp	garlic salt	5 mL
1 tsp	dried onion flakes	5 mL
½ tsp	dried basil	2 mL
½ tsp	dried thyme	2 mL
½ tsp	dried parsley	2 mL
½ tsp	freshly ground black pepper	2 mL

1. In a bowl, whisk together buttermilk, sour cream, sugar, bell peppers, salt, garlic salt, onion flakes, basil, thyme, parsley and pepper until smooth.

Red French Tomato Dressing

Makes 1 cup (250 mL)

Paris has so many bistros. I had lunch one summer that served a zesty dressing like this one.

½ cup	Traditional Mayonnaise (page 100) or store-bought	125 mL
¼ cup	freshly squeezed lemon juice	60 mL
¼ cup	extra virgin olive oil	60 mL
2	cloves garlic, minced	2
2 tsp	Bold Chili Sauce (page 115) or store-bought	10 mL
1 tsp	sea salt	5 mL
1 tsp	dried tomato powder (see Tip, left)	5 mL
½ tsp	dry mustard	2 mL
½ tsp	Hungarian paprika	2 mL
¼ tsp	freshly ground black pepper	1 mL

1. In a bowl, whisk together mayonnaise, lemon juice, oil, garlic, chili sauce, salt, tomato powder, dry mustard, paprika and pepper.

Tip

Dried tomato powder is made of the sweetest red tomatoes, dried and ground into a fine powder. It adds a nice fresh tomato flavor without adding moisture to the dressing (see Sources, page 274).

Roasted Garlic Dressing

**Makes ¾ cup
(175 mL)**

*This dressing is
perfect for garlic
lovers.*

Tip

To roast garlic: Preheat
oven to 400°F (200°C).
Cut about ¼ inch
(0.5 cm) off the top of
the bulb and drizzle
with 1 tsp (5 mL)
olive oil. Wrap in foil
and roast until golden
brown and very soft,
30 to 35 minutes. Let
cool, turn upside down
and press cloves out
of bulb.

- **Food processor**

4 oz	cream cheese, softened	125 g
¼ cup	Traditional Mayonnaise (page 100) or store-bought	60 mL
8	cloves roasted garlic (see Tip, left)	8
½ tsp	Hungarian paprika	2 mL
½ tsp	sea salt	2 mL
¼ tsp	hot pepper flakes	1 mL

1. In a food processor fitted with a metal blade, process cream cheese, mayonnaise, garlic, paprika, salt and hot pepper flakes until smooth, about 2 minutes.

Roasted Honey Garlic Dressing

**Makes 1 cup
(250 mL)**

*This dressing is
one of my sister's
favorites.*

- **Food processor**

4 oz	cream cheese, softened	125 g
¼ cup	sour cream	60 mL
¼ cup	buttermilk	60 mL
8	cloves roasted garlic (see Tip, above)	8
2 tsp	liquid honey	10 mL
1 tsp	dried onion flakes	5 mL
½ tsp	sea salt	2 mL
¼ tsp	hot pepper flakes	1 mL

1. In a food processor fitted with a metal blade, process cream cheese, sour cream, buttermilk, garlic, honey, onion flakes, salt and hot pepper flakes until smooth, about 2 minutes.

Roquefort Dressing

Makes 1 cup (250 mL)

The blue cheese for this dressing is cured in the caves of Roquefort, France.

½ cup	Traditional Mayonnaise (page 100) or store-bought	125 mL
¼ cup	buttermilk	60 mL
1½ tsp	Worcestershire sauce	7 mL
¼ tsp	garlic powder	1 mL
2 oz	Roquefort cheese, crumbled	60 g

1. In a bowl, whisk together mayonnaise, buttermilk, Worcestershire sauce and garlic powder until smooth. Fold in Roquefort.

Sesame Ginger Dressing

Makes ¾ cup (175 mL)

If you're having Chinese food, serve a salad with this dressing.

½ cup	Traditional Mayonnaise (page 100) or store-bought	125 mL
¼ cup	buttermilk	60 mL
1½ tsp	liquid honey	7 mL
2 tsp	Worcestershire sauce	10 mL
1 tsp	freshly grated gingerroot	5 mL
1 tsp	sesame seeds	5 mL
¼ tsp	garlic powder	1 mL

1. In a bowl, whisk together mayonnaise, buttermilk, honey, Worcestershire sauce, ginger, sesame seeds and garlic powder until smooth.

Spicy Hot Love Dressing

Makes 1½ cups (375 mL)

This dressing is so simple, you're fated to fall for it.

1 cup	Traditional Mayonnaise (page 100) or store-bought	250 mL
¼ cup	sour cream	60 mL
¼ cup	plain yogurt (see Tip, page 70)	60 mL
1 tsp	hot pepper flakes	5 mL
½ tsp	cayenne pepper	2 mL

1. In a bowl, combine mayonnaise, sour cream, yogurt, hot pepper flakes and cayenne.

Tarragon Cream Dressing

**Makes 1 cup
(250 mL)**

*Toss this dressing
with romaine leaves
then top it all with
chopped red onions.*

Tip

Depending on the
brand, you may need
to drain the yogurt to
avoid a watery dressing.

½ cup	Traditional Mayonnaise (page 100) or store-bought	125 mL
¼ cup	plain yogurt (see Tip, left)	60 mL
¼ cup	buttermilk	60 mL
1 tbsp	dried tarragon	15 mL
2 tsp	reduced-sodium soy sauce	10 mL
¼ tsp	garlic powder	1 mL

1. In a bowl, whisk together mayonnaise, yogurt, buttermilk, tarragon, soy sauce and garlic powder until smooth.

Thousand Island Dressing

**Makes 1¾ cups
(425 mL)**

*This is the "secret
sauce" that's
found on fast food
hamburgers.*

- **Food processor**

1	hard-boiled egg (see Tips, page 138)	1
1 cup	Traditional Mayonnaise (page 100) or store-bought	250 mL
¼ cup	Bold Chili Sauce (page 115) or store-bought	60 mL
¼ cup	pimento-stuffed olives	60 mL
1	sweet pickle, cut in half	1
1½ tsp	dried onion flakes	7 mL
1½ tsp	freshly squeezed lemon juice	7 mL
1 tsp	dried parsley	5 mL
⅛ tsp	sea salt	0.5 mL
⅛ tsp	freshly ground black pepper	0.5 mL

1. In a food processor bowl fitted with a metal blade, pulse egg, mayonnaise, chili sauce, olives, pickle, onion flakes, lemon juice, parsley, salt and pepper until desired texture. For a chunky dressing, pulse about 10 times; for a smooth dressing, process for about 1 minute. Refrigerate for at least 1 hour to allow the flavors to develop.

Tomato Basil Dressing

**Makes ¹⁄₂ cup
(125 mL)**

*When serving
an Italian pasta
dish, toss the
accompanying salad
with this dressing.*

- **Food processor**

4 oz	cream cheese, softened	125 g
2 tbsp	Traditional Mayonnaise (page 100) or store-bought	30 mL
2	cloves garlic, coarsely chopped	2
2 tsp	Bold Chili Sauce (page 115) or store-bought	10 mL
1 tsp	sea salt	5 mL
1 tsp	dried tomato powder (see Tip, page 84)	5 mL
1 tsp	dried basil	5 mL
¹⁄₂ tsp	Hungarian paprika	2 ml
¹⁄₄ tsp	freshly ground black pepper	1 mL

1. In a food processor fitted with a metal blade, process cream cheese, mayonnaise, garlic, chili sauce, salt, tomato powder, basil, paprika and pepper until smooth, about 2 minutes.

Wasabi Sour Cream Dressing

**Makes ³⁄₄ cup
(175 mL)**

*Use this dressing
with grated
cabbages and
carrots.*

¹⁄₂ cup	Traditional Mayonnaise (page 100) or store-bought	125 mL
¹⁄₄ cup	sour cream	60 mL
1¹⁄₂ tsp	liquid honey	7 mL
1 tsp	Worcestershire sauce	5 mL
¹⁄₄ tsp	wasabi powder	1 mL

1. In a bowl, whisk together mayonnaise, sour cream, honey, Worcestershire sauce and wasabi powder.

Zesty Tomato Onion Dressing

Makes ½ cup (125 mL)

Hearty dishes are complemented by this zesty dressing.

Tip

Dried tomato powder is made of the sweetest red tomatoes, dried and ground into a fine powder. It adds a nice fresh tomato flavor without adding moisture to the dressing (see Sources, page 274).

- **Food processor**

4 oz	cream cheese, softened	125 g
2 tbsp	Traditional Mayonnaise (page 100) or store-bought	30 mL
2	cloves garlic, coarsely chopped	2
1 tbsp	dried onion flakes	15 mL
2 tsp	Spicy Chili Sauce (page 117) or store-bought	10 mL
1 tsp	sea salt	5 mL
1 tsp	dried tomato powder (see Tip, left)	5 mL
½ tsp	Hungarian paprika	2 mL
¼ tsp	freshly ground black pepper	1 mL

1. In a food processor fitted with a metal blade, process cream cheese, mayonnaise, garlic, onion flakes, chili sauce, salt, tomato powder, paprika and pepper until smooth, about 2 minutes.

Lower-Fat Dressings

"Lower fat" does not need to mean less flavor. I think salads are one of the easiest dishes in which you can achieve optimal flavor with lower-fat ingredients. Use a tasty lower-fat dressing and watch what you top your salads with. Try carrot shavings, instead of grated cheeses, and a few toasted nuts in place of croutons.

Balsamic Vinaigrette

Makes 1 cup (250 mL)

Here's a light and easy vinaigrette.

½ cup	balsamic vinegar	125 mL
3 tbsp	Low-Fat No-Egg Mayonnaise (page 105) or store-bought	45 mL
3 tbsp	hot water	45 mL
3 tbsp	freshly squeezed orange juice	45 mL
¼ tsp	dried basil	1 mL
¼ tsp	dried oregano	1 mL
¼ tsp	sea salt	1 mL
¼ tsp	granulated sugar	1 mL

1. In a bowl, whisk together vinegar, mayonnaise, hot water, orange juice, basil, oregano, salt and sugar. Refrigerate in a sealed container for 2 hours prior to serving.

Buttermilk Dressing

Makes ¾ cup (175 mL)

Here's a lighter version of the popular dressing.

½ cup	buttermilk	125 mL
¼ cup	Low-Fat No-Egg Mayonnaise (page 105) or store-bought	60 mL
1 tbsp	white wine vinegar	15 mL
2 tsp	Dijon Mustard (page 112) or store-bought	10 mL
1 tsp	chopped fresh chives	5 mL
1	clove garlic, minced	1
½ tsp	granulated sugar	2 mL
¼ tsp	sea salt	1 mL
¼ tsp	freshly ground black pepper	1 mL

1. In a bowl, whisk together buttermilk, mayonnaise, vinegar, mustard, chives, garlic, sugar, salt and pepper until blended.

Chile and Lime Dressing

Makes 1 cup (250 mL)

Try this dressing as a dip with baked corn chips.

1	can (4½ oz/127 mL) chopped green chiles, drained	1
¼ cup	chopped fresh cilantro	60 mL
1 tsp	grated lime zest	5 mL
¼ cup	freshly squeezed lime juice	60 mL
¼ cup	hot water	60 mL
2	cloves garlic, minced	2
2 tsp	liquid honey	10 mL
1 tsp	freshly ground black pepper	5 mL

1. In a bowl, whisk together chiles, cilantro, lime zest and juice, hot water, garlic, honey and pepper until blended. Refrigerate in a sealed container for 2 hours prior to use.

Citrus Vinaigrette

Makes ½ cup (125 mL)

Drizzle this vinaigrette on freshly sliced pears.

¼ cup	white wine vinegar	60 mL
1 tbsp	grated lemon zest	15 mL
2 tbsp	freshly squeezed lemon juice	30 mL
2 tbsp	freshly squeezed orange juice	30 mL
1 tbsp	canola oil	15 mL
1	clove garlic, minced	1
½ tsp	Dijon Mustard (page 112) or store-bought	2 mL
⅛ tsp	garlic salt	0.5 mL
⅛ tsp	freshly ground black pepper	0.5 mL

1. In a bowl, whisk together vinegar, lemon zest and juice, orange juice, oil, garlic, mustard, garlic salt and pepper until blended.

Creamy Herb Dressing

Makes 2¼ cups (550 mL)

Here's a thick dressing with a light pink color.

Tip

Make sure you drain the cottage cheese or you will have a watery dressing.

- **Food processor**

1	red bell pepper, seeded and chopped	1
2 cups	nonfat cottage cheese, drained (see Tip, left)	500 mL
¼ cup	fresh basil	60 mL
3	cloves garlic, coarsely chopped	3
1 tbsp	freshly squeezed lemon juice	15 mL
1 tbsp	chopped fresh chives	15 mL
½ tsp	sea salt	2 mL
¼ tsp	freshly ground black pepper	1 mL

1. In a food processor fitted with a metal blade, process bell pepper, cottage cheese, basil, garlic, lemon juice, chives, salt and pepper until smooth.

Creamy Yogurt Herb Dressing

Makes ½ cup (125 mL)

The plum sauce adds a hint of sweetness.

Tip
Make sure you drain the yogurt or you will have a watery dressing.

Variation
Replace the plum sauce with strawberry jam.

½ cup	plain nonfat yogurt (see Tip, left)	125 mL
1 tbsp	balsamic vinegar	15 mL
1 tsp	plum sauce	5 mL
½ tsp	onion powder	2 mL
¼ tsp	dried tarragon	1 mL
¼ tsp	dried Italian seasoning	1 mL
⅛ tsp	sea salt	0.5 mL

1. In a bowl, whisk together yogurt, vinegar, plum sauce, onion powder, tarragon, Italian seasoning and salt until blended. Refrigerate in a sealed container for 2 hours prior to use.

Cucumber Dressing

Makes ½ cup (125 mL)

Napa cabbage perfectly suits this dressing.

- **Food processor**

1 cup	plain nonfat yogurt (see Tip, above)	250 mL
½	cucumber, peeled, seeded and cut into chunks	½
1 tsp	freshly squeezed lemon juice	5 mL
1 tsp	fresh dill	5 mL
1	clove garlic	1
½ tsp	sea salt	2 mL
½ tsp	ground white pepper	2 mL

1. In a food processor fitted with a metal blade, process yogurt, cucumber, lemon juice, dill, garlic, salt and white pepper until smooth, about 1 minute.

Fat-Free Honey Dijon Dressing

¼ cup	Dijon Mustard (page 112) or store-bought	60 mL
¼ cup	white wine vinegar	60 mL
5 tbsp	liquid honey	75 mL
2 tbsp	instant skim milk powder	30 mL
1 tsp	onion powder	5 mL
½ tsp	dry mustard	2 mL

1. In a bowl, whisk together mustard, vinegar, honey, milk powder, onion powder and dry mustard until blended. Refrigerate in a sealed container for 2 hours prior to use.

Fat-Free Zesty Herb Dressing

⅔ cup	hot water	150 mL
¼ cup	white wine vinegar	60 mL
1 tbsp	chopped fresh dill	15 mL
1 tsp	granulated sugar	5 mL
¼ tsp	garlic powder	1 mL
¼ tsp	dry mustard	1 mL
¼ tsp	freshly ground black pepper	1 mL

1. In a bowl, whisk together hot water, vinegar, dill, sugar, garlic powder, dry mustard and pepper until blended. Refrigerate in a sealed container for 2 hours prior to use.

Garlic Caesar Dressing

Makes ¼ cup (60 mL)

Here's a lower-fat version for Caesar salads.

5	cloves garlic, finely minced	5
1 tbsp	freshly squeezed lemon juice	15 mL
2 tsp	balsamic vinegar	10 mL
1 tsp	red wine vinegar	5 mL
1 tsp	warm water	5 mL
½ tsp	dry mustard	2 mL
2	drops hot pepper sauce	2

1. In a bowl, combine garlic, lemon juice, balsamic and red wine vinegars, warm water, dry mustard and hot pepper sauce until blended.

Honey Basil Vinaigrette

Makes ½ cup (125 mL)

Make this speedy dressing with a few simple ingredients.

¼ cup	balsamic vinegar	60 mL
2 tbsp	liquid honey	30 mL
¼ tsp	dried basil	1 mL
¼ tsp	dried oregano	1 mL
¼ tsp	sea salt	1 mL
¼ tsp	freshly ground black pepper	1 mL

1. In a bowl, whisk together vinegar, honey, basil, oregano, salt and pepper until smooth. Refrigerate in a sealed container for 2 hours prior to use.

Honey Mustard Dressing

¼ cup	Dijon Mustard (page 112) or store-bought	60 mL
¼ cup	liquid honey	60 mL
¼ cup	white wine vinegar	60 mL
2 tbsp	instant skim milk powder	30 mL
1 tsp	onion powder	5 mL
½ tsp	dry mustard	2 mL
¼ cup	canola oil	60 mL

1. In a bowl, whisk together mustard, honey, vinegar, milk powder, onion powder and dry mustard. While vigorously whisking, pour in oil in a thin steady stream until smooth.

Lemon Herb Dressing

¼ cup	white wine vinegar	60 mL
1 tbsp	grated lemon zest	15 mL
3 tbsp	freshly squeezed lemon juice	45 mL
2	cloves garlic, minced	2
1 tsp	chopped fresh tarragon	5 mL
1 tsp	chopped fresh rosemary	5 mL
½ tsp	Dijon Mustard (page 112) or store-bought	2 mL
⅛ tsp	garlic salt	0.5 mL
⅛ tsp	freshly ground black pepper	0.5 mL

1. In a bowl, whisk together vinegar, lemon zest and juice, garlic, tarragon, rosemary, mustard, garlic salt and pepper until blended.

Lemon Yogurt Dressing

Tip

To make yogurt cheese: Place 3 cups (750 mL) plain nonfat yogurt in a cheesecloth-lined sieve set over a bowl. Place in the refrigerator and let it drain overnight (discard the liquid).

1½ cups	yogurt cheese (see Tip, left)	375 mL
1 cup	buttermilk	250 mL
2 tbsp	white wine vinegar	30 mL
2	cloves garlic, minced	2
1 tsp	dried dill	5 mL
1 tsp	grated lemon zest	5 mL
⅛ tsp	sea salt	0.5 mL
⅛ tsp	freshly ground black pepper	0.5 mL

1. In a bowl, whisk together yogurt cheese, buttermilk, vinegar, garlic, dill, lemon zest, salt and pepper until blended.

Low-Fat Blue Cheese Dressing

Variation

Use any feta or Gorgonzola instead of the blue cheese.

1⅓ cups	1% milk	325 mL
1 tsp	apple cider vinegar	5 mL
⅓ cup	Low-Fat No-Egg Mayonnaise (page 105) or store-bought	75 mL
⅓ cup	plain nonfat yogurt	75 mL
1 tsp	white wine vinegar	5 mL
1 tsp	Dijon Mustard (page 112) or store-bought	5 mL
½ tsp	dried parsley	2 mL
¼ tsp	dried tarragon	1 mL
¼ tsp	sea salt	1 mL
¼ tsp	freshly ground black pepper	1 mL
¼ tsp	granulated sugar	1 mL
⅛ tsp	garlic powder	0.5 mL
4 oz	blue cheese, crumbled	125 g

1. In a bowl, combine milk and cider vinegar. Let stand until thickened, about 2 minutes. Whisk in mayonnaise, yogurt, white wine vinegar, mustard, parsley, tarragon, salt, pepper, sugar and garlic powder. Toss in blue cheese. Refrigerate in a sealed container for 2 hours prior to use.

Low-Fat Paris Dressing

Makes ¼ cup (60 mL)

Here's a perfect light dressing for a bed of endive.

2 tbsp	freshly squeezed lemon juice	30 mL
2 tsp	white wine vinegar	10 mL
¼ tsp	sea salt	1 mL
¼ tsp	granulated sugar	1 mL
⅛ tsp	mild dry mustard	0.5 mL
⅛ tsp	freshly ground black pepper	0.5 mL
1 tbsp	olive oil	15 mL

1. In a bowl, whisk together lemon juice, vinegar, salt, sugar, dry mustard and pepper. While whisking, pour in oil in a thin steady stream until smooth.

Miso Dressing

Makes 1 cup (250 mL)

A bowl of miso soup begins the day in Japan, then reappears in soups, sauces and marinades, and as an energizing afternoon beverage. Derived from fermented soybeans, miso is very nutritious. Try this dressing over chopped napa cabbage.

⅓ cup	white miso	75 mL
⅓ cup	natural rice vinegar (see Tip, page 52)	75 mL
⅓ cup	granulated sugar	75 mL
3 tbsp	dry mustard	45 mL
1 tsp	freshly squeezed lemon juice	5 mL

1. In a bowl, whisk together miso, vinegar, sugar, dry mustard and lemon juice until blended.

Olive Vinaigrette

Makes ⅓ cup (75 mL)

Here's a perfect vinaigrette to try on Greek salads.

¼ cup	balsamic vinegar	60 mL
3 tbsp	pitted and finely chopped niçoise olives	45 mL
1 tbsp	liquid honey	15 mL
1½ tsp	prepared mustard	7 mL
1 tsp	finely chopped fresh cilantro	5 mL
1 tsp	finely·chopped shallots	5 mL

1. In a bowl, whisk together vinegar, olives, honey, mustard, cilantro and shallots until blended.

Parmesan Dressing

Makes 2 cups (500 mL)

This dressing may be lower in fat but it's got lots of flavor.

Tip
Make sure you drain the yogurt or you will have a watery dressing.

1⅓ cups	1% milk	325 mL
1 tsp	apple cider vinegar	5 mL
⅓ cup	Low-Fat No-Egg Mayonnaise (page 105) or store-bought	75 mL
⅓ cup	plain nonfat yogurt (see Tip, left)	75 mL
¼ tsp	white wine vinegar	1 mL
1 tsp	Dijon Mustard (page 112) or store-bought	5 mL
½ tsp	dried parsley	2 mL
¼ tsp	sea salt	1 mL
¼ tsp	freshly ground black pepper	1 mL
¼ tsp	granulated sugar	1 mL
⅛ tsp	garlic powder	0.5 mL
¾ cup	freshly grated Parmesan cheese (about 3 oz/90 g)	175 mL

1. In a bowl, whisk together milk and cider vinegar. Let stand until thickened, about 2 minutes. Whisk in mayonnaise, yogurt, white wine vinegar, mustard, parsley, salt, pepper, sugar and garlic powder. Toss in Parmesan. Refrigerate in a sealed container for 2 hours prior to use.

Peppercorn Dressing

Makes ⅔ cup (150 mL)

You can also use this dressing as a low-cal dipping sauce for celery or vegetables.

• **Food processor**

⅓ cup	Low-Fat No-Egg Mayonnaise (page 105) or store-bought	75 mL
⅓ cup	plain nonfat yogurt (see Tip, page 94)	75 mL
2 tbsp	white wine vinegar	30 mL
1 tsp	whole black peppercorns	5 mL
½ tsp	dried parsley	2 mL
¼ tsp	dried tarragon	1 mL
¼ tsp	sea salt	1 mL
¼ tsp	freshly ground black pepper	1 mL
¼ tsp	granulated sugar	1 mL
⅛ tsp	garlic powder	0.5 mL

1. In a food processor fitted with a metal blade, process mayonnaise, yogurt, vinegar, peppercorns, parsley, tarragon, salt, pepper, sugar and garlic powder until smooth, about 2 minutes. Refrigerate in a sealed container for 2 hours prior to use.

Ranch Buttermilk Dressing

Makes 2 cups (500 mL)

Here's a flavorful lower calorie version of this popular dressing.

1⅓ cups	nonfat milk	325 mL
2 tsp	apple cider vinegar	10 mL
⅔ cup	Low-Fat No-Egg Mayonnaise (page 105) or store-bought	150 mL
4 tsp	white wine vinegar	20 mL
1 tsp	Dijon Mustard (page 112) or store-bought	5 mL
¾ tsp	dried dill	3 mL
½ tsp	dried parsley	2 mL
½ tsp	minced dried garlic	2 mL
¼ tsp	sea salt	1 mL
¼ tsp	freshly ground black pepper	1 mL
¼ tsp	granulated sugar	1 mL

1. In a bowl, combine milk and cider vinegar. Let stand until thickened, about 3 minutes. Whisk in mayonnaise, white wine vinegar, mustard, dill, parsley, garlic, salt, pepper and sugar until smooth.

Raspberry Yogurt Dressing

**Makes 1 cup
(250 mL)**

*Dip fresh berries into
this yogurt dressing
for a sweet treat.*

Tip
Make sure you drain
the yogurt or you will
have a watery dressing.

1 cup	raspberry-flavored nonfat yogurt (see Tip, left)	250 mL
2 tbsp	white wine vinegar	30 mL
2	cloves garlic, minced	2
1 tsp	dried tarragon	5 mL
1/8 tsp	sea salt	0.5 mL
1/8 tsp	freshly ground black pepper	0.5 mL

1. In a bowl, whisk together yogurt, vinegar, garlic, tarragon, salt and pepper until blended.

Sesame Orange Dressing

**Makes 1 cup
(250 mL)**

*Serve this dressing
with shredded
cabbage and orange
segments.*

Tip
Natural rice vinegar,
also called unseasoned
rice vinegar, has no
added sugar or salt,
and I prefer it over the
seasoned variety.

1/3 cup	warm water	75 mL
1/4 cup	natural rice vinegar (see Tip, left)	60 mL
1/4 cup	sesame oil	60 mL
2 tsp	freshly squeezed orange juice	10 mL
1 tsp	apple juice concentrate	5 mL
1 tsp	reduced-sodium soy sauce	5 mL
1 1/2 tsp	Dijon Mustard (page 112) or store-bought	7 mL
1/4 tsp	garlic powder	1 mL
1/4 tsp	onion powder	1 mL
1/8 tsp	cayenne pepper	0.5 mL

1. In a bowl, combine warm water, vinegar, sesame oil, orange juice, apple juice concentrate, soy sauce, mustard, garlic powder, onion powder and cayenne pepper until blended.

Lemon Dijon Vinaigrette (page 42), Pomegranate Vinaigrette (page 46) and Orange Cinnamon Vinaigrette (page 45) *(clockwise from front)*

Grapefruit Radicchio Salad (page 122)

Spinach and Avocado Salad (page 125)

Salad Niçoise (page 150)

Fresh Vegetable Pasta Salad (page 154)

Sesame Noodle Salad (page 162)

Tabbouleh with Tomatoes and Dried Fruit Salad (page 181)

Pepper Bean Salad (page 195)

Shallot Dressing

Makes 1¼ cups (300 mL)

A light drizzle of this dressing is perfect for butterhead lettuce.

⅔ cup	warm water	150 mL
1 tsp	arrowroot powder	5 mL
1 tbsp	Dijon Mustard (page 112) or store-bought	15 mL
¼ cup	minced shallots	60 mL
¼ cup	sherry wine vinegar	60 mL

1. In a bowl, whisk together warm water and arrowroot powder until smooth. Whisk in mustard, shallots and vinegar.

Tarragon Buttermilk Dressing

Makes ⅔ cup (150 mL)

This dressing is so good, you'll think you're eating a rich full calorie dressing.

⅓ cup	Low-Fat No-Egg Mayonnaise (page 105) or store-bought	75 mL
⅓ cup	buttermilk	75 mL
1 tsp	Dijon Mustard (page 112) or store-bought	5 mL
1 tsp	dried tarragon	5 mL
¼ tsp	sea salt	1 mL
¼ tsp	freshly ground black pepper	1 mL
⅛ tsp	garlic powder	0.5 mL

1. In a bowl, whisk together mayonnaise, buttermilk, mustard, tarragon, salt, pepper and garlic powder. Refrigerate in a sealed container for 2 hours prior to use.

Tomato Vinaigrette

Makes 1 cup (250 mL)

I like to pour this vinaigrette over cooked asparagus.

2	Roma (plum) tomatoes, seeded and diced	2
2 tbsp	white wine vinegar	30 mL
½ tsp	dried basil	2 mL
½ tsp	dried thyme	2 mL
½ tsp	Dijon Mustard (page 112) or store-bought	2 mL

1. In a saucepan over low heat, bring tomatoes, vinegar, basil, thyme and mustard to a light boil, stirring, about 4 minutes. Use vinaigrette warm or cool.

Yogurt Dressing

Makes 2½ cups (625 mL)

I like using this dressing on Greek salads or in lamb sandwiches.

Tip

To make yogurt cheese: Place 3 cups (750 mL) plain nonfat yogurt in a cheesecloth-lined sieve set over a bowl. Place in the refrigerator and let it drain overnight (discard the liquid).

1½ cups	yogurt cheese (see Tip, left)	375 mL
1 cup	buttermilk	250 mL
2 tbsp	white wine vinegar	30 mL
2	cloves garlic, minced	2
1 tsp	dried dill	5 mL
⅛ tsp	sea salt	0.5 mL
⅛ tsp	freshly ground black pepper	0.5 mL

1. In a bowl, combine yogurt cheese, buttermilk, vinegar, garlic, dill, salt and pepper until blended.

Zesty Oil-Free Dressing

Makes ¾ cup (175 mL)

Use this dressing on salads, or drizzle it on sandwiches for lower-calorie subs.

¼ cup	freshly squeezed lemon juice	60 mL
¼ cup	apple cider vinegar	60 mL
¼ cup	unsweetened apple juice	60 mL
½ tsp	dried oregano	2 mL
½ tsp	dry mustard	2 mL
½ tsp	onion powder	2 mL
½ tsp	dried basil	2 mL
⅛ tsp	dried thyme	0.5 mL
⅛ tsp	dried rosemary	0.5 mL

1. In a bowl, whisk together lemon juice, vinegar, apple juice, oregano, dry mustard, onion powder, basil, thyme and rosemary until smooth.

Condiments

Mayonnaises

You can walk down the condiment aisle at the grocery store and see many brands and varieties, in jar after jar. I can't even pronounce many of the ingredients in these jars, let alone understand how they can last for months — or years — in the refrigerator. When you make your own condiments you know exactly what's in each, and how long it will last. Once you make mayonnaise, you will never purchase it again.

Traditional Mayonnaise

Makes 1 cup (250 mL)

If you've never tasted fresh homemade mayonnaise you are in for a treat. Fresh mayonnaise is so silky and nothing like its stepsister in the jar.

Tip
If egg yolks are not processed for the full 2 minutes, they will not emulsify correctly when the oil is incorporated.

Variation
Try flavored oils in place of the plain vegetable oil to enhance your dishes.

● **Food Processor**

2	egg yolks, at room temperature, or ¼ cup (60 mL) pasteurized eggs (liquid or in the shell) (see Tips, page 101)	2
2 tbsp	white wine vinegar	30 mL
1 tsp	dry mustard	5 mL
1 tsp	sea salt	5 mL
1 tsp	granulated sugar	5 mL
½ tsp	ground white pepper	2 mL
1 cup	vegetable oil	250 mL

1. In a food processor fitted with a metal blade, process egg yolks, vinegar, dry mustard, salt, sugar and white pepper until smooth, for 2 minutes (see Tip, left). With the processor running, slowly drizzle oil through the small hole in the feed tube until it has been incorporated into the mayonnaise (see Tips, page 102).

2. When all the oil is drizzled into egg mixture, remove processor lid and, with a rubber spatula, scrape down the sides and bottom, which sometimes collect residue, as necessary, to incorporate all of the mixture. Replace lid and process for about 15 seconds.

Cajun Mayonnaise

Tips

This recipe contains
raw egg yolks. If you
are concerned about
the safety of using raw
eggs, use pasteurized
eggs in the shell or
pasteurized liquid
whole eggs, instead.

Mayonnaise keeps
well, covered and
refrigerated, for up
to 5 days. If using
pasteurized eggs, it
will keep for up to
2 weeks.

- **Blender**

½ cup	green onions, finely chopped	125 mL
2	egg yolks, at room temperature, or ¼ cup (60 mL) pasteurized eggs (liquid or in the shell) (see Tips, left)	2
1 tbsp	freshly squeezed lemon juice	15 mL
1 tsp	sea salt	5 mL
1	clove garlic, minced	1
⅛ tsp	hot pepper sauce	0.5 mL
1 cup	vegetable oil	250 mL

1. In a blender, combine green onions, egg yolks, lemon juice, salt, garlic and hot pepper sauce. Blend for 2 minutes (see Tip, page 100). With the motor running, slowly drizzle oil through the small hole in the feed tube until it has been incorporated into the mayonnaise (see Tips, page 102).

2. When all the oil is drizzled into egg mixture, remove processor lid and, with a rubber spatula, scrape down the sides and bottom, which sometimes collect residue, as necessary to incorporate all of the mixture. Replace lid and blend for about 30 seconds.

Fresh Dill Mayonnaise

Tips

Mayonnaise keeps well, covered and refrigerated, for up to 5 days. If using pasteurized eggs, it will keep for up to 1 week.

I do not advise making a double batch of this mayonnaise unless you use it within a week, since the dill will turn dark after that.

If your food processor has a feed tube with the drip feature (a small hole in the bottom of the tube), fill the tube with oil and let it drizzle in, refilling the tube with oil as it drains until all of the oil is incorporated. Alternatively, pour a thin, steady stream of oil slowly into the feed tube. Adding the oil too quickly can cause the mayonnaise to separate.

Variation

Try the same amount of rosemary in place of the dill.

- **Food Processor**

3	egg yolks, at room temperature, or ⅓ cup (75 mL) pasteurized eggs (liquid or in the shell) (see Tips, page 101)	3
3 tbsp	sherry wine vinegar	45 mL
2 tsp	mustard seeds	10 mL
2 tsp	sea salt	10 mL
1½ tsp	granulated sugar	7 mL
1 tsp	ground white pepper	5 mL
1 cup	peanut oil	250 mL
2 tbsp	loosely packed fresh dill	30 mL

1. In a food processor fitted with a metal blade, process egg yolks, vinegar, mustard seeds, salt, sugar and white pepper until smooth, for 2 minutes (see Tips, page 103). With the motor running, slowly drizzle oil through the small hole in the feed tube until it has been incorporated into the mayonnaise (see Tips, left).

2. When all the oil is drizzled into egg mixture, remove processor lid and, with a rubber spatula, scrape down the sides and bottom, which sometimes collect residue, as necessary to incorporate all of the mixture. Add dill. Replace lid and process for about 15 seconds.

Chipotle Mayonnaise

Makes 1 cup (250 mL)

A dollop of this tasty mayonnaise on the side of any meat dish will enhance the flavor.

Tips

If egg yolks are not processed for the full 2 minutes they will not emulsify correctly when the oil is incorporated.

Mayonnaise keeps well, covered and refrigerated, for up to 5 days. If using pasteurized eggs, it will keep for up to 2 weeks.

If you have any of the adobo sauce left from the chiles you can fold it into the mayonnaise to make a great dip for chips.

Variation

You can add $\frac{1}{8}$ tsp (0.5 mL) cayenne pepper for more heat.

- **Food processor**

2	egg yolks, at room temperature, or $\frac{1}{4}$ cup (60 mL) pasteurized eggs (liquid or in the shell) (see Tips, page 101)	2
2 tbsp	white wine vinegar	30 mL
1 tsp	dry mustard	5 mL
1 tsp	sea salt	5 mL
1 tsp	granulated sugar	5 mL
$\frac{1}{2}$ tsp	ground white pepper	2 mL
$\frac{1}{4}$ tsp	ground nutmeg	1 mL
$\frac{3}{4}$ cup	vegetable oil	175 mL
2	chipotle peppers in adobo sauce, drained and seeded	2

1. In a food processor fitted with a metal blade, process egg yolks, vinegar, dry mustard, salt, sugar, white pepper and nutmeg until smooth, for 2 minutes (see Tips, left). With the motor running, slowly drizzle oil through the small hole in the feed tube until it has been incorporated into the mayonnaise (see Tips, page 102).

2. When all the oil is drizzled into egg mixture, remove processor lid and, with a rubber spatula, scrape down the sides and bottom, which sometimes collect residue, as necessary to incorporate all of the mixture. Add chipotle peppers. Replace lid and process for about 10 seconds.

No-Egg Mayonnaise

Makes 1⅓ cups (325 mL)

This is a perfect creamy mayonnaise when you can't have eggs.

Tip

Mayonnaise keeps well, covered and refrigerated, for up to 5 days.

- **Blender**

½ cup	soft tofu, drained	125 mL
2 tbsp	white wine vinegar	30 mL
½ tsp	dry mustard	2 mL
½ tsp	mustard seeds	2 mL
½ tsp	sea salt	2 mL
¾ cup	vegetable oil, divided	175 mL

1. In a blender, combine tofu, vinegar, dry mustard, mustard seeds, salt and ¼ cup (60 mL) of the vegetable oil. Blend for 2 minutes.

2. With the blender running, slowly drizzle remaining ½ cup (125 mL) of oil in a very thin stream through the hole in the lid until it has been incorporated into the mayonnaise (see Tips, page 102).

Avocado Mayonnaise

Makes 1 cup (250 mL)

Here's another no-egg mayonnaise that I also like to use as a spread.

Tip

To determine if your avocado is ripe: Hold it in the palm of your hand and press. The avocado should feel like a tomato that has a little "give."

- **Food processor**

1	ripe avocado, cut into quarters (see Tip, left)	1
2 tbsp	freshly squeezed lime juice	30 mL
2 tbsp	chopped fresh cilantro	30 mL
¼ tsp	sea salt	1 mL
¼ tsp	freshly ground black pepper	1 mL
2 tbsp	extra virgin olive oil	30 mL

1. In a food processor fitted with a metal blade, process avocado, lime juice, cilantro, salt and pepper until smooth.

2. With the motor running, slowly drizzle oil through the small hole in the feed tube until it has been incorporated into mayonnaise (se Tips, page 102). Use within a few hours.

Low-Fat No-Egg Mayonnaise

*When you need to
make a low-fat and
no-egg mayonnaise
for dressings, you
won't get much
better than this.*

Tip
Mayonnaise keeps
well, covered and
refrigerated, for up
to 1 week.

Variation
Add 1 tsp (5 mL)
Spicy Chili Sauce
(page 117) to make a
spicy mayonnaise.

1 cup	cold water	250 mL
1 tbsp	cornstarch	15 mL
2 tbsp	extra virgin olive oil	30 mL
2 tbsp	white wine vinegar	30 mL
2 tbsp	plain nonfat yogurt	30 mL
1 tsp	Dijon Mustard (page 112) or store-bought	5 mL
$\frac{1}{2}$ tsp	prepared horseradish	2 mL

1. In a small saucepan over medium heat, whisk together cold water and cornstarch. Whisk continuously until mixture comes to a boil and turns clear, about 3 minutes.

2. Pour mixture into a heatproof bowl and whisk in olive oil, vinegar, yogurt, mustard and horseradish until blended. Let cool before serving.

Ketchups and Mustards

Easy Ketchup

**Makes 2 cups
(500 mL)**

*Making your own
ketchup may seem
a bit over the top
but it's worth it. It's
easy to make, and
the homemade
version is so much
more delicious
than supermarket
varieties, which
are loaded with
corn syrup.*

Tip
Ketchup keeps well,
tightly covered and
refrigerated, for up to
2 weeks.

- **Blender or food processor**

1	can (28 oz/796 mL) crushed tomatoes	1
2 tbsp	extra virgin olive oil	30 mL
1	onion, chopped	1
1 tbsp	tomato paste	15 mL
$2/3$ cup	lightly packed brown sugar	150 mL
$1/2$ cup	apple cider vinegar	125 mL
$1/2$ tsp	sea salt	2 mL

1. In a blender, purée tomatoes until smooth.

2. In a heavy saucepan, heat oil over medium heat. Add onion and cook, stirring, until softened and translucent, about 8 minutes.

3. Add puréed tomatoes, tomato paste, brown sugar, vinegar and salt. Simmer, stirring occasionally, until very thick, about 1 hour. (Stir more frequently toward end of cooking to prevent scorching.)

4. Add ketchup to blender in 2 batches and purée until smooth. Let cool.

Country Ketchup

Tip
Ketchup keeps well,
tightly covered and
refrigerated, for up to
2 weeks.

- **Food mill**

4 lbs	Roma (plum) tomatoes, quartered	2 kg
½	onion, chopped	½
⅛ tsp	cayenne pepper	0.5 mL
½ cup	granulated sugar	125 mL
½ cup	white wine vinegar	125 mL
2 tsp	sea salt	10 mL
½ tsp	ground cinnamon	2 mL
½ tsp	dill seeds	2 mL
¼ tsp	ground cloves	1 mL

1. In a Dutch oven over medium heat, bring tomatoes, onion and cayenne to a boil and cook, stirring occasionally, until tomatoes are softened, about 15 minutes. Transfer tomatoes to a food mill fitted with a fine plate and press to extract juice into a medium saucepan. Discard solids.

2. Stir in sugar. Place saucepan over medium-high heat and bring to a boil. Reduce heat to low and simmer, stirring occasionally, until thick enough to mound on a spoon, about 45 minutes.

3. In a small saucepan over medium heat, bring vinegar, salt, cinnamon, dill seeds and cloves to a boil. Let stand for 5 minutes. Stir in tomato sauce and cook until bubbling. Let cool.

Chunky Ketchup

*I like to eat this
ketchup on toasted
bread that's topped
with cheese — sort
of a quick pizza
for one.*

Tip

Ketchup keeps well,
tightly covered and
refrigerated, for up to
3 days.

- Preheat oven to 475°F (240°C)
- Baking sheet, lined with parchment paper
- Food processor

12 oz	Roma (plum) tomatoes, cut in half lengthwise, seeded and juice removed	375 g
1/4	large green bell pepper	1/4
1	onion, sliced	1
2 tbsp	extra virgin olive oil	30 mL
1 tbsp	apple cider vinegar	15 mL
2 tsp	lightly packed brown sugar	10 mL
2 tsp	dried parsley	10 mL
1 tsp	dry mustard	5 mL
1/2 tsp	dried thyme	2 mL
1/2 tsp	sea salt	2 mL
1/2 tsp	freshly ground black pepper	2 mL
1/8 tsp	garlic powder	0.5 mL
1/8 tsp	ground cinnamon	0.5 mL

1. On prepared baking sheet, place tomatoes, skin side up, green pepper and onion. Brush very lightly with olive oil. Roast in preheated oven until lightly browned, about 15 minutes. Let cool slightly.

2. In a food processor fitted with a metal blade, pulse tomatoes, pepper and onion about 10 times, until chunky. Place chunky vegetables in a bowl. Stir in vinegar, brown sugar, parsley, dry mustard, thyme, salt, pepper, garlic powder and cinnamon. Let cool.

Roasted Red Pepper Ketchup

Here's a sweet ruby red ketchup with the added flavor of red peppers.

Tips

Ketchup keeps well, tightly covered and refrigerated, for up to 2 weeks.

If you prefer smooth ketchup, purée it in a blender or food processor until it's the desired texture.

1	can (14 oz/398 mL) diced tomatoes with juice	1
1	jar (7 oz/210 mL) roasted red bell peppers, drained	1
1	red onion, chopped	1
½ cup	dry red wine	125 mL
6 tbsp	lightly packed brown sugar	90 mL
3	cloves garlic, minced	3
2	large dried ancho chiles, seeded and coarsely chopped	2
1	bay leaf	1
2 tbsp	tomato paste	30 mL
2 tbsp	red wine vinegar	30 mL
1 tbsp	fennel seeds	15 mL
1½ tsp	ground cumin	7 mL

1. In large heavy saucepan over high heat, combine tomatoes with juice, red peppers, red onion, wine, brown sugar, garlic, ancho chiles, bay leaf, tomato paste, vinegar, fennel seeds and cumin and bring to a boil. Reduce heat and simmer, stirring occasionally, until reduced to 3 cups (750 mL), about 30 minutes. Let cool. Discard bay leaf.

No-Sugar Ketchup

**Makes 2 cups
(500 mL)**

*Use this ketchup
when you want
to cut calories —
most store-bought
ketchups are packed
with sugars.*

Tip
Ketchup keeps well,
tightly covered and
refrigerated, for up to
1 week.

3 cups	tomato juice	750 mL
1/4 cup	apple cider vinegar	60 mL
1/4 cup	sugar substitute, such as Splenda	60 mL
1 1/2 tsp	dried green pepper flakes	7 mL
1/2 tsp	dried onion flakes	2 mL
1/4 tsp	freshly ground black pepper	1 mL
1/8 tsp	dried rosemary	0.5 mL
1/8 tsp	dried thyme	0.5 mL
1/8 tsp	dried basil	0.5 mL
1/8 tsp	dried parsley	0.5 mL

1. In a large saucepan over medium heat, combine tomato juice, vinegar, sugar substitute, green pepper flakes, onion flakes, black pepper, rosemary, thyme, basil and parsley and bring to a boil. Reduce heat and simmer, stirring occasionally, until thickened, about 1 hour. Let cool.

Spiced Ketchup

**Makes 1/2 cup
(125 mL)**

*Here's a spicy
ketchup for added
punch.*

Tip
Ketchup keeps well,
tightly covered and
refrigerated, for up to
2 weeks.

1/2 cup	Country Ketchup (page 107) or store-bought	125 mL
1/3 cup	freshly squeezed orange juice	75 mL
1	dried habanero chile	1
1 tbsp	light (fancy) molasses	15 mL
1/2 tsp	Worcestershire sauce	2 mL
1/4 tsp	whole cloves	1 mL

1. In a small saucepan over medium-high heat, combine ketchup, orange juice, habanero, molasses, Worcestershire sauce and cloves. Simmer stirring occasionally, for 5 minutes. Strain through a fine mesh sieve into a bowl, discarding habanero and cloves. Let cool.

Fast and Easy Mustard

Makes 1⅔ cups (400 mL)

Why purchase prepared mustard when you can make it yourself? It's quick and easy, and you'll know exactly what's in it.

Tip

Mustard keeps well, covered and refrigerated, for up to 3 weeks.

1 cup	dry mustard	250 mL
⅓ cup	cold water	75 mL
⅓ cup	red wine vinegar	75 mL

1. In a bowl, whisk together dry mustard, cold water and vinegar until smooth.
2. Refrigerate for at least 2 days to allow the flavors to develop prior to serving.

Honey Mustard Sauce

Makes 1 cup (250 mL)

I use this as a quick-to-make dipping sauce for scallops or shrimp.

Tip

Sauce keeps well, covered and refrigerated, for up to 3 weeks.

1 cup	liquid honey	250 mL
2 tbsp	prepared mustard	30 mL
1 tsp	hot pepper flakes	5 mL
1 tsp	sea salt	5 mL

1. In a small bowl, whisk together honey, mustard, hot pepper flakes and salt.

Dijon Mustard

2 cups	dry white wine	500 mL
1 cup	chopped onion	250 mL
2 tbsp	liquid honey	30 mL
2	cloves garlic, minced	2
½ cup	dry mustard	125 mL
1 tbsp	vegetable oil	15 mL
2 tsp	sea salt	10 mL
4	drops hot pepper sauce	4

1. In a medium saucepan over medium heat, combine wine, onion, honey and garlic and bring to a boil. Reduce heat and simmer for 5 minutes. Pour into a heatproof bowl and let cool.

2. Strain through a fine mesh sieve back into the saucepan. Whisk in dry mustard until smooth. Whisk in oil, salt and hot pepper sauce. Cook over medium heat, stirring, until thickened, about 5 minutes. Let cool.

Honey Yellow Mustard

½ cup	dry mustard	125 mL
⅓ cup	white wine vinegar	75 mL
1 tsp	liquid honey	5 mL
½ tsp	sea salt	2 mL

1. In a bowl, whisk together dry mustard, vinegar, honey and salt.

2. Refrigerate for at least 2 days to allow the flavors to develop prior to serving.

Coarse Brown Mustard

Makes ⅔ cup (150 mL)

Spread this mustard on ham slices or pork chops.

Tip
Mustard keeps well, covered and refrigerated, for up to 3 weeks.

½ cup	dry mustard	125 mL
⅓ cup	apple cider vinegar	75 mL
2 tbsp	brewed espresso	30 mL
2 tsp	mustard seeds	10 mL
½ tsp	salt	2 mL

1. In a bowl, whisk together dry mustard, vinegar, espresso, mustard seeds and salt.

2. Refrigerate for at least 2 days to allow the flavors to develop prior to serving.

Honey Stone-Ground Mustard

Makes 1½ cups (375 mL)

Sometimes you need a mustard with texture. This one has it.

Tip
Mustard keeps well, covered and refrigerated, for up to 3 weeks.

1 cup	dry mustard	250 mL
1 cup	dry white wine	250 mL
½ cup	chopped onion	125 mL
3 tbsp	white wine vinegar	45 mL
3	cloves garlic, minced	3
2 tsp	mustard seeds	10 mL
1 tsp	granulated sugar	5 mL
¾ tsp	sea salt	3 mL
1	bay leaf	1
½ tsp	whole allspice	2 mL
½ cup	liquid honey	125 mL

1. In a medium saucepan over medium heat, whisk together dry mustard, wine, onion, 6 tbsp (90 mL) water, vinegar, garlic, mustard seeds, sugar, salt, bay leaf and allspice and bring to a boil. Reduce heat and boil, stirring, until reduced by half, about 12 minutes. Strain through a large mesh strainer, discarding bay leaf and allspice. Stir in honey. Let cool.

Creole Mustard

Makes ¾ cup (175 mL)

In New Orleans, I noticed that all the city's restaurants have a Creole mustard — now you can make a quick and easy version at home.

Tip

Sauce keeps well, covered and refrigerated, for up to 3 weeks.

½ cup	dry mustard	125 mL
⅓ cup	red wine vinegar	75 mL
2 tsp	mustard seeds	10 mL
½ tsp	sea salt	2 mL
¼ tsp	cayenne pepper	1 mL
5	drops hot pepper sauce	5

1. In a bowl, whisk together dry mustard, vinegar, mustard seeds, salt, cayenne pepper and hot pepper sauce.

2. Refrigerate for at least 2 days to allow the flavors to develop prior to serving.

Chili Sauces and Relishes

Bold Chili Sauce

**Makes 3 cups
(750 mL)**

*This bold and spicy
sauce is all you need
on hot dogs or steak
burgers.*

Tip
Sauce keeps well,
covered and
refrigerated, for up
to 1 week.

- **Preheat oven to 400°F (200°C)**
- **Baking sheet, lined with parchment paper**
- **Food processor or blender**

16	dried guajillo chiles	16
2 tbsp	canola oil	30 mL
6	cloves garlic	6
1½ tbsp	extra virgin olive oil	22 mL
1½ tsp	granulated sugar	7 mL
1 tsp	dried oregano	5 mL
1 tsp	sea salt	5 mL
¼ tsp	freshly ground black pepper	1 mL
⅛ tsp	ground cumin	0.5 mL
3 cups	beef broth	750 mL

1. Place chiles on prepared baking sheet. Brush with
   canola oil. Roast in preheated oven until softened, about
   15 minutes. Split the chiles and remove the seeds. Place
   in a bowl with enough hot water to cover and soak for
   10 minutes. Drain and transfer to a food processor fitted
   with a metal blade and process until smooth. Add garlic,
   olive oil, sugar, oregano, salt, pepper and cumin and
   process for 15 seconds.

2. Transfer mixture to a medium saucepan over medium
   heat. Add beef broth and simmer, stirring occasionally,
   until thickened, for 30 minutes. Let cool.

Smoked Chili Sauce

**Makes about
2 cups (500 mL)**

*This sauce is so
versatile, you can
use it as a barbecue
sauce or in many
of the recipes
mentioned in
this book.*

Tips

Sauce keeps well,
covered and
refrigerated, for up
to 3 weeks.

Using two types of
vinegar prevents a
bitter aftertaste.

Variation

Omit the chipotle
peppers for a basic
chili sauce.

- **Food processor or blender**

1 cup	rice vinegar	250 mL
1 cup	apple cider vinegar	250 mL
2 tsp	ground cloves	10 mL
1 tsp	ground allspice	5 mL
1	onion, cut into quarters	1
10	cloves garlic	10
1 cup	lightly packed brown sugar	250 mL
1½ cups	Easy Ketchup (page 106) or store-bought	375 mL
1	can (7 oz/210 mL) chipotle peppers in adobo sauce, drained	1
2 tbsp	fresh cilantro	30 mL
1 tbsp	Worcestershire sauce	15 mL

1. In a deep saucepan over medium heat, combine rice vinegar, cider vinegar, cloves and allspice. Bring to a gentle boil. Set aside.

2. In a food processor fitted with a metal blade, process onion, garlic, brown sugar, ketchup, chipotle peppers, cilantro and Worcestershire sauce until finely chopped, about 30 seconds. Add to vinegar mixture and bring to a gentle boil, stirring occasionally, over medium heat. Reduce heat and boil gently, stirring often, until thickened, about 1 hour. Let cool.

Spicy Chili Sauce

**Makes 2 cups
(500 mL)**

*Here's a perfect
condiment for a
hamburger or beef
sandwich.*

Tip
Sauce keeps well,
covered and
refrigerated, for up
to 1 week.

• **Food processor or blender**

1	can (7 oz/210 mL) chipotle peppers in adobo sauce with liquid	1
1	onion, cut into wedges	1
12	cloves garlic	12
1 cup	lightly packed brown sugar	250 mL
2 cups	white wine vinegar	500 mL
1 cup	Easy Ketchup or Country Ketchup (pages 106 and 107) or store-bought	250 mL
1/4 cup	extra virgin olive oil	60 mL
1/4 cup	light (fancy) molasses	60 mL
1 tbsp	Worcestershire sauce	15 mL
2 tsp	ground cloves	10 mL
2 tsp	ground coriander	10 mL
1 tsp	hot pepper sauce	5 mL
1 tsp	ground cinnamon	5 mL
1 tsp	ground allspice	5 mL
1/8 tsp	sea salt	0.5 mL

1. In a food processor fitted with a metal blade, process chipotle peppers in adobe sauce, onion and garlic until puréed, about 1 minute. Add brown sugar and purée until smooth. Set aside.

2. In a medium saucepan over medium heat, combine vinegar, ketchup, olive oil, molasses, Worcestershire sauce, cloves, coriander, hot pepper sauce, cinnamon and allspice. Cook, stirring occasionally, until reduced by half, 14 to 16 minutes. Stir in puréed chipotle mixture. Reduce heat to low and cook, stirring occasionally, until thickened, for 1 hour. Season with salt. Let cool.

Tarragon Pickle Relish

Tip
Relish keeps
well, covered and
refrigerated, for up
to 1 week.

1½ cups	apple cider vinegar	375 mL
2 tbsp	granulated sugar	30 mL
1 tsp	mustard seeds	5 mL
1 tsp	coriander seeds	5 mL
8	large sour dill pickles, finely diced	8
2 tbsp	chopped fresh dill	30 mL
1	small red bell pepper, finely diced	1
1	small yellow bell pepper, finely diced	1
1	small onion, finely diced	1
1 tsp	dried tarragon	5 mL

1. In a medium saucepan over medium heat, combine vinegar, sugar, mustard seeds and coriander seeds and bring to a boil. Boil until syrupy and reduced by half, about 20 minutes.

2. Remove from heat. Stir in pickles, dill, red and yellow bell peppers, onion and tarragon. Toss to coat. Let cool.

Classic Salads

Classic Salads

Making these classic salads is a great way to start learning traditional combinations. I prefer to make all of my salads fresh each time, but, if you have any leftovers, place them in a covered container and refrigerate. If I'm taking salad to a party, I travel with the dressing in a separate container, then toss it all together just before serving. On a hot day, I use cold packs to keep the salad cool while traveling.

Arugula and Cilantro Salad

Serves 4

Here's a peppery and slightly sweet salad.

Variation

I like to sprinkle this salad with large shavings of Parmesan cheese.

1½ cups	arugula	375 mL
1½ cups	baby spinach leaves	375 mL
½ cup	fresh cilantro leaves	125 mL
¼ cup	chopped Italian flat-leaf parsley	60 mL
½ cup	Lucca Vinaigrette (page 43)	125 mL

1. In a large bowl, combine arugula, spinach, cilantro and parsley.
2. Divide greens evenly onto 4 plates. Drizzle vinaigrette evenly over each.

Fresh Flower Garden Salad

Serves 4

Years ago I used to teach an array of classes using fresh flowers; this was one of the students' favorite recipes.

Tips

Make sure you use flowers clearly labeled "not sprayed with pesticides" or use those you've grown yourself, chemical-free.

Do not coat the flowers with the dressing; if you do, they will wilt quickly.

4 cups	chopped romaine lettuce (about 1 head)	1 L
1 cup	torn red leaf lettuce	250 mL
¼ cup	chopped Italian flat-leaf parsley	60 mL
¼ cup	Sherry Vinaigrette (page 50)	60 mL
	Sea salt and freshly ground black pepper	
8	nasturtium flowers (see Tips, left)	8
¼ cup	pansy flowers (see Tips, left)	60 mL

1. In a large bowl, combine romaine, red leaf lettuce and parsley. Drizzle with vinaigrette and toss to coat.

2. Divide dressed greens evenly onto 4 plates. Season with salt and pepper to taste. Garnish with nasturtium and pansy flowers.

Garlic Greens with Raspberries

Serves 4

This simple salad is the perfect side for grilled meats.

4 cups	salad greens	1 L
3	cloves garlic, minced	3
½ cup	fresh raspberries	125 mL
½ cup	Raspberry Vinaigrette (page 47) or store-bought	125 mL
	Sea salt and freshly ground black pepper	

1. In a large bowl, toss together greens, garlic and raspberries.

2. Divide evenly onto 4 plates. Drizzle vinaigrette evenly over each. Season with salt and pepper to taste.

Grapefruit Radicchio Salad

Serves 6

*Serve this tangy
citrus and
bitter-leaf salad as
an accompaniment
to spicy foods.*

4 cups	radicchio leaves, torn if large	1 L
2 cups	torn red leaf lettuce	500 mL
2	large grapefruits, segmented	2
1/2 cup	chopped red onion	125 mL
1	can (4 oz/125 mL) water chestnuts, drained and cut into strips	1
1/4 cup	chopped Italian flat-leaf parsley	60 mL
1/4 cup	chopped fresh basil	60 mL
1/4 cup	Radda Vinaigrette (page 47)	60 mL
	Sea salt and freshly ground black pepper	

1. Arrange radicchio and red leaf lettuce on a serving platter. Top with grapefruit segments, red onion, water chestnuts, parsley and basil. Drizzle with vinaigrette. Season with salt and pepper to taste.

Mixed Greens with Herbs Salad

Serves 4

*Shop for an array of
fresh herbs for this
flavorful salad.*

4 cups	salad greens	1 L
1/2 cup	chopped fresh herbs, such as chervil, tarragon, dill, basil, mint, sorrel and/or cilantro	125 mL
1/4 cup	Parmesan Vinaigrette (page 45)	60 mL

1. Pat greens and herbs dry with paper towels or spin in a salad spinner to make sure they are very dry. Place in a large bowl. Drizzle with vinaigrette and toss to coat. Divide evenly onto 4 plates.

Simple Orange and Endive Salad

Serves 6

The flavors of this simple salad complement any seafood dish.

Tip
Don't chop Belgian endive too early or it will brown. Also, keep it wrapped in paper towels so it doesn't turn green and bitter.

3 cups	chopped Belgian endive (see Tip, left)	750 mL
3	oranges, segmented	3
	Freshly squeezed juice of 1 orange	
2 tbsp	extra virgin olive oil	30 mL
	Sea salt and freshly ground black pepper	
½ cup	chopped pecans, toasted (see Tip, page 71)	125 mL

1. Arrange endive on a serving platter. Top with orange segments.

2. In a bowl, whisk together orange juice and oil. Season with salt and pepper to taste. Drizzle over salad. Sprinkle with pecans.

Egg and Parma Ham Caesar Salad

Serves 4

Here's an easy and satisfying Caesar salad with crunch.

1	head romaine lettuce, cut into pieces	1
2	hard-boiled eggs (see Tips, page 138), sliced	2
6 oz	Parma ham, cut into small pieces	175 g
1 cup	Garlic Croutons (page 270) or store-bought	250 mL
½ cup	Caesar Dressing (page 53) or store-bought	125 mL
	Sea salt and freshly ground black pepper	

1. In a large bowl, combine romaine, eggs, ham and croutons. Drizzle with dressing. Season with salt and pepper to taste.

Classic Egg Salad

8	hard-boiled eggs, coarsely chopped (see Tips, page 138)	8
½	red onion, minced	½
¼ cup	Traditional Mayonnaise (page 100) or store-bought	60 mL
2 tbsp	Dijon Mustard (page 112) or store-bought	30 mL
1 tsp	dried dill	5 mL
1 tsp	Hungarian paprika	5 mL
½ tsp	sea salt	2 mL
½ tsp	freshly ground black pepper	2 mL

1. In a bowl, using a fork, stir together eggs, red onion, mayonnaise, mustard, dill, paprika, salt and pepper until blended. Use immediately or tightly cover and refrigerate for up to 3 days.

Onion and Egg Salad

8	hard-boiled eggs, coarsely chopped (see Tips, page 138)	8
1 cup	chopped onion	250 mL
¼ cup	Traditional Mayonnaise (page 100) or store-bought	60 mL
1 tbsp	chopped Italian flat-leaf parsley	15 mL
2 tsp	Dijon Mustard (page 112) or store-bought	10 mL
	Sea salt and freshly ground black pepper	

1. In a large bowl, using a fork, combine eggs, onion, mayonnaise, parsley and mustard. Season with salt and pepper to taste. Use immediately or tightly cover and refrigerate for up to 2 days.

Spinach and Avocado Salad

Tip
You can use any citrus juice to keep the avocado bright green.

1	large ripe avocado, diced (see Tip, left and page 131)	1
1 tbsp	freshly squeezed lime juice	15 mL
4 cups	baby spinach leaves	1 L
½ cup	chopped green onions	125 mL
1 cup	cherry tomatoes, cut in half	250 mL
1 cup	sliced radishes	250 mL
½ cup	Italian Herb Vinaigrette (page 42) or store-bought	125 mL

1. In a small bowl, coat avocado with lime juice. Set aside.

2. In a large bowl, toss together spinach, green onions, tomatoes, radishes and vinaigrette. Divide evenly onto 4 plates. Top with avocado.

Spinach and Mushroom Salad

2 cups	baby spinach leaves	500 mL
2	large heirloom tomatoes, quartered and seeded	2
12 oz	sliced button mushrooms	375 g
1 cup	Roasted Corn (page 271)	250 mL
½ cup	red onion slices	125 mL
½ cup	Chenin Blanc Vinaigrette (page 39)	125 mL
	Sea salt and freshly ground black pepper	

1. Divide spinach evenly onto 4 plates. Set aside.

2. In a medium bowl, toss together tomatoes, mushrooms, corn, red onion slices and vinaigrette. Divide evenly on top of spinach. Season with salt and pepper to taste.

Toasted Seed Green Salad

Serves 4

Seeds lend nutrition, crunch and flavor to salads.

4 cups	salad greens	1 L
¼ cup	loosely packed fresh basil chiffonade (see Tip, page 132)	60 mL
2 tbsp	Spicy Sunflower Seeds (page 273)	30 mL
2 tbsp	chopped Italian flat-leaf parsley	30 mL
½ cup	Cilantro and Lime Vinaigrette (page 40)	125 mL
	Sea salt and freshly ground black pepper	

1. In a large bowl, toss together salad greens, basil, sunflower seeds, parsley and vinaigrette to coat.

2. Divide evenly onto 4 plates. Season with salt and pepper to taste.

The "Wedge"

Serves 4

The "Wedge" has recently begun to resurface as a "new" type of salad. I first ate a wedge at the Bullock's Wilshire Tea Room in Los Angeles in the early 70s. It now houses the Southwestern Law School.

1	head iceberg lettuce, cut into 4 wedges, core removed	1
½ cup	Blue Cheese Dressing (page 61) or store-bought	125 mL
½ cup	crisply cooked bacon pieces	125 mL
½ cup	grape tomatoes, cut in half	125 mL
	Freshly ground black pepper	

1. Place a wedge of lettuce on each of 4 plates. Pour dressing over one tip of each wedge and sprinkle with bacon. Add a few tomato halves. Season with pepper to taste.

Wild Rocket Salad with Herbs

Serves 4

In England, arugula is called "rocket," and it's a familiar ingredient in the gourmet salads offered up by many London eateries. Luckily, you can enjoy one of my favorites without flying across the pond.

Tip

Choose young greens for this salad — they're the most flavorful.

⅓ cup	extra virgin olive oil	75 mL
2 tbsp	freshly squeezed lemon juice	30 mL
	Sea salt and freshly ground black pepper	
2 cups	arugula (rocket)	500 mL
2 cups	torn romaine lettuce	500 mL
½ cup	chopped Italian flat-leaf parsley	125 mL
2 tbsp	chopped fresh dill	30 mL

1. In a bowl, whisk together olive oil and lemon juice. Add salt and pepper to taste.

2. Divide arugula, romaine, parsley and dill evenly onto 4 plates. Drizzle with dressing.

Blue Cheese Peanut Coleslaw

Serves 6

The rich bite of blue cheese combined with creamy peanut dressing makes this coleslaw a picnic favorite.

Tip

I like to shred the carrots and cut the cabbage by hand instead of purchasing precut vegetables. It just tastes better this way to me, but if you're in a hurry I understand.

Variation

For a different flavor, you can substitute any cheese for the blue cheese.

½ cup	Traditional Mayonnaise (page 100) or store-bought	125 mL
2 tbsp	freshly squeezed lemon juice	30 mL
½ tsp	freshly ground black pepper	2 mL
½ tsp	sea salt	2 mL
¼ tsp	granulated sugar	1 mL
1	onion, diced	1
1	green bell pepper, diced	1
2 cups	grated carrots	500 mL
12 oz	cabbage (about ½ head), grated	375 g
4 oz	blue cheese, crumbled	125 g
1	package (8 oz/250 g) unsalted roasted peanuts, crushed	1

1. In a large salad bowl, whisk together mayonnaise, lemon juice, pepper, salt and sugar until blended. Add onion, bell pepper, carrots and cabbage and stir to coat with dressing. Add blue cheese and peanuts. Refrigerate, tightly covered, for at least 1 hour to allow the flavors to develop prior to serving or for up to 3 days.

Cabbage Salad with Olives

Serves 6

On the Greek island of Santorini, I found many cafés featuring salads with the surprising combination of cabbage and olives. It works.

5 cups	grated cabbage (about 1 head)	1.25 L
1 cup	kalamata olives, pitted and finely chopped	250 mL
½ cup	Roasted Garlic Vinaigrette (page 48)	125 mL
	Sea salt and freshly ground black pepper	

1. In a large bowl, toss together cabbage, olives and vinaigrette. Let stand for about 1 hour to allow the flavors to develop prior to serving. Season with salt and pepper to taste.

Pesto Coleslaw

A rich basil flavor makes this slaw a new favorite.

Tip

To toast pine nuts: Place nuts in a single layer on a baking sheet in a preheated 350°F (180°C) oven for 6 to 8 minutes, or until fragrant and golden, stirring once or twice.

• **Food processor**

4 cups	shredded cabbage	1 L
1 cup	grated carrots	250 mL
½ cup	chopped green onions	125 mL
1 tbsp	chopped Italian flat-leaf parsley	15 mL
1 cup	pine nuts, toasted (see Tip, left)	250 mL
1 cup	Traditional Mayonnaise (page 100) or store-bought	250 mL
½ cup	lightly packed fresh basil leaves	125 mL
	Sea salt and freshly ground white pepper	

1. In a large bowl, combine cabbage, carrots, green onions, parsley and pine nuts. Set aside.

2. In a food processor fitted with a metal blade, process mayonnaise and basil until smooth, about 5 seconds. Pour over cabbage mixture and toss to coat. Season with salt and pepper to taste.

Carrot and Ginger Salad

Serves 4

This salad is brightly colored and full of flavor, so it's a great addition to any festive table.

Tip

To peel gingerroot without a vegetable peeler, use the edge of a large spoon to scrape off the skin.

2 cups	grated carrots	500 mL
2 tbsp	extra virgin olive oil	30 mL
1 tbsp	freshly grated gingerroot (see Tip, left)	15 mL
1 tbsp	poppy seeds	15 mL
	Sea salt and freshly ground black pepper	

1. In a medium bowl, combine carrots, oil, ginger and poppy seeds. Season with salt and pepper to taste. Cover and refrigerate for about 30 minutes to allow flavors to develop. Serve at room temperature.

Carrot and Raisin Salad

Serves 8

At my elementary school I happily ate carrot and raisin salad every week. Here is my adult variation.

Tip

To toast almonds: Place nuts in a single layer on a baking sheet in a preheated 350°F (180°C) oven for 11 to 13 for whole, 10 to 12 minutes for chopped, or until fragrant and golden, stirring once or twice.

½ cup	Traditional Mayonnaise (page 100) or store-bought	125 mL
1 tsp	freshly squeezed lime juice	5 mL
½ tsp	sea salt	2 mL
½ tsp	freshly ground black pepper	2 mL
4 cups	grated carrots	1 L
1 cup	golden raisins	250 mL
1	apple, such as Pippin, Granny Smith or Rome, peeled and cubed	1
½ cup	sliced almonds, toasted (see Tip, left)	125 mL

1. In a large bowl, whisk together mayonnaise, lime juice, salt and pepper. Add carrots, raisins, apple and almonds and mix to coat. Cover and refrigerate until chilled for at least 1 hour, or for up to 2 days.

Carrot, Raisin and Dried Apricot Salad

Serves 4

This salad is rich with raisins, flavorful apricots and a creamy dressing.

Tip

If raisins are dried out and not plump, you can soak in hot water for a few minutes, then drain before using.

12 oz	cabbage (about ½ head), grated	375 g
1 cup	grated carrots	250 mL
¾ cup	golden raisins	175 mL
½ cup	chopped red onion	125 mL
½ cup	diced celery	125 mL
½ cup	chopped dried apricots	125 mL
½ cup	Traditional Mayonnaise (page 100) or store-bought	125 mL
2 tsp	chopped fresh mint	10 mL
	Sea salt and freshly ground white pepper	

1. In a large bowl, combine cabbage, carrots, raisins, red onion, celery, apricots, mayonnaise and mint. Season with salt and white pepper to taste.

Artichoke Salad

Serves 4

This is an easy salad when you need a fast first course.

Tip

For the freshest taste, rinse artichokes after draining and pat dry with paper towels.

4 cups	salad greens	1 L
1	jar (13.75 oz/390 mL) marinated artichoke hearts, drained (see Tip, left)	1
2	cloves garlic, minced	2
3 tbsp	minced Italian flat-leaf parsley	45 mL
2 tbsp	extra virgin olive oil	30 mL
	Freshly ground black pepper	

1. Divide greens evenly onto 4 plates. Set aside.

2. In a medium bowl, combine artichoke hearts, garlic and parsley. Divide evenly over salad greens. Drizzle with oil, then sprinkle with pepper to taste.

Bean and Avocado Salad

Serves 8

This salad is perfect for a brunch when you need something fast and hearty.

Tips

If you don't add the avocado, you can keep this salad in a sealed container for up to 4 days. Dice and add the avocado just before serving.

To determine if your avocado is ripe: Hold it in the palm of your hand and press. The avocado should feel like a tomato that has a little "give."

1 tbsp	extra virgin olive oil	15 mL
½ cup	chopped onion	125 mL
4	cloves garlic, minced	4
2	jalapeño peppers, seeded and minced	2
2	Roma (plum) tomatoes, diced	2
2 tsp	chopped fresh oregano	10 mL
2 tsp	ground cumin	10 mL
1 tsp	ground coriander	5 mL
1	can (14 to 19 oz/398 to 540 mL) red kidney beans, drained and rinsed	1
1	can (14 to 19 oz/398 to 540 mL) white beans, drained and rinsed	1
1	can (14 to 19 oz/398 to 540 mL) chickpeas (garbanzo beans), drained and rinsed	1
1	ripe avocado, diced (see Tips, left)	1

1. In a shallow saucepan, heat oil over medium heat. Add onion and sauté until softened, about 3 minutes. Add garlic, jalapeños, tomatoes, oregano, cumin and coriander and sauté for 3 minutes. Add a little water if mixture gets too dry and starts sticking to pan.

2. Transfer mixture to a large bowl and let cool. Stir in kidney beans, white beans, chickpeas and avocado to combine.

Caprese Salad

Serves 4 to 6

This simple fresh salad from Italy makes a lovely appetizer or side dish.

Tip

To chiffonade basil: Stack the leaves with the largest on the bottom. Roll them up tightly, jelly-roll fashion, then finely slice across the roll. This prevents the basil from being bruised in the cutting, and prematurely darkening.

1 tbsp	red wine vinegar	15 mL
1 tbsp	balsamic vinegar	15 mL
1 tsp	sea salt	5 mL
$\frac{1}{2}$ tsp	granulated sugar	2 mL
$\frac{1}{2}$ tsp	freshly ground black pepper	2 mL
$\frac{1}{2}$ cup	extra virgin olive oil	125 mL
6	Roma (plum) tomatoes, sliced	6
1 lb	ball mozzarella, cut into $\frac{1}{4}$-inch (0.5 cm) thick slices	500 g
$\frac{1}{2}$ cup	loosely packed fresh basil chiffonade (see Tip, left)	125 mL

1. In a bowl, whisk together red wine and balsamic vinegars, salt, sugar and pepper. Whisk in oil.

2. Divide sliced tomatoes and mozzarella evenly onto plates. Drizzle with dressing. Sprinkle with basil.

Panzanella Salad

Tip

The heirloom tomatoes add a great look to this salad, but if none are readily available, then use all Roma (plum) tomatoes instead.

Salad

8 oz	bacon	250 g
4 cups	Italian bread, cut into 1-inch (2.5 cm) cubes and dried overnight	1 L
2 tbsp	canola oil	30 mL
3	Roma (plum) tomatoes, seeded and diced	3
2	heirloom tomatoes, seeded and cut into small pieces (see Tip, left)	2
2 cups	chopped romaine lettuce	500 mL

Dressing

¼ cup	red wine vinegar	60 mL
¼ tsp	sea salt	1 mL
¼ tsp	freshly ground black pepper	1 mL
3 tbsp	extra virgin olive oil	45 mL
1 tbsp	shredded fresh mint	15 mL
1 tbsp	shredded fresh basil	15 mL
1 tsp	chopped fresh tarragon	5 mL

1. *Salad:* In a large deep skillet over medium-high heat, cook bacon until evenly browned and crisp. Leaving drippings in pan, transfer bacon to paper towels to drain. Crumble and set aside. In a large bowl, toss together bread cubes and bacon drippings from pan, to soak up fat.

2. Add canola oil and Roma and heirloom tomatoes to pan and cook until browned, about 5 minutes. Set aside.

3. *Dressing:* In a bowl, whisk together vinegar, salt and pepper. Whisk in olive oil.

4. *Assemble:* In a large bowl, toss together bacon, bread cubes, tomatoes, dressing and lettuce to coat. Garnish with mint, basil and tarragon.

Papaya, Tomato and Onion Salad

Serves 6

I like to present this colorful salad on a large platter and let my guests serve themselves.

Tip

I like to use a mandoline to slice my onion and cucumber for this salad. That way, the slices are precisely the same thickness.

3	large heirloom tomatoes, thinly sliced	3
2	large papaya, sliced	2
1 cup	sliced red onion	250 mL
1 cup	thinly sliced cucumber (see Tip, left)	250 mL
½ cup	Cabernet Sauvignon Vinaigrette (page 38)	125 mL
	Sea salt and freshly ground black pepper	

1. Arrange tomatoes, papayas, red onion and cucumber on a serving platter. Drizzle with vinaigrette. Sprinkle with salt and pepper to taste.

Greek Salad

Serves 6

This light salad is perfect for a spring day.

3 tbsp	extra virgin olive oil	45 mL
1½ tbsp	freshly squeezed lemon juice	22 mL
1	clove garlic, minced	1
½ tsp	dried oregano	2 mL
¼ tsp	sea salt	1 mL
¼ tsp	freshly ground black pepper	1 mL
1	cucumber	1
3	Roma (plum) tomatoes, cut into wedges	3
1	small red onion, cut into rings	1
½	green bell pepper, sliced	½
4 oz	feta cheese, crumbled	125 g
½ cup	kalamata olives, pitted	125 mL
	Freshly ground black pepper	

1. In a bowl, whisk together oil, lemon juice, garlic, oregano, salt and pepper.

2. Cut cucumber in half lengthwise. Scoop out seeds and slice cucumber into half-moons. In a large salad bowl, combine cucumber, tomatoes, red onion, bell pepper, feta and olives. Just before serving, pour on dressing and toss gently to combine. Garnish with a little black pepper.

Roasted Butternut Eggplant Salad

Serves 4

England has many communities drawn from countries all over the Middle East. In one such London neighborhood, I discovered this vibrant salad.

Tip

Many cooks salt sliced eggplant and let it stand for about 30 minutes, rinse it quickly and thoroughly, then pat it dry with paper towels prior to use. This reduces bitterness (especially in more mature eggplants) and prevents the eggplant from becoming soggy or absorbing too much oil or grease during cooking. This is optional and may not be necessary with firm fresh young eggplants from a farmers' market, but might be a good idea if you see lots of moisture seeping from the slices.

- **Preheat barbecue grill to medium**

2	medium eggplants, sliced (see Tip, left)	2
2 tsp	sea salt	10 mL
1/2 cup	extra virgin olive oil	125 mL
2 lbs	butternut squash, peeled and sliced	1 kg
1 tsp	Hungarian paprika	5 mL
6 oz	feta cheese, crumbled	175 g
1/2 cup	pistachios, toasted and chopped	125 mL
	Sea salt and freshly ground black pepper	

1. Place eggplant slices on a tray in a single layer and sprinkle with salt. Let stand for 30 minutes. Rinse and pat dry with paper towels.

2. Brush oil all over eggplant and squash slices. On preheated grill, sear eggplant and squash slices, about 3 minutes per side. Arrange on a serving dish. Sprinkle with paprika, feta and pistachios. Season with salt and pepper to taste.

Green Mango Salad

1 lb	green mangos, cut into slivers	500 g
½ cup	finely chopped fresh cilantro	125 mL
1	jalapeño pepper, seeded and finely chopped	1
2 tbsp	granulated sugar	30 mL
2 tsp	grated lime zest	10 mL
2 tsp	freshly squeezed lime juice	10 mL
	Sea salt	

1. In a large bowl, combine mangos, cilantro, jalapeño, sugar and lime zest and juice. Let stand for about 30 minutes to allow flavors to develop. Season with salt to taste.

Mango and Apple Salad

Dressing

½ cup	plain yogurt (see Tip, left)	125 mL
1 tsp	chopped fresh dill	5 mL
1 tsp	prepared horseradish	5 mL
	Sea salt and freshly ground black pepper	

Salad

2	apples, such as Red or Golden Delicious, peeled and diced	2
2	mangos, diced	2
½ cup	chopped celery	125 mL
1 tbsp	chopped fresh dill	15 mL

1. *Dressing:* In a small bowl, combine yogurt, dill and horseradish. Season with salt and pepper to taste. Set aside.

2. *Salad:* In a large bowl, toss together apples, mangos and celery. Add dressing and toss to coat.

3. Divide evenly onto 4 plates. Garnish with dill.

Waldorf Salad

Serves 4

The first Waldorf salad was created in 1893 by Oscar Tschirky, the maître d'hôtel of the Waldorf Astoria hotel in New York City. There have been many variations, but this is pretty close to the original.

3 tbsp	Traditional Mayonnaise (page 100) or store-bought	45 mL
1 tbsp	freshly squeezed lemon juice	15 mL
1 tsp	sea salt	5 mL
1/2 tsp	ground white pepper	2 mL
1/2 cup	chopped walnuts, toasted	125 mL
1/2 cup	diced celery	125 mL
1/2 cup	red seedless grapes, sliced	125 mL
1	small cooking apple, chopped	1
4 cups	salad greens	1 L

1. In a bowl, whisk together mayonnaise and lemon juice. Add salt and white pepper. Fold in walnuts, celery, grapes and apple.

2. Divide greens evenly onto 4 plates. Top with walnut mixture.

Waldorf Parma Salad

Serves 4

This hybrid combines flavors from New York and Italy.

3	apples, such as Rome, Delicious or Jonagold, peeled and shredded	3
8 oz	Parma ham, sliced into strips	250 g
3	stalks celery, julienned	3
1/2 cup	Traditional Mayonnaise (page 100) or store-bought	125 mL
2 cups	torn butterhead lettuce	500 mL
1 cup	shredded radicchio leaves	250 mL
1/2 cup	chopped walnuts, toasted	125 mL
	Sea salt and freshly ground black pepper	

1. In a medium bowl, combine apples, ham, celery and mayonnaise to coat.

2. Divide lettuce and radicchio evenly onto 4 plates. Top with apple mixture. Sprinkle with walnuts. Season with salt and pepper to taste.

Bacon and New Potato Salad

Smoky crunchy bacon boosts creamy potato salad up a notch.

Tips

To cook potatoes: Place whole potatoes in a pot of cold salted water; bring to a simmer over medium heat and cook until fork-tender Do not allow to boil or the skins will burst and allow potato flesh to absorb water. If desired, peel slightly cooled potatoes, then cut into bite-size pieces.

To cook hard-boiled eggs: Arrange a single layer of eggs in a saucepan and add enough cold water to cover by 1 inch (2.5 cm). Bring to a boil over high heat. Remove from heat and, without draining the water, cover and let stand for 10 minutes. With a slotted spoon, carefully transfer each egg into a large bowl of ice water. Let cool completely for at least 5 minutes. Remove eggshells under cool running water.

6 oz	smoked bacon, preferably applewood, cut into small pieces	175 g
4	hard-boiled eggs (see Tips, left)	4
1 cup	Traditional Mayonnaise (page 100) or store-bought	250 mL
1 cup	diced celery	250 mL
2 tbsp	Dijon Mustard (page 112) or store-bought	30 mL
1 tbsp	minced Italian flat-leaf parsley	15 mL
2 lbs	white fingerling potatoes, cooked and cut into bite-size pieces (see Tips, left, and page 140) Sea salt and freshly ground white pepper	1 kg

1. In a saucepan over medium heat, cook bacon until crisp, about 8 minutes. Drain on paper towels.

2. In a large bowl, using a fork, mash together eggs, mayonnaise, celery, mustard and parsley. Stir in potatoes and bacon. Season with salt and white pepper to taste.

Deli Potato Salad

A summer picnic isn't complete without potato salad. Try this one for your next event.

Tips

You can make this 1 day prior to serving.

If you're taking it to a picnic, nestle it into cold packs enroute, then keep the serving bowl on ice in the hot sun.

3 lbs	white fingerling potatoes, cooked and cut into quarters (see Tips, page 138)	1.5 kg
4	hard-boiled eggs, chopped (see Tips, page 138)	4
1 cup	chopped red onion	250 mL
1 cup	diced celery	250 mL
½ cup	chopped green olives	125 mL
¼ cup	chopped Italian flat-leaf parsley	60 mL
¾ cup	Traditional Mayonnaise (page 100) or store-bought	175 mL
¼ cup	extra virgin olive oil	60 mL
¼ cup	red wine vinegar	60 mL
2 tbsp	Honey Stone-Ground Mustard (page 113) or store-bought	30 mL
	Sea salt and freshly ground black pepper	
	Hungarian paprika	

1. In a large bowl, combine potatoes, eggs, red onion, celery, olives and parsley.

2. In a small bowl, whisk together mayonnaise, oil, vinegar and mustard. Pour over potato mixture and stir to coat completely. Season with salt and pepper to taste. Transfer to a serving bowl and sprinkle with paprika.

Feta Potato Salad

I could eat a potato salad every day, and this one is no exception.

Tip

If you can find the tiny fingerling potatoes that are truly finger-size, you don't have to cut them.

Variation

For a stronger flavor, try replacing the feta with blue cheese or Stilton.

½ cup	chopped green onions	125 mL
½ cup	black olives, pitted and chopped	125 mL
¼ cup	chopped Italian flat-leaf parsley	60 mL
1 tbsp	drained capers	15 mL
6 oz	feta, crumbled	175 g
1½ lbs	white fingerling potatoes, cooked and cut into bite-size pieces (see Tip, left, and page 141)	750 g
½ cup	Traditional Mayonnaise (page 100) or store-bought	125 mL
	Sea salt and freshly ground white pepper	

1. In a large bowl, combine green onions, olives, parsley, capers and feta. Stir in potatoes and mayonnaise to coat. Season with salt and white pepper to taste.

Potato Radish Salad

Serves 4

Crunchy radishes contrast with creamy potatoes to make this a delightful summer salad.

1 lb	small new potatoes	500 g
¼ cup	extra virgin olive oil	60 mL
2 tbsp	red wine vinegar	30 mL
2 tsp	Honey Yellow Mustard (page 112) or store-bought	10 mL
½ cup	thinly sliced radishes	125 mL
2 tbsp	chopped fresh chives	30 mL
	Sea salt and freshly ground white pepper	

1. Place potatoes in a large pot of cold salted water. Bring to a simmer over medium heat and cook until fork tender, about 20 minutes. Drain well. If potatoes are large, slice in half.

2. Transfer potatoes to a bowl. Stir in oil, vinegar, mustard, radishes and chives to coat. Season with salt and white pepper to taste.

Spicy Potato Salad

Serves 8

This makes a lively sidekick for a po' boy sandwich!

Tips

To cook potatoes: Place whole potatoes in a pot of cold salted water; bring to a simmer over medium heat and cook until fork-tender Do not allow to boil or the skins will burst and allow potato flesh to absorb water. If desired, peel slightly cooled potatoes, then cut into bite-size pieces.

To cook hard-boiled eggs: Arrange a single layer of eggs in a saucepan and add enough cold water to cover by 1 inch (2.5 cm). Bring to a boil over high heat. Remove from heat and, without draining the water, cover and let stand for 10 minutes. With a slotted spoon, carefully transfer each egg into a large bowl of ice water. Let cool completely for at least 5 minutes. Remove eggshells under cool running water.

2 lbs	small fingerling potatoes, cooked and sliced (see Tips, left, and page 140)	1 kg
3	hard-boiled eggs, chopped (see Tips, left)	3
1	green bell pepper, diced	1
½ cup	chopped green onions	125 mL
1 cup	Traditional Mayonnaise (page 100) or store-bought	250 mL
¼ cup	Tarragon Pickle Relish (page 118) or store-bought relish	60 mL
1 tbsp	Dijon Mustard (page 112) or store-bought	15 mL
1 tbsp	hot pepper sauce	15 mL
Pinch	cayenne pepper	Pinch
	Sea salt and freshly ground black pepper	

1. In a medium bowl, combine potatoes, eggs, bell pepper, green onions, mayonnaise, relish, mustard, hot pepper sauce and cayenne. Stir to coat potatoes. Season with salt and pepper to taste.

New Orleans Spicy Potato Salad

Serves 6

You can't get any spicier than New Orleans spicy. This memorable salad was served at that city's famous jazz festival one year.

Tips

To cook potatoes: Place whole potatoes in a pot of cold salted water; bring to a simmer over medium heat and cook until fork-tender Do not allow to boil or the skins will burst and allow potato flesh to absorb water. If desired, peel slightly cooled potatoes, then cut into bite-size pieces.

To cook hard-boiled eggs: Arrange a single layer of eggs in a saucepan and add enough cold water to cover by 1 inch (2.5 cm). Bring to a boil over high heat. Remove from heat and, without draining the water, cover and let stand for 10 minutes. With a slotted spoon, carefully transfer each egg into a large bowl of ice water. Let cool completely for at least 5 minutes. Remove eggshells under cool running water.

2 lbs	white fingerling potatoes, cooked and cut into bite-size pieces (see Tips, left, and page 140)	1 kg
3	hard-boiled eggs, chopped (see Tips, left)	3
2	red bell peppers, diced	2
½ cup	chopped green onions	125 mL
½ cup	chopped shallots	125 mL
1	jalapeño pepper, seeded and diced	1
1	clove garlic, minced	1
1 cup	Traditional Mayonnaise (page 100) or store-bought	250 mL
¼ cup	Tarragon Pickle Relish (page 118) or store-bought relish	60 mL
1 tbsp	Dijon Mustard (page 112) or store-bought	15 mL
1 tsp	hot pepper sauce	5 mL
1 tsp	chopped Italian flat-leaf parsley	5 mL
	Sea salt and freshly ground black pepper	

1. In a medium bowl, stir together potatoes, eggs, bell peppers, green onions, shallots, jalapeño, garlic, mayonnaise, relish, mustard, hot pepper sauce and parsley to coat. Season with salt and pepper to taste.

Asparagus and Bacon Salad

Serves 4

You can serve this as a main dish for lunch or as a side for dinner.

Tip

Don't chop Belgian endive too early or it will brown. Also, keep it wrapped in paper towels so it doesn't turn green and bitter.

1½ lbs	asparagus, sliced on the diagonal	750 g
8 oz	smoked bacon, preferably applewood, sliced	250 g
2 cups	chopped Belgian endive (see Tip, left)	500 mL
½ cup	Creamy French Honey Dressing (page 67)	125 mL
	Sea salt and freshly ground white pepper	

1. Fill a shallow saucepan or skillet with ½ inch (1 cm) water and bring to a simmer over medium heat. Add asparagus and cook for 3 minutes. Have a bowl of ice water nearby. Drain asparagus, then immediately submerge in ice water to set color and stop cooking, about 3 minutes. Transfer with tongs to a bowl.

2. In same pan over medium heat, cook bacon until crisp, about 8 minutes. Drain on paper towels. Crumble bacon.

3. In a salad bowl, toss together endive and bacon. Add asparagus. Drizzle with dressing and toss to coat. Season with salt and white pepper to taste.

Brown Derby Cobb Salad

Serves 8

The Brown Derby
was a celebrated
watering hole
in Los Angeles,
frequented by movie
and television stars.
This salad was
made famous by the
restaurant owner,
Robert Cobb.

Tips

*To determine if your
avocado is ripe:* Hold
it in the palm of your
hand and press. The
avocado should feel
like a tomato that has
a little "give."

You can store the
dressing for up
to 1 week in the
refrigerator.

Dressing

¾ cup	red wine vinegar	175 mL
1 tbsp	Worcestershire sauce	15 mL
2 tsp	freshly squeezed lemon juice	10 mL
1 tsp	granulated sugar	5 mL
1 tsp	freshly ground black pepper	5 mL
1 tsp	Dijon Mustard (page 112) or store-bought	5 mL
¾ tsp	sea salt	3 mL
1	clove garlic, minced	1
1 cup	extra virgin olive oil	250 mL
1 cup	canola oil	250 mL

Salad

4 cups	finely chopped iceberg lettuce (about ½ head)	1 L
2 cups	finely chopped watercress (about ½ bunch)	500 mL
1 cup	finely chopped chicory (about 1 small bunch)	250 mL
4 cups	finely chopped romaine lettuce (about ½ head)	1 L
2	vine-ripened tomatoes, seeded and diced	2
1 lb	cooked boneless skinless chicken breasts, diced	500 g
8 oz	bacon, crisply cooked and crumbled	250 g
1	ripe avocado, diced (see Tips, left)	1
3	hard-boiled eggs, finely chopped (see Tip, right)	3
2 tbsp	chopped fresh chives	30 mL
½ cup	crumbled Roquefort cheese	125 mL

Tip

To cook hard-boiled eggs:
Arrange a single layer
of eggs in a saucepan
and add enough cold
water to cover by
1 inch (2.5 cm). Bring
to a boil over high heat.
Remove from heat and,
without draining the
water, cover and let
stand for 10 minutes.
With a slotted spoon,
carefully transfer each
egg into a large bowl
of ice water. Let cool
completely for at least
5 minutes. Remove
eggshells under cool
running water.

1. *Dressing:* In a widemouthed jar with a tight-fitting lid, combine vinegar, $\frac{1}{4}$ cup (60 mL) water, Worcestershire sauce, lemon juice, sugar, pepper, mustard, salt and garlic. Shake for 1 minute. Add olive and canola oils and shake well until emulsified, about 1 minute. Use immediately or cover tightly and refrigerate until ready to use. Shake before using.

2. *Salad:* In a large shallow bowl or deep plate, toss together iceberg lettuce, watercress, chicory and romaine with enough of the dressing to coat.

3. Divide salad greens evenly onto 8 plates. Arrange tomatoes in a strip across center of greens. Arrange chicken on top. Sprinkle with bacon, avocado, eggs, chives and Roquefort.

Chicken Gruyère Salad

Serves 4

Besides eating this as a salad, I also like to place it between toasted bread for a sandwich.

2 tbsp	Traditional Mayonnaise (page 100) or store-bought	30 mL
1 tbsp	Dijon Mustard (page 112) or-store-bought	15 mL
1 tsp	white wine vinegar	5 mL
1 tsp	sea salt	5 mL
1 tsp	freshly ground black pepper	5 mL
1	3-lb (1.5 kg) deli-roasted chicken, skin and bones removed, shredded into bite-size pieces	1
8 oz	Gruyère cheese, cut into cubes	250 g
1	apple, such as Pippin, Granny Smith or Rome, peeled and finely chopped	1
1 cup	diced celery	250 mL
1 tbsp	sesame seeds	15 mL
2 cups	salad greens	500 mL
	Sea salt and freshly ground black pepper	

1. In a large bowl, combine mayonnaise, mustard, vinegar, salt and pepper. Add chicken, Gruyère, apple, celery and sesame seeds, and toss to coat.

2. Arrange salad greens on a serving platter. Top with chicken mixture. Season with salt and pepper to taste.

Roasted Chicken Pecan Salad

¹/₂ cup	Traditional Mayonnaise (page 100) or store-bought	125 mL
2 tbsp	Dijon Mustard (page 112) or store-bought	30 mL
2 tbsp	Tarragon Pickle Relish (page 118) or store-bought relish	30 mL
1 cup	chopped pecans, toasted	250 mL
¹/₂ cup	dried cherries or raisins	125 mL
2 tbsp	chopped fresh tarragon	30 mL
1	3-lb (1.5 kg) deli-roasted chicken, skin and bones removed, shredded into bite-size pieces	1
2 cups	salad greens	500 mL

1. In a large bowl, combine mayonnaise, mustard and relish. Add pecans, cherries, tarragon and chicken, and toss to coat. Serve on a bed of greens.

Spicy Chicken Salad

1	3-lb (1.5 kg) deli-roasted chicken, bones and skin removed, shredded into bite-size pieces	1.5 kg
8 oz	elbow macaroni, cooked, rinsed and drained	250 g
1	red bell pepper, seeded and finely chopped	1
3	stalks celery, chopped	3
¹/₄ cup	chopped shallots	60 mL
2 tbsp	liquid honey	30 mL
1 tbsp	Creole Mustard (page 114)	15 mL
1 tsp	grated lemon zest	5 mL
1 tbsp	freshly squeezed lemon juice	15 mL
2 cups	salad greens	500 mL
	Sea salt and freshly ground black pepper	

1. In a large bowl, combine chicken, macaroni, bell pepper, celery, shallots, honey, mustard and lemon zest and juice.

2. Arrange greens on a large platter. Top with chicken mixture. Season with salt and pepper to taste.

Salad Olivier

Serves 6

This salad was invented by a French chef, M. Olivier, who served it in Moscow in the late 1800s. It is known worldwide by many names including Salade Olivier, Russian Salad or Sour Russian Potato Salad.

2½ cups	cubed boneless skinless cooked chicken	625 mL
4	medium boiling potatoes, cooked, peeled and cubed	4
1 cup	frozen peas, cooked	250 mL
2	hard-boiled eggs, coarsely chopped (see Tips, page 138)	2
1	small onion, finely chopped	1
1	large carrot, diced	1
2 tbsp	dill pickle relish, drained	30 mL
1 tbsp	drained capers	15 mL
¾ cup	Traditional Mayonnaise (page 100) or store-bought	175 mL
¼ cup	sour cream	60 mL
1 tbsp	Dijon Mustard (page 112) or store-bought	15 mL
2 tsp	freshly squeezed lemon juice	10 mL
½ tsp	sea salt	2 mL
½ tsp	freshly ground black pepper	2 mL
½ tsp	dried dill	2 mL
1	head Boston lettuce	1
1	Roma (plum) tomato, cut into small wedges	1
⅛ tsp	Hungarian paprika	0.5 mL

1. In a large bowl, combine chicken, potatoes, peas, eggs, onion, carrot, relish and capers. Fold gently just to mix.

2. In another bowl, whisk together mayonnaise, sour cream, mustard, lemon juice, salt, pepper and dill. Pour over chicken mixture and gently combine. Cover and refrigerate for at least 1 hour to allow the flavors to develop prior to serving or for up to 4 days.

3. To serve, mound lettuce leaves on a large platter and top with chicken mixture. Garnish with tomato wedges. Sprinkle with paprika.

Hamburger Salad

Serves 4

*All that can go into
a hamburger can go
into this entrée salad.*

Tip

Taco seasoning is a
blend of paprika, salt,
dried onion flakes,
tomato powder, cumin,
garlic, oregano, black
pepper, cocoa powder
and allspice.

2 tsp	canola oil	10 mL
½ cup	chopped red onion	125 mL
2 lbs	lean ground beef or turkey	1 kg
1 tsp	taco seasoning (see Tip, left)	5 mL
2 cups	salad greens	500 mL
2	Roma (plum) tomatoes, diced	2
4 oz	blue cheese, crumbled	125 g
½ cup	Thousand Island Dressing (page 82) or store-bought	125 mL
1 tsp	sesame seeds	5 mL
	Sea salt and freshly ground black pepper	

1. In a skillet, heat oil over medium heat. Add red onion and sauté until soft, about 5 minutes. Add ground beef and taco seasoning and cook, breaking up with a spoon, until no longer pink, about 8 minutes. Let cool.

2. Divide salad greens, tomatoes and blue cheese evenly onto 4 plates or arrange them on a platter for a buffet serving. Top with ground beef mixture. Drizzle with dressing and sprinkle with sesame seeds. Season with salt and pepper to taste.

Salad Niçoise

Serves 6

This simple salad is served in bistros throughout France.

Tips

To cook potatoes: Place whole potatoes in a pot of cold salted water; bring to a simmer over medium heat and cook until fork-tender Do not allow to boil or the skins will burst and allow potato flesh to absorb water. If desired, peel slightly cooled potatoes, then cut into bite-size pieces.

To cook hard-boiled eggs: Arrange a single layer of eggs in a saucepan and add enough cold water to cover by 1 inch (2.5 cm). Bring to a boil over high heat. Remove from heat and, without draining the water, cover and let stand for 10 minutes. With a slotted spoon, carefully transfer each egg into a large bowl of ice water. Let cool completely for at least 5 minutes. Remove eggshells under cool running water.

1	large head Boston lettuce	1
1 lb	green beans, cooked and cooled	500 g
1½ tbsp	minced shallots	22 mL
½ cup	Italian Herb Vinaigrette or Red Balsamic Vinaigrette with Kalamata Olives (pages 42 and 48)	125 mL
¼ tsp	sea salt	1 mL
¼ tsp	freshly ground black pepper	1 mL
4	Roma (plum) tomatoes, cut into wedges	4
4	small fingerling potatoes, cooked and sliced (see Tips, left, and page 140)	4
1	can (6 oz/170 g) solid white tuna, drained	1
6	hard-boiled eggs, halved (see Tips, left)	6
⅓ cup	small black niçoise olives	75 mL
3 tbsp	minced Italian flat-leaf parsley	45 mL
2 tbsp	drained capers	30 mL

1. Arrange lettuce leaves on a serving platter. In a large bowl, toss together beans, shallots, 2 or 3 large spoonfuls of vinaigrette, salt and pepper.

2. Baste tomatoes with a spoonful of vinaigrette. Place potatoes in the center of the platter and arrange a mound of beans at either end, with tomatoes and small mounds of tuna at strategic intervals. Ring platter with halves of hard-boiled eggs, sunny-side up. Spoon more vinaigrette over all. Scatter with olives, parsley and capers.

Pasta Salads

Pasta Salads

Filling and satisfying, pasta salads are also flexible, so you can bump up their flavor with almost any additional ingredients you fancy. It's important to start by carefully checking the directions on each package of pasta, though. Different brands and types require cooking for different lengths of time, and freshly made pasta usually cooks much faster than dried.

To cook pasta, bring a large pot of salted water to a roaring boil over high heat. Stir in the pasta to ensure that it's completely submerged. Start timing after the water returns to a boil. Drain and rinse, then proceed with the recipe.

If you're preparing a cold pasta dish, toss the drained pasta with a few spoonfuls of canola oil to prevent it from sticking together, then let it cool before adding the other ingredients. If the recipe doesn't specify cooling the pasta, however, you can toss it with the oil, then prepare and serve the salad either warm or cold.

Avocado and Corn Pasta Salad

Serves 4

Bright colors, combined with contrasts in textures and flavors, make this salad a crowd-pleaser.

8 oz	fusilli pasta, cooked and drained	250 g
1½ cups	Roasted Corn (page 271)	375 mL
2	ripe avocados, diced (see Tip, page 153)	2
1 tsp	freshly squeezed lemon juice	5 mL
½ cup	diced red bell pepper	125 mL
½ cup	black olives, pitted and chopped	125 mL
½ cup	chopped green onions	125 mL
½ cup	Sherry Vinaigrette (page 50)	125 mL
¼ cup	oil-packed sun-dried tomatoes, finely chopped	60 mL

1. In a large bowl, combine pasta, corn, avocados, lemon juice, bell pepper, olives, green onions, vinaigrette and sun-dried tomatoes.

Cold Creamy Pasta Salad

Tip

To determine if your avocado is ripe: Hold it in the palm of your hand and press. The avocado should feel like a tomato that has a little "give."

Dressing

½ cup	sour cream	125 mL
⅓ cup	Traditional Mayonnaise (page 100) or store-bought	75 mL
2 tsp	chopped fresh dill	10 mL
2 tsp	freshly cracked black peppercorns	10 mL
½ cup	freshly grated Parmesan cheese	125 mL

Salad

8 oz	rotini pasta, cooked, drained and cooled	250 g
2	ripe avocados, sliced (see Tip, left)	2

1. *Dressing:* In a large bowl, whisk together sour cream, mayonnaise, dill, pepper and Parmesan. Let stand to allow flavors to develop, about 20 minutes.

2. *Salad:* Add pasta to dressing and toss to coat. Arrange on a serving platter. Top with avocados.

Farmhouse Pasta Salad

8 oz	penne pasta, cooked and drained	250 g
8 oz	green beans, blanched and chilled	250 g
1 cup	cherry tomatoes, cut in half	250 mL
½ cup	freshly grated Parmesan cheese	125 mL
¼ cup	chopped green onions	60 mL
2 tbsp	drained capers	30 mL
¼ cup	Lemon Dijon Vinaigrette (page 42)	60 mL

1. In a large bowl, combine pasta, green beans, tomatoes, Parmesan, green onions and capers. Drizzle with vinaigrette and toss to coat.

Fresh Vegetable Pasta Salad

Tip
If fresh basil is not in season, use 1 tbsp (15 mL) dried instead.

¼ cup	canola oil	60 mL
1 cup	diced carrots	250 mL
1 cup	diced green zucchini	250 mL
1 cup	diced yellow summer squash, such as zucchini	250 mL
½ cup	finely chopped onion	125 mL
8 oz	penne pasta, cooked and drained	250 g
2	Roma (plum) tomatoes, diced	2
½ cup	chopped fresh basil (see Tip, left)	125 mL

1. In a large skillet, heat oil over medium heat. Add carrots, zucchini, squash and onion. Sauté until tender-crisp, about 2 minutes. Toss with pasta. Arrange on a serving platter and garnish with tomatoes and basil.

Black Bean and Red Pepper Pasta Salad

Serves 6

I like to serve this with a crusty bread or Italian focaccia for a complete meal.

Tip

To smash garlic: Peel each clove. Using one flat side of a chef's knife blade, smash the clove, then chop, if necessary.

Salad

1 lb	fusilli pasta, cooked and drained	500 g
1	can (14 to 19 oz/398 to 540 mL) black beans, drained and rinsed	1
12 oz	roasted red bell peppers, drained and chopped	375 g
6 oz	shiitake mushrooms, stems removed, caps sliced	175 g
6 oz	button mushrooms, sliced	175 g
½ cup	golden raisins	125 mL
½ cup	chopped green onions	125 mL
2 tbsp	chopped fresh basil	30 mL
1 tbsp	chopped fresh tarragon	15 mL

Dressing

3 tbsp	balsamic vinegar	45 mL
2 tbsp	extra virgin olive oil	30 mL
2	cloves garlic, smashed (see Tip, left)	2
	Sea salt and freshly ground black pepper	

1. *Salad:* In a large bowl, combine pasta, beans, bell peppers, shiitake and button mushrooms, raisins, green onions, basil and tarragon. Set aside.

2. *Dressing:* In a small bowl, whisk together balsamic vinegar, olive oil and garlic. Drizzle over pasta mixture and toss to coat. Season with salt and pepper to taste.

Olive Pasta Salad

Serves 6

The variety of French olives and sun-dried tomatoes make this a visual treat.

Tip

To smash garlic: Peel each clove. Using one flat side of a chef's knife blade, smash the clove, then chop, if necessary.

1 lb	farfalle (bow tie) pasta, cooked and drained	500 g
1/3 cup	picholine olives, pitted and chopped	75 mL
1/3 cup	niçoise olives, pitted and chopped	75 mL
1/3 cup	oil-packed sun-dried tomatoes, drained and finely chopped	75 mL
1/4 cup	finely chopped Italian flat-leaf parsley	60 mL
2 tbsp	drained capers	30 mL
2	cloves garlic, smashed (see Tip, left)	2
1/4 cup	balsamic vinegar	60 mL
	Sea salt and freshly ground black pepper	

1. In a large bowl, combine pasta, picholine and niçoise olives, sun-dried tomatoes, parsley, capers, garlic and vinegar. Season with salt and pepper to taste.

Provençal Pasta Salad

Serves 6

Many cafés line the Croisette in Cannes. You can sit and watch the yachts on the Mediterranean while you're savoring salads just like this one.

Tip

I have not included any salt or pepper for this salad because the capers add their own saltiness. Taste before seasoning, then add just what you think is needed.

1 lb	penne pasta, cooked and drained	500 g
1	can (14 oz/398 mL) green beans, drained	1
1/2 cup	chopped roasted red bell pepper	125 mL
2 tbsp	chopped Italian flat-leaf parsley	30 mL
1 tbsp	drained capers	15 mL
1/2 tsp	herbes de Provence	2 mL
1/4 cup	French Dressing (page 54) or store-bought	60 mL
3 oz	goat cheese, crumbled	90 g

1. In a large bowl, combine pasta, green beans, bell pepper, parsley, capers and herbes de Provence. Drizzle with dressing and toss to coat. Sprinkle with goat cheese.

Roasted Mushroom Pasta Salad

Tips

You can also roast your mushrooms in a roasting basket on an outdoor grill.

To toast pine nuts: Place nuts in a single layer on a baking sheet in a preheated 350°F (180°C) oven for 6 to 8 minutes, or until fragrant and golden, stirring once or twice.

- **Baking sheet, lined with parchment paper**
- **Preheat oven to 400°F (200°C)**

1 lb	button mushrooms, stemmed and quartered	500 g
1 tbsp	extra virgin olive oil	15 mL
1 tsp	freshly squeezed lemon juice	5 mL
8 oz	orzo pasta, cooked and drained	250 g
¾ cup	diced red bell pepper	175 mL
¼ cup	shredded fresh mint	60 mL
¼ cup	pine nuts, toasted (see Tip, left)	60 mL
	Sea salt and freshly ground black pepper	
6 oz	Parmesan cheese, grated	175 g

1. On prepared baking sheet, combine mushrooms, oil and lemon juice and arrange in a single layer. Roast in preheated oven for 15 minutes. Let cool.

2. In a bowl, combine pasta, mushrooms and cooking juices, bell pepper, mint and pine nuts. Season with salt and pepper to taste. Sprinkle with Parmesan.

Roasted Vegetable Pasta Salad

Serves 6

I like to use fresh garden vegetables if possible, but in the dead of winter roasting improves any vegetable.

Tip

Many cooks salt sliced eggplant and let it stand for about 30 minutes, rinse it quickly and thoroughly, then pat it dry with paper towels prior to use. This reduces bitterness (especially in more mature eggplants) and prevents the eggplant from becoming soggy or absorbing too much oil or grease during cooking. This is optional and may not be necessary with firm fresh young eggplants from a farmers' market, but might be a good idea if you see lots of moisture seeping from the slices.

- Baking sheet, lined with parchment paper
- Preheat oven to 400°F (200°C)

1 cup	diced red bell pepper	250 mL
1 cup	diced yellow bell pepper	250 mL
1	medium eggplant, cut into cubes (see Tip, left)	1
1 cup	yellow summer squash, such as zucchini, sliced	250 mL
¼ cup	extra virgin olive oil	60 mL
¼ tsp	sea salt	1 mL
¼ tsp	freshly ground black pepper	1 mL
12 oz	farfalle (bow tie) pasta, cooked and drained	375 g
½ cup	shredded fresh basil	125 mL
4	cloves garlic, minced	4
2 tbsp	balsamic vinegar	30 mL
4 oz	Gorgonzola cheese, crumbled	125 g

1. On prepared baking sheet, combine red and yellow bell peppers, eggplant, squash, oil, salt and pepper, and arrange in a single layer. Roast in preheated oven for 15 minutes. Let cool.

2. In a large bowl, combine roasted vegetables and cooking juices, pasta, basil, garlic, vinegar and Gorgonzola.

Three-Herb Pasta Salad

Make this pasta salad in the morning so all of the flavors have time to develop by the time you're ready to serve it for lunch or dinner.

Tip

I prefer to use a small round or shell-shaped pasta, such as little wheels or elbow-shaped, that is easily coated by the creamy sauce.

- **Food processor**

8 oz	cream cheese, softened	250 g
½ cup	Traditional Mayonnaise (page 100) or store-bought	125 mL
½ cup	buttermilk	125 mL
2 tbsp	freshly squeezed lemon juice	30 mL
1 tbsp	chopped fresh dill	15 mL
1 tbsp	chopped fresh tarragon	15 mL
1 tsp	chopped fresh rosemary	5 mL
1 tbsp	dried onion flakes	15 mL
1 tbsp	freshly ground black pepper	15 mL
½ tsp	garlic powder	2 ml
1 lb	pasta, cooked and drained (see Tip, left)	500 g

1. In a food processor fitted with a metal blade, process cream cheese, mayonnaise, buttermilk and lemon juice until smooth, about 2 minutes. Add dill, tarragon, rosemary, onion flakes, pepper and garlic powder. Process until well blended. Add dressing to cooked pasta and toss to coat. Cover and refrigerate for at least 2 hours prior to serving or for up to 3 days.

Whole Wheat Pasta Salad with Fresh Vegetables

8 oz	whole wheat linguini pasta, broken into 2- to 3-inch (5 to 7.5 cm) pieces, cooked and drained	250 g
½ cup	grated carrots	125 mL
1 cup	broccoli florets	250 mL
1 cup	baby green peas	250 mL
½ cup	diced green bell pepper	125 mL
½ cup	diced celery	125 mL
¼ cup	chopped green onions	60 mL
2	Roma (plum) tomatoes, diced	2
2 tbsp	Citrus Vinaigrette (page 87)	30 mL

1. In a large bowl, combine pasta, carrots, broccoli, peas, bell pepper, celery, green onions and tomatoes. Drizzle with vinaigrette and toss to coat.

Pear Pasta Salad

Tip
Purchase blue cheese in a wedge and crumble off what you need with a fork.

Variation
Try apples in place of pears.

8 oz	farfalle (bow tie) pasta, cooked and drained	250 g
2	pears, thinly sliced	2
½ cup	Glazed Hot Pecans (page 270)	125 mL
½ cup	golden raisins	125 mL
½ cup	chopped green onions	125 mL
½ cup	diced red bell pepper	125 mL
¼ cup	chopped Italian flat-leaf parsley	60 mL
¼ cup	Italian Herb Vinaigrette (page 42) or store-bought	60 mL
4 cups	fresh spinach leaves, torn, stems removed	1 L
4 oz	blue cheese, crumbled (see Tip, left)	125 g

1. In a large bowl, combine pasta, pears, pecans, raisins, green onions, bell pepper and parsley. Drizzle with vinaigrette and toss to coat. Arrange spinach on a serving platter. Top with pasta mixture and sprinkle with blue cheese.

Hot-and-Sour Noodle Salad

Serves 6

*Crisp vegetables
and soft noodles
livened up with a
chile-pepper kick will
make this salad a
family favorite.*

1 lb	rice noodles, cooked and drained	500 g
1 cup	chopped fresh cilantro	250 mL
2	Roma (plum) tomatoes, diced	2
1 cup	Roasted Corn (page 271)	250 mL
1 cup	roasted peanuts	250 mL
½ cup	chopped green onions	125 mL
½ cup	chopped red bell pepper	125 mL
2	jalapeño peppers, seeded and finely chopped	2
2 tbsp	reduced-sodium soy sauce	30 mL
1 tsp	liquid honey	5 mL

1. In a large bowl, combine noodles, cilantro, tomatoes, corn, peanuts, green onions, bell pepper and jalapeños.

2. In a small bowl, whisk together soy sauce and honey. Add to pasta and toss to coat.

Pineapple and Peach Ginger Noodle Salad

Serves 4

*Here's a perfect
"island" salad for a
spring brunch.*

1	can (14 oz/398 mL) diced pineapple	1
¼ cup	lightly packed brown sugar	60 mL
¼ cup	freshly squeezed lime juice	60 mL
¼ cup	coconut milk	60 mL
2 tbsp	fish or oyster sauce	30 mL
2 tbsp	freshly grated gingerroot	30 mL
2	cloves garlic, minced	2
1 tsp	freshly ground black pepper	5 mL
10 oz	udon noodles, cooked and drained	300 g
2 cups	chopped peaches	500 mL

1. In a medium saucepan over medium heat, stir together pineapple and brown sugar until sugar is completely dissolved and beginning to caramelize, about 8 minutes. Let cool.

2. In a salad bowl, combine lime juice, coconut milk and fish sauce. Whisk in ginger, garlic and pepper. Add noodles, pineapple and peaches. Toss to coat.

Sesame Noodle Salad

Here's a salad that's
nutty with toasted
sesame seeds.

Tip

To toast sesame seeds:
Place seeds on a baking
sheet and toast in
a preheated 350°F
(180°C) oven for 5 to
7 minutes, or until
fragrant and golden,
stirring once or twice.

Dressing

2 tbsp	toasted sesame oil	30 mL
1 tbsp	canola oil	15 mL
2 tsp	reduced-sodium soy sauce	10 mL
1	clove garlic, minced	1
	Sea salt and freshly ground white pepper	

Salad

12 oz	egg noodles, cooked, drained and cooled	375 g
1½ cups	snow peas, blanched	375 mL
½ cup	julienned carrots	125 mL
2	Roma (plum) tomatoes, diced	2
½ cup	chopped green onions	125 mL
¼ cup	chopped fresh cilantro	60 mL
2 tsp	sesame seeds, toasted (see Tip, left)	10 mL

1. *Dressing:* In a jar with a tight-fitting lid, combine sesame and canola oils, soy sauce and garlic. Add salt and white pepper to taste and shake vigorously. Set aside.

2. *Salad:* In a large bowl, combine noodles, snow peas, carrots, tomatoes, green onions, cilantro and sesame seeds. Drizzle with dressing and toss to coat.

Rice Noodle and Tofu Salad

Tip

If you cannot find fried tofu, purchase firm tofu, instead. Press as much water out of it as you can, then fry it in canola oil until all sides are light brown, about 2 minutes per side. Remove and drain on paper towels.

8 oz	rice noodles, cooked, drained and cooled	250 g
12 oz	deep-fried tofu, cut into cubes (see Tip, left)	375 g
1 cup	chopped fresh cilantro	250 mL
1/2 cup	chopped green onions	125 mL
2 tbsp	reduced-sodium soy sauce	30 mL
1 tbsp	toasted sesame oil	15 mL
1 1/2 tsp	hot pepper flakes	7 mL
1 tsp	grated lemon zest	5 mL
1 tsp	freshly squeezed lemon juice	5 mL
1/2 cup	sesame seeds, toasted (see Tip, page 162)	125 mL

1. In a large bowl, combine noodles, tofu, cilantro, green onions, soy sauce, oil, hot pepper flakes, lemon zest and juice, and sesame seeds.

Thai Noodle Salad

Here's a fresh vegetable salad that's packed with peanut flavor. Although North Americans often eat sprouts raw, I noticed in Asia that sprouts are frequently blanched.

Tip
Cook the noodles first, then remove them with tongs and use the same pot of boiling water for the vegetables.

12 oz	rice noodles, cooked, drained and cooled (see Tip, left)	375 g
2 cups	asparagus tips	500 mL
1 cup	diced red bell pepper	250 mL
1 cup	corn kernels	250 mL
1 cup	bean sprouts	250 mL
1 cup	chopped carrots	250 mL
1	can (8 oz/227 mL) water chestnuts, drained and chopped	1
½ cup	Thai Peanut Dressing (page 59) or store-bought	125 mL
½ cup	roasted peanuts	125 mL

1. In a large pot of boiling salted water, cook asparagus, bell pepper, corn, bean sprouts, carrots and water chestnuts until slightly softened, 2 to 4 minutes. With a slotted spoon, transfer vegetables to a bowl of ice water to set color and stop cooking.

2. In a serving bowl, combine noodles and vegetables. Drizzle with dressing and toss to coat. Garnish with peanuts.

Roasted Tomato Pasta Salad

Serves 4

Sweet tomatoes straight from your garden make this salad even better.

- Baking sheet, lined with parchment paper
- Preheat oven to 400°F (200°C)

6	Roma (plum) tomatoes, sliced	6
2 tbsp	extra virgin olive oil	30 mL
½ tsp	sea salt	2 mL
12 oz	rotelle pasta, cooked and drained	375 g
½ cup	chopped fresh basil	125 mL
½ cup	chopped green onions	125 mL
½ cup	chopped black olives	125 mL
½ cup	chopped cucumber	125 mL

1. On prepared baking sheet, combine tomatoes, olive oil and salt and arrange in a single layer. Roast in preheated oven for 15 minutes. Let cool.

2. In a bowl, combine tomatoes and cooking juices, pasta, basil, green onions, olives and cucumber.

Heirloom Tomatoes with Basil Pasta Salad

8 oz	orecchiette pasta, cooked and drained	250 g
1 lb	heirloom tomatoes, seeded and chopped	500 g
1/4 cup	chopped fresh basil	60 mL
1/4 cup	black olives, pitted and chopped	60 mL
1	clove garlic, minced	1
2 tbsp	extra virgin olive oil	30 mL
	Sea salt and freshly ground black pepper	
6 oz	feta cheese	175 g

1. In a bowl, combine pasta, tomatoes, basil, olives and garlic. Drizzle with oil and toss to coat. Season with salt and pepper to taste. Crumble feta on top.

Roma Tomatoes and Avocado Pasta Salad

12 oz	farfalle (bow tie) pasta, cooked, drained and cooled	375 g
12 oz	mozzarella cheese, cut into cubes	375 g
6	Roma (plum) tomatoes, diced	6
2	ripe avocados, diced (see Tip, left)	2
1/4 cup	pine nuts, toasted (see Tip, page 205)	60 mL
1/2 cup	Chenin Blanc Vinaigrette (page 39)	125 mL

1. In a large bowl, combine pasta, mozzarella, tomatoes, avocados and pine nuts. Drizzle with vinaigrette and toss to coat. Cover and refrigerate until chilled, about 25 minutes, before serving.

Summer Pasta Salad

8 oz	penne pasta, cooked and drained	250 g
5 oz	mozzarella cheese, diced	150 g
4	Roma (plum) tomatoes, diced	4
½ cup	black olives, pitted and sliced	125 mL
½ cup	chopped fresh basil	125 mL
2 tbsp	Radda Vinaigrette (page 47)	30 mL

1. In a large bowl, combine pasta, mozzarella, tomatoes, olives and basil. Drizzle with vinaigrette and toss to coat.

Caprese Pasta Salad

8 oz	cappelletti or gnocchi pasta, cooked and drained	250 g
8 oz	mozzarella cheese, cut into cubes	250 g
2	Roma (plum) tomatoes, diced	2
1 cup	chopped fresh basil	250 mL
¼ cup	Lemon Dijon Vinaigrette (page 42)	60 mL
	Sea salt and freshly ground black pepper	

1. In a large bowl, combine pasta, mozzarella, tomatoes and basil. Drizzle with vinaigrette and toss to coat. Season with salt and pepper to taste.

Gorgonzola Pecan Pasta Salad

Serves 4

This is a fast and easy salad with lots of flavor.

Tip

To toast pecans: Place nuts in a single layer on a baking sheet in a preheated 350°F (180°C) oven for 10 to 12 minutes for halves, 8 to 10 minutes for chopped, or until fragrant and golden, stirring once or twice.

6 tbsp	canola oil	90 mL
2 tbsp	red wine vinegar	30 mL
8 oz	penne pasta, cooked and drained	250 g
8 oz	Gorgonzola, crumbled	250 g
1 cup	chopped pecans, toasted	250 mL
2 cups	salad greens (see Tip, left)	500 mL

1. In a large bowl, whisk together oil and vinegar. Add pasta, Gorgonzola and pecans, and toss to coat. Place on a bed of salad greens.

Chicken and Snow Peas with Lemon Dijon Salad

Serves 4

Make this a complete meal by pairing the salad with servings of soup.

8 oz	mini penne pasta, cooked, drained and cooled	250 g
2 cups	shredded cooked chicken	500 mL
1 cup	cooked snow peas	250 mL
1 cup	grated carrots	250 mL
1 cup	sliced button mushrooms	250 mL
1/4 cup	chopped crisply cooked bacon	60 mL
1/4 cup	chopped fresh cilantro	60 mL
1/2 cup	Lemon Dijon Vinaigrette (page 42)	125 mL
	Sea salt and freshly ground black pepper	

1. In a large bowl, combine pasta, chicken, snow peas, carrots, mushrooms, bacon, cilantro and vinaigrette. Season with salt and pepper to taste. Cover and refrigerate until chilled, about 25 minutes, before serving.

Chicken with Tomatoes and Basil Pasta Salad

Serves 4

Try using any leftover chicken for this salad, then enjoy the accent of fresh and sweet tomato sauce.

Tip

If green beans are in season then by all means use them. Blanch the beans in boiling water for 4 minutes. Remove the beans with a slotted spoon and place in a bowl of ice water to cool and set the color, then cut into bite-size pieces.

8 oz	small pasta shells, cooked and drained	250 g
2 cups	shredded cooked chicken	500 mL
2	Roma (plum) tomatoes, diced	2
½ cup	chopped fresh basil	125 mL
1	can (14 oz/398 mL) green beans, drained (see Tip, left)	1
¼ cup	black olives, pitted and chopped	60 mL
2 tbsp	Country Ketchup (page 107) or store-bought	30 mL
1 tbsp	extra virgin olive oil	15 mL

1. In a large bowl, combine pasta, chicken, tomatoes, basil, green beans and olives. Set aside.

2. In a small bowl, whisk together ketchup and oil. Drizzle over pasta mixture and toss to coat.

Pasta Salad with Salami, Corn and Basil

1 lb	small pasta shells, cooked, drained and cooled	500 g
8 oz	salami, skinned and cut into cubes	250 g
8 oz	mozzarella cheese, cut into cubes	250 g
1 cup	Roasted Corn (page 271)	250 mL
1 cup	chopped fresh basil	250 mL
¾ cup	chopped red onion	175 mL
½ cup	Ligurian olives, pitted and chopped (see Tip, left)	125 mL
½ cup	Radda Vinaigrette (page 47)	125 mL

1. In a large bowl, combine pasta, salami, mozzarella, corn, basil, red onion and olives. Drizzle with vinaigrette and toss to coat.

2. Refrigerate for 1 hour to allow the flavors to develop prior to serving.

Gnocchi Mediterranean Salad

8 oz	gnocchi pasta, cooked and drained	250 g
4 oz	salami, chopped	125 g
½ cup	niçoise olives, pitted and chopped	125 mL
½ cup	chopped red onion	125 mL
½ cup	chopped fresh basil	125 mL
¼ cup	Caesar Dressing (page 53) or store-bought	60 mL
	Sea salt and freshly ground black pepper	

1. In a bowl, combine gnocchi, salami, olives, red onion and basil. Drizzle with dressing and toss to coat. Season with salt and pepper to taste.

Ham and Cheese Pasta Salad

Tip

Depending on the brand, you may need to drain the yogurt to avoid a watery dressing.

Salad

8 oz	small elbow macaroni, cooked and drained	250 g
8 oz	cooked ham, cut into cubes	250 g
4 oz	sharp Cheddar cheese, cut into cubes	125 g
¼ cup	chopped Italian flat-leaf parsley	60 mL

Dressing

¾ cup	plain yogurt (see Tip, left)	175 mL
¼ cup	Traditional Mayonnaise (page 100) or store-bought	60 mL
1 tbsp	Dijon Mustard (page 112) or store-bought	15 mL
	Sea salt and freshly ground black pepper	

1. *Salad:* In a large bowl, combine macaroni, ham, Cheddar and parsley. Set aside.

2. *Dressing:* In a bowl, whisk together yogurt, mayonnaise and mustard. Stir into macaroni mixture to coat. Season with salt and pepper to taste.

Hawaiian Salad

Serves 4

This salad uses foods, such as pineapples and macadamia nuts, that are native to Hawaii, so it's perfect for your next luau.

Tip

To toast macadamia nuts: Place nuts in a single layer on a baking sheet in a preheated 350°F (180°C) oven for 10 to 12 minutes for halves, 8 to 10 minutes for chopped, or until fragrant and golden, stirring once or twice.

Variation

Substitute ½ cup (125 mL) of any chopped toasted nuts for the macadamias.

Salad

8 oz	whole wheat penne pasta, cooked and drained	250 g
4 oz	cooked ham, cut into cubes	125 g
1	can (8 oz/227 mL) crushed pineapple, drained	1
¾ cup	chopped celery	175 mL
½ cup	diced green bell pepper	125 mL
½ cup	chopped macadamia nuts, toasted (see Tip, left)	125 mL

Dressing

½ cup	plain yogurt (see Tip, page 170)	125 mL
1 tbsp	apple cider vinegar	15 mL
1 tsp	Dijon Mustard (page 112) or store-bought	5 mL
1 tsp	granulated sugar	5 mL
	Sea salt and freshly ground black pepper	

1. *Salad:* In a large bowl, combine pasta, ham, pineapple, celery, bell pepper and macadamia nuts. Set aside.

2. *Dressing:* In a bowl, whisk together yogurt, vinegar, mustard and sugar. Drizzle over pasta mixture and toss to coat. Season with salt and pepper to taste.

Bean Noodle and Crab Salad

Bean thread noodles, also called cellophane noodles or harusame, can be fried to give them crunch or simply boiled as you prefer. Either way, they complement Pacific Rim flavors.

Salad

8 oz	bean thread noodles, cooked, drained and cooled	250 g
8 oz	cooked shelled crabmeat, drained and flaked	250 g
1 cup	sliced papaya	250 mL
1/2 cup	chopped mango	125 mL
1/4 cup	chopped shallots	60 mL
2 tsp	freshly grated gingerroot	10 mL
1 tsp	ground coriander	5 mL
1/2 tsp	chopped fresh chives	2 mL

Dressing

2 tbsp	freshly squeezed lime juice	30 mL
1 tbsp	Bold Chili Sauce (page 115) or store-bought	15 mL
2 tsp	fish or oyster sauce	10 mL
1/2 cup	canola oil	125 mL
1 tsp	sesame oil	5 mL

1. *Salad:* In a large bowl, combine noodles, crabmeat, papaya, mango, shallots, ginger, coriander and chives. Set aside.

2. *Dressing:* In a small bowl, whisk together lime juice, chili sauce and fish sauce. Whisk in canola and sesame oils until blended. Drizzle over crab and noodle mixture and toss to coat. Cover and refrigerate until chilled, about 25 minutes, before serving.

Smoked Salmon Pasta Salad

2 tbsp	extra virgin olive oil	30 mL
½ cup	chopped fresh fennel	125 mL
½ cup	chopped green onions	125 mL
6 oz	hot-smoked salmon, flaked	175 g
3 tbsp	chopped fresh dill	45 mL
½ cup	Traditional Mayonnaise (page 100) or store-bought	125 mL
2 tbsp	heavy or whipping (35%) cream	30 mL
2 tsp	freshly squeezed lime juice	10 mL
1 lb	small pasta shells, cooked and drained	500 g
	Sea salt and freshly ground black pepper	

1. In a skillet, heat oil over medium heat. Add fennel and green onions and sauté until lightly browned, about 4 minutes.

2. Transfer fennel mixture to a large bowl and let cool. Add salmon, dill, mayonnaise, cream and lime juice. Add pasta and toss to coat. Season with salt and pepper to taste.

French Pasta Salad

8 oz	penne pasta, cooked and drained	250 g
1	can (14 to 15 oz/398 to 425 mL) green beans, drained	1
1	can (6 oz/170 g) tuna, drained	1
3	Roma (plum) tomatoes, diced	3
½ cup	black olives, pitted and finely chopped	125 mL
1	can (2 oz/60 g) oil-packed anchovies, chopped	1
¼ cup	chopped Italian flat-leaf parsley	60 mL
	Sea salt and freshly ground black pepper	

1. In a large bowl, combine pasta, green beans, tuna, tomatoes, olives, anchovies with oil and parsley. Season with salt and pepper to taste.

Mediterranean Pasta Salad

Serves 4

In 2006 I took a Mediterranean cruise and discovered cafés with remarkable pasta salads at every island stop. Here is one from the Greek isle of Santorini.

8 oz	penne pasta, cooked and drained	250 g
2	Roma (plum) tomatoes, diced	2
1/2 cup	chopped fresh basil	125 mL
1	can (6 oz/170 g) tuna, drained and rinsed	1
1	hard-boiled egg, chopped (see Tips, page 138)	1
1	can (2 oz/60 g) anchovy fillets, drained and chopped	1
2 tsp	drained capers	10 mL
1/2 cup	Cabernet Sauvignon Vinaigrette (page 38)	125 mL

1. In a large bowl, combine pasta, tomatoes, basil, tuna, egg, anchovies and capers. Drizzle with vinaigrette and toss to coat.

Fast and Easy Shrimp Pasta Salad

Serves 4

When you need an easy dish, this is it.

8 oz	vermicelli pasta, cooked, drained and cooled	250 g
8 oz	cooked small salad shrimp	250 g
1/2 cup	chopped green onions	125 mL
1/2 cup	grated carrots	125 mL
1/4 cup	green olives, pitted and chopped	60 mL
1/2 cup	Radda Vinaigrette (page 47)	125 mL

1. In a large bowl, combine pasta, shrimp, green onions, carrots, olives and vinaigrette. Let stand for at least 30 minutes to allow the flavors to develop. Cover and refrigerate until chilled, about 25 minutes, before serving.

Thai Prawn Noodle Salad

Serves 6

Walking the food stalls in Bangkok, I found a veritable feast of noodle dishes. Here is a recipe that was given to me by the street vendor after I'd eaten it for lunch one day.

Tip

When seeding and dicing chile peppers, wear rubber gloves.

8 oz	egg noodles, cooked and drained	250 g
1½ lbs	cooked medium shrimp, peeled	750 g
2 cups	chopped mango	500 mL
1 cup	grated carrots	250 mL
¼ cup	shredded cucumber	60 mL
½ cup	chopped red onion	125 mL
3 tbsp	chopped peanuts	45 mL
2 tbsp	chopped fresh cilantro	30 mL
2 tsp	grated lime zest	10 mL
1	red chile pepper, seeded and minced (see Tip, left)	1
	Sea salt and freshly ground black pepper	

1. In a large bowl, combine noodles, shrimp, mango, carrots, cucumber, red onion, peanuts, cilantro, lime zest and chile pepper. Season with salt and pepper to taste.

Shrimp Noodle Salad

Serves 6

Here's a tasty Asian twist on shrimp and slaw.

Tips

When seeding and dicing chile peppers, wear rubber gloves.

If you are taking this salad to a party or plan to serve it later in the day, keep the salad and dressing separate and toss just prior to serving.

Variation

Use cubed tofu or scallops in place of the shrimp.

Salad

12 oz	cooked jumbo shrimp, peeled	375 g
8 oz	vermicelli rice noodles, cooked and drained	250 g
1 cup	cubed papaya	250 mL
1/2 cup	chopped green onions	125 mL
1/2 cup	chopped cucumber	125 mL
1/2 cup	shredded fresh basil	125 mL
1/2 cup	grated purple cabbage	125 mL
1	red chile pepper, seeded and finely chopped (see Tips, left)	1

Dressing

2 tbsp	oyster or fish sauce	30 mL
2 tbsp	freshly squeezed lime juice	30 mL
1 tbsp	lightly packed brown sugar	15 mL
1 tsp	hot pepper sauce	5 mL

1. *Salad:* In a large bowl, combine shrimp, rice noodles, papaya, green onions, cucumber, basil, cabbage and chile pepper. Set aside.

2. *Dressing:* In a bowl, whisk together oyster sauce, lime juice, brown sugar and hot pepper sauce until blended. Drizzle over shrimp mixture and toss to coat.

Whole-Grain and Bean Salads

Whole-Grain and Bean Salads

I'm a real fan of whole grains and beans, and not just because they're popular with nutritionists. They make my salads nutty, crunchy and full of flavor, adding a whole new dimension — as well as goodness — to the recipes. Try these combinations, then experiment with your own favorite grains and beans.

Bulgur Salad

Serves 4

This salad has a toasty taste from the bulgur.

1¼ cups	coarse bulgur	300 mL
1 cup	chicken broth	250 mL
1 tsp	sea salt	5 mL
⅛ tsp	ground cumin	0.5 mL
⅛ tsp	ground cinnamon	0.5 mL
Pinch	cayenne pepper	Pinch
1 cup	diced red bell pepper	250 mL
1 cup	diced yellow bell pepper	250 mL
2	Roma (plum) tomatoes, seeded and diced	2
¼ cup	diced shallots	60 mL
¼ cup	black olives, pitted and chopped	60 mL
3 tbsp	chopped fresh basil	45 mL
3 tbsp	chopped Italian flat-leaf parsley	45 mL
3 tbsp	chopped walnuts, toasted	45 mL
½ cup	extra virgin olive oil	125 mL
2 tbsp	balsamic vinegar	30 mL
	Sea salt and freshly ground black pepper	

1. Place bulgur in a heatproof bowl. In a saucepan over medium heat, bring chicken broth, salt, cumin, cinnamon and cayenne to a simmer. Pour over bulgur. Stir well and set aside until liquid is absorbed, about 30 minutes.

2. In a bowl, combine red and yellow bell peppers, tomatoes, shallots, olives, basil, parsley, walnuts, oil and vinegar.

3. Squeeze out excess liquid from bulgur, pressing firmly with your hands, and add to bell pepper mixture. Toss to evenly combine. Season with salt and pepper to taste.

Bulgur Tomato Salad

Serves 6

I ate this great salad in a deli in the Lincoln Park area of Chicago.

2 cups	coarse bulgur	500 mL
2 cups	boiling water	500 mL
1½ cups	frozen baby green peas (8 oz/250 g)	375 mL
1 cup	grape tomatoes, cut in half	250 mL
1 cup	chopped onion	250 mL
1 cup	chopped red bell pepper	250 mL
3 tbsp	chopped Italian flat-leaf parsley	45 mL
2 tbsp	extra virgin olive oil	30 mL
1 tbsp	red wine vinegar	15 mL
½ tsp	dried thyme	2 mL
	Sea salt and freshly ground black pepper	

1. In a large heatproof bowl, soak bulgur in boiling water. Stir well and set aside until liquid is absorbed, about 30 minutes. Squeeze out excess liquid from bulgur, pressing firmly with your hands.

2. In a small saucepan of boiling water, cook peas for 4 minutes. Drain. Add to bulgur. Add tomatoes, onion, bell pepper, parsley, oil, vinegar and thyme. Toss to evenly combine. Let stand for 20 minutes. Season with salt and pepper to taste.

Tabbouleh Salad

This Lebanese staple is a refreshing and healthy summer salad and a wonderful way to use mint.

Tip

If using coarse bulgur, increase the boiling-water soaking time to 30 minutes.

1/3 cup	fine bulgur (see Tip, left)	75 mL
1 cup	boiling water	250 mL
1/4 cup	freshly squeezed lemon juice	60 mL
2	cloves garlic, minced	2
1/2 tsp	sea salt	2 mL
1/2 tsp	freshly ground black pepper	2 mL
1	bunch fresh mint, chopped (about 1 cup/250 mL)	1
4 cups	chopped Italian flat-leaf parsley	1 L
1/2 cup	chopped green onions	125 mL
3	tomatoes, seeded and diced	3
1/4 cup	extra virgin olive oil	60 mL
1	head romaine lettuce	1

1. In a large heatproof bowl, combine bulgur and boiling water. Stir well and set aside until bulgur is softened, about 15 minutes. Squeeze out excess liquid, pressing firmly with your hands. Add lemon juice, garlic, salt and pepper. Let stand until bulgur is tender, about 30 minutes. Squeeze out excess liquid.

2. Add mint, parsley, green onions and tomatoes to bulgur mixture. Toss with oil to coat. Serve with small romaine lettuce leaves on the side for scoops.

Tabbouleh with Tomatoes and Dried Fruit Salad

Serves 6

This Middle Eastern salad is rich with color and flavor.

1½ cups	coarse bulgur	375 mL
2 cups	boiling water	500 mL
3	Roma (plum) tomatoes, seeded and diced	3
2	cloves garlic, minced	2
1 cup	chopped zucchini	250 mL
½ cup	chopped green onions	125 mL
½ cup	dried apricots, finely chopped	125 mL
¼ cup	golden raisins	60 mL
2 tbsp	freshly squeezed lemon juice	30 mL
1 tsp	chopped fresh mint	5 mL
	Sea salt and freshly ground black pepper	

1. In a large heatproof bowl, combine bulgur and boiling water. Stir well and set aside until liquid is absorbed, about 30 minutes. Squeeze out excess liquid, pressing firmly with your hands. Transfer to a bowl.

2. Add tomatoes, garlic, zucchini, green onions, apricots, raisins, lemon juice and mint and toss to evenly combine. Season with salt and pepper to taste.

Cracked Wheat with Nut Salad

Serves 4

Make this a day before you serve it, to allow all of the flavors to mingle and marry.

Tip

To toast almonds: Place nuts in a single layer on a baking sheet in a preheated 350°F (180°C) oven for 11 to 13 for whole, 10 to 12 minutes for chopped, or until fragrant and golden, stirring once or twice.

1 cup	coarse bulgur	250 mL
1 cup	boiling water	250 mL
1 cup	diced green bell pepper	250 mL
½ cup	sliced cucumber	125 mL
¼ cup	chopped almonds, toasted (see Tip, left)	60 mL
1 tsp	grated lemon zest	5 mL
2 tsp	freshly squeezed lemon juice	10 mL
1	large navel orange, peeled and segmented	1
	Sea salt and freshly ground black pepper	

1. In a large heatproof bowl, combine bulgur and boiling water. Stir well and set aside until liquid is absorbed, about 30 minutes. Squeeze out excess liquid, pressing firmly with your hands. Add bell pepper, cucumber, almonds, lemon zest and juice and orange segments and toss to evenly combine. Season with salt and pepper to taste.

Couscous Salad

Tip

I like to make this salad a day prior to use, then cover and refrigerate, to allow the flavors to develop.

Salad

2 cups	couscous	500 mL
2½ cups	boiling chicken broth	625 mL
1 cup	chopped zucchini	250 mL
½ cup	black olives, pitted and chopped	125 mL
¼ cup	chopped almonds, toasted	60 mL

Dressing

¼ cup	canola oil	60 mL
1 tsp	grated lemon zest	5 mL
1 tbsp	freshly squeezed lemon juice	15 mL
1 tbsp	chopped fresh cilantro	15 mL
Pinch	ground cumin	Pinch
Pinch	cayenne pepper	Pinch

1. *Salad:* In a heatproof bowl, combine couscous and chicken broth. Cover and let stand for 10 minutes. Fluff with a fork.

2. Stir in zucchini, olives and almonds. Set aside.

3. *Dressing:* In a small bowl, whisk together oil, lemon zest and juice, cilantro, cumin and cayenne. Drizzle over couscous and toss to coat.

Roasted Eggplant Couscous Salad

Tip

Many cooks salt sliced eggplant and let it stand for about 30 minutes, rinse it quickly and thoroughly, then pat it dry with paper towels prior to use. This reduces bitterness (especially in more mature eggplants) and prevents the eggplant from becoming soggy or absorbing too much oil or grease during cooking. This is optional and may not be necessary with firm fresh young eggplants from a farmers' market, but might be a good idea if you see lots of moisture seeping from the slices.

- **Roasting pan**
- **Preheat oven to 425°F (220°C)**

3	medium eggplants, cut into cubes (see Tip, left)	3
2 tbsp	extra virgin olive oil	30 mL
1 cup	couscous	250 mL
¼ cup	chopped fresh mint	60 mL
	Sea salt and freshly ground black pepper	

1. Toss eggplants with oil. Transfer to a roasting pan and arrange in a single layer. Roast in preheated oven, stirring occasionally, until golden brown, 7 to 12 minutes. Transfer to a large bowl and set aside.

2. In a saucepan over high heat, bring 1¾ cups (425 mL) water to a boil. Stir in couscous. Remove from heat and let stand for 5 minutes. Fluff with a fork and let cool.

3. Add couscous and mint to eggplants and toss with a fork to combine. Season with salt and pepper to taste.

Brown Rice Salad with Fruit and Vegetables

Tip

To peel gingerroot without a vegetable peeler, use the edge of a large spoon to scrape off the skin.

2 cups	cooked long- or short-grain brown rice, cold	500 mL
1 cup	corn kernels, thawed if frozen	250 mL
½ cup	diced red bell pepper	125 mL
1	can (8 oz/227 mL) crushed pineapple, drained	1
¼ cup	golden raisins	60 mL
1	clove garlic, minced	1
1 tsp	freshly grated gingerroot (see Tip, left)	5 mL
1 tbsp	reduced-sodium soy sauce	15 mL
1 tbsp	canola oil	15 mL
	Sea salt and freshly ground black pepper	

1. In a bowl, combine rice, corn, bell pepper, pineapple, raisins, garlic and ginger.

2. Drizzle soy sauce and oil over rice mixture and toss to combine. Season with salt and pepper to taste.

Easy Rice Salad

Serves 6

If you have leftover rice, you can skip Step 1 and get this on the table even faster.

Tip

When seeding and dicing chile peppers, wear rubber gloves.

Salad

1½ cups	long-grain brown rice, rinsed and drained	375 mL
½ cup	chopped green onions	125 mL
½ cup	diced green bell pepper	125 mL
½ cup	diced red bell pepper	125 mL
¼ cup	chopped Italian flat-leaf parsley	60 mL
1	serrano chile pepper, seeded and finely chopped (see Tip, left)	1
1	Roma (plum) tomato, seeded and diced	1

Dressing

¼ cup	extra virgin olive oil	60 mL
1 tbsp	freshly squeezed lemon juice	15 mL
1 tsp	Dijon mustard (page 112) or store-bought	5 mL
	Sea salt and freshly ground black pepper	

1. *Salad:* In a saucepan over medium heat, bring 3 cups (750 mL) water to a boil. Stir in rice. Reduce heat to low. Cover and cook for 50 minutes. Transfer to a bowl and let cool. Fluff with a fork.

2. In a large bowl, combine green onions, green and red bell peppers, parsley, chile pepper and tomato. Gently stir in rice with a fork.

3. *Dressing:* In a bowl, whisk together olive oil, lemon juice and mustard. Drizzle over rice mixture and toss to combine. Season with salt and pepper to taste.

Spanish Rice Salad

Serves 6

If I am making rice for dinner, I double the batch, so I have enough to assemble this salad for lunch the next day.

Salad

1½ cups	brown rice, rinsed and drained	375 mL
½ cup	chopped red bell pepper	125 mL
½ cup	chopped green bell pepper	125 mL
½ cup	chopped green onions	125 mL
3	Roma (plum) tomatoes, seeded and diced	3
2 tbsp	chopped fresh cilantro	30 mL

Dressing

2 tbsp	canola oil	30 mL
1 tbsp	white wine vinegar	15 mL
I tsp	Dijon Mustard (page 112) or store-bought	5 mL
	Sea salt and freshly ground black pepper	

1. *Salad:* In a saucepan over medium heat, bring 3 cups (750 mL) water to a boil. Stir in rice. Reduce heat to low. Cover and simmer for 50 minutes. Transfer to a bowl, fluff with a fork and let cool.

2. Add red and green bell peppers, green onions, tomatoes and cilantro. Set aside.

3. *Dressing:* In a small bowl, whisk together canola oil, vinegar and mustard. Drizzle over rice mixture and toss to combine. Season with salad and pepper to taste.

Thai Rice Salad

Tip

Use the lower tender part of the lemongrass as the darker ends are more fibrous.

3 cups	vegetable broth	750 mL
½ cup	diced onion	125 mL
1 tbsp	grated lime zest	15 mL
1 tbsp	chopped fresh lemongrass (see Tip, left)	15 mL
1 tsp	freshly grated gingerroot	5 mL
1 tbsp	extra virgin olive oil	15 mL
1½ tsp	coriander seeds	7 mL
1½ tsp	cumin seeds	7 mL
1¼ cups	long-grain brown rice, rinsed	300 mL
¼ cup	chopped fresh cilantro	60 mL
¼ cup	chopped green onions	60 mL

1. In a large saucepan, combine vegetable broth, onion, lime zest, lemongrass, ginger, oil, and coriander and cumin seeds. Bring to a boil over medium heat. Stir in rice. Reduce heat to low. Cover and cook for 50 minutes. Transfer to a bowl and fluff with a fork. Let cool.

2. Stir in cilantro and green onions.

Bean and Blue Cheese Salad

Tip

To toast pecans: Place nuts in a single layer on a baking sheet in a preheated 350°F (180°C) oven for 10 to 12 minutes for halves, 8 to 10 minutes for chopped, or until fragrant and golden, stirring once or twice.

1 cup	dried cannellini or white kidney beans	250 mL
½ cup	chopped onion	125 mL
1	bay leaf	1
1 tsp	chopped fresh thyme	5 mL
1	serrano chile pepper, seeded and finely chopped	1
3 tbsp	chopped Italian flat-leaf parsley	45 mL
¼ cup	chopped pecans, toasted (see Tip, left)	60 mL
8 oz	blue cheese, crumbled	250 g
2 tbsp	Radda Vinaigrette (page 47)	30 mL
	Sea salt and freshly ground black pepper	

1. In a bowl, cover beans with water and soak overnight.

2. Drain beans. In a saucepan over medium heat, cover beans with fresh cold water and bring to a boil. Boil for 10 minutes, then reduce heat to low. Add onion, bay leaf, thyme and chile pepper and simmer until beans are tender, about 30 minutes. Drain beans and discard bay leaf. Transfer to a large bowl. Let cool to room temperature, about 20 minutes.

3. Mix in parsley, pecans and blue cheese. Drizzle with vinaigrette and toss to coat. Season with salt and pepper to taste.

Bean and Feta Salad

Serves 4

Serve this salad with toasted pita bread.

Tip
If using canned fava beans, drain and rinse, then proceed to Step 2.

12 oz	frozen fava beans (see Tip, left)	375 g
¼ cup	extra virgin olive oil	60 mL
3	Roma (plum) tomatoes, smashed	3
4	cloves garlic, smashed (see Tip, page 155)	4
4 oz	feta cheese, crumbled	125 g
⅓ cup	green olives, pitted and chopped	75 mL
3 tbsp	chopped fresh dill	45 mL
	Sea salt and freshly ground black pepper	

1. In a large pot of boiling salted water, cook beans until just tender or according to package directions. Drain, place on paper towels and let cool.

2. In a skillet, heat oil over medium heat. Add tomatoes and garlic and sauté until tomatoes are softened, about 3 minutes. Add feta and cook for 1 minute. Transfer to a bowl. Add beans, olives and dill and toss to combine. Season with salt and pepper to taste.

Fava Bean Salad

Serves 4

Here's a salad of light fava beans with the flavors of citrus.

1	can (14 to 19 oz/398 to 540 mL) fava beans, drained and rinsed	1
2	lemons, peeled and segmented	2
¼ cup	chopped fresh cilantro	60 mL
3 tbsp	extra virgin olive oil	45 mL
2 tbsp	freshly squeezed lemon juice	30 mL
2	cloves garlic, minced	2
2 tsp	Hungarian paprika	10 mL
	Sea salt and freshly ground black pepper	

1. In a bowl, combine beans, lemon segments, cilantro, oil, lemon juice, garlic and paprika. Season with salt and pepper to taste.

2. Make this salad at least 1 hour, or up to 8 hours, prior to serving to allow the flavors to develop.

Black Bean Salad

Serves 4

I like to serve this salad with chips, as an appetizer.

Tip

If your cans of beans are larger than 14 oz (398 mL), use a total 3 cups (750 mL) drained and rinsed canned black beans.

2	cans (each 14 oz/398 mL) black beans, drained and rinsed (see Tip, left)	2
1 cup	chopped red onion	250 mL
2	serrano chile peppers, seeded and chopped	2
1	canned chipotle pepper in adobo sauce, drained and chopped	1
½ cup	chopped fresh cilantro	125 mL
2 tbsp	extra virgin olive oil	30 mL
1 tsp	grated lime zest	5 mL
2 tsp	freshly squeezed lime juice	10 mL

1. In a bowl, combine black beans, red onion, chile peppers, chipotle, cilantro, oil and lime zest and juice. Cover and refrigerate for at least 6 hours to allow the flavors to develop prior to serving.

Brown Bean Salad

Serves 4

*I like to serve
this hearty salad
alongside chicken
or fish in the fall and
winter months.*

Tip

Swedish brown beans
are smaller brown
buttery beans. They
may be difficult to find
at the local grocery
store, so check the
international aisle of
supermarkets or use
pinto beans.

Variation

Use red kidney beans
or lima beans in
place of brown beans
for another look
and flavor.

1	can (14 to 19 oz/398 to 540 mL) Swedish brown beans or pinto beans, drained and rinsed (see Tip, left)	1
½ cup	chopped red onion	125 mL
2	hard-boiled eggs, chopped (see Tips, page 138)	2
4	cloves garlic, minced	4
⅓ cup	chopped Italian flat-leaf parsley	75 mL
¼ cup	Tarragon Pickle Relish (page 118) or store-bought relish	60 mL
¼ cup	chopped green onions	60 mL
¼ cup	extra virgin olive oil	60 mL
½ tsp	dried thyme	2 mL
½ tsp	ground cumin	2 mL
	Sea salt and freshly ground black pepper	

1. In a large bowl, combine brown beans, red onion, eggs, garlic, parsley, relish, green onions, oil, thyme and cumin. Season with salt and pepper to taste.

Endive and Blue Cheese Salad (page 210)

Sun-Dried Tomato and Pepper Salad (page 219)

Vietnamese Beef Salad (page 226)

Asian Chicken Salad (page 232)

Shrimp and Melon Salad (page 250)

Crab and Arugula Salad (page 258)

Watermelon and Feta Salad (page 265)

Grapes and Gorgonzola Salad (page 266)

Chickpea Salad

You can have this salad on the table in minutes.

Tip

If you can't find a 28-oz (796 mL) can of chickpeas, use two 14-oz (398 mL) cans or a total 3 cups (750 mL) drained and rinsed canned chickpeas.

1	can (28 oz/796 mL) chickpeas, drained and rinsed (see Tip, left)	1
½ cup	finely chopped green onions	125 mL
2	Roma (plum) tomatoes, seeded and diced	2
½ cup	diced red onion	125 mL
½ cup	chopped black olives	125 mL
2 tbsp	chopped Italian flat-leaf parsley	30 mL
1 tbsp	drained capers	15 mL

1. In a large bowl, combine chickpeas, green onions, tomatoes, red onion, olives, parsley and capers.

Green Bean and Tomato Salad

Serves 4

They may be at their best harvested fresh from the garden, but the red tomatoes and green beans in this superfast salad will brighten up your table any time of year.

1 lb	green beans	500 g
4	Roma (plum) tomatoes, seeded and diced	4
½ cup	chopped green onions	125 mL
2 tbsp	pine nuts, toasted	30 mL
1 tbsp	chopped fresh tarragon	15 mL
½ cup	Parmesan Vinaigrette (page 45)	125 mL

1. In a large pot of boiling salted water, blanch green beans until just tender, about 4 minutes. Drain and transfer to a bowl of ice water to set color and stop cooking. Drain when cooled.

2. In a large bowl, toss together beans, tomatoes, green onions, pine nuts, tarragon and vinaigrette.

Lentil and Cabbage Salad

Crunchy cabbage salad can be a complete meal simply by serving it with crusty bread.

1 cup	brown lentils, rinsed	250 mL
1	onion, quartered	1
1 tbsp	olive oil	15 mL
1/2 cup	chopped red onion	125 mL
3	cloves garlic, minced	3
1 tbsp	chopped fresh thyme	15 mL
3 cups	shredded cabbage	750 mL
1 tbsp	red wine vinegar	15 mL
1 tsp	grated lemon zest	5 mL
2 tsp	freshly squeezed lemon juice	10 mL
	Sea salt and freshly ground black pepper	

1. In a large pot, combine lentils, 3 cups (750 mL) cold water and quartered onion. Bring to a boil over medium heat. Boil for 10 minutes. Reduce heat to low and simmer until lentils are tender, 15 to 20 minutes. Drain and discard onion. Set aside.

2. In a skillet, heat oil over medium heat. Add red onion, garlic and thyme and sauté until softened, about 5 minutes. Add cabbage and sauté until slightly wilted but still crunchy, about 3 minutes. Stir in cooked lentils, vinegar and lemon zest and juice. Season with salt and pepper to taste. Serve warm or let cool.

Lima Bean Salad

Tip
When seeding and dicing chile peppers, wear rubber gloves.

1	can (14 to 19 oz/398 to 540 mL) lima beans, drained and rinsed	1
½ cup	diced onion	125 mL
1	jalapeño pepper, seeded and diced (see Tip, left)	1
2 tbsp	chopped Italian flat-leaf parsley	30 mL
2 tbsp	canola oil	30 mL
1 tbsp	balsamic vinegar	15 mL
½ tsp	sea salt	2 mL

1. In a bowl, combine beans, onion, jalapeño, parsley, oil, vinegar and salt. Let stand for 1 hour to allow the flavors to develop prior to serving.

Pepper Bean Salad

1	can (14 to 19 oz/398 to 540 mL) red kidney beans, drained and rinsed	1
1	can (14 to 19 oz/398 to 540 mL) black-eyed peas, drained and rinsed	1
1	can (14 to 19 oz/398 to 540 mL) chickpeas, drained and rinsed	1
½ cup	chopped red bell pepper	125 mL
½ cup	sliced radishes	125 mL
¼ cup	chopped green onions	60 mL
½ cup	Parmesan Vinaigrette (page 45)	125 mL

1. In a large bowl, combine kidney beans, black-eyed peas, chickpeas, bell pepper, radishes, green onions and vinaigrette. Let stand for 30 minutes to allow the flavors to develop prior to serving.

Pinto Bean Salad

Tips

If your cans of pinto beans are larger than 14 oz (398 mL), use a total 3 cups (750 mL) drained and rinsed canned beans.

Don't skip washing the tomatillos after husking them. There is a sticky substance on the skins that you need to remove.

2	cans (each 14 oz/398 mL) pinto beans, drained and rinsed (see Tips, left)	2
4	tomatillos, washed, seeded and diced (see Tips, left)	4
2 to 3	canned chipotle peppers in adobo sauce, drained and chopped	2 to 3
2	red chile peppers, seeded and chopped	2
3	cloves garlic, minced	3
1 cup	chopped red onion	250 mL
	Sea salt and freshly ground black pepper	

1. In a large bowl, combine pinto beans, tomatillos, chipotles to taste, red chile peppers, garlic and red onion. Season with salt and pepper to taste.

Spicy Bean Salad

Serves 8

This bean salad pairs perfectly with anything hot off the grill.

1	can (14 to 19 oz/398 to 540 mL) black-eyed peas, drained and rinsed	1
1	can (14 to 19 oz/398 to 540 mL) chickpeas, drained and rinsed	1
1	can (14 to 19 oz/398 to 540 mL) kidney beans, drained and rinsed	1
½ cup	chopped onion	125 mL
1 tbsp	sesame oil	15 mL
1 tbsp	freshly squeezed lemon juice	15 mL
2	cloves garlic, minced	2
1 tsp	ground cumin	5 mL
1 tsp	freshly ground black pepper	5 mL
1 tsp	sea salt	5 mL
½ tsp	ground coriander	2 mL
¼ tsp	hot pepper flakes	1 mL

1. In a bowl, combine black-eyed peas, chickpeas, kidney beans, onion, oil, lemon juice, garlic, cumin, black pepper, salt, coriander and hot pepper flakes.

2. Let stand for 1 hour to allow the flavors to develop prior to serving.

Three-Bean Salad

Serves 8

Here's a satisfying and simple-to-make salad.

1	can (14 to 19 oz/398 to 540 mL) red kidney beans, drained and rinsed	1
1	can (14 to 19 oz/398 to 540 mL) lima beans, drained and rinsed	1
1	can (10 to 14 oz/284 to 398 mL) green beans, drained and rinsed	1
1 cup	chopped yellow bell pepper	250 mL
½ cup	chopped green onions	125 mL
½ cup	grated carrot	125 mL
2 tbsp	extra virgin olive oil	30 mL
2 tbsp	red wine vinegar	30 mL
1 tbsp	dried minced onions	15 mL
½ cup	cashews, finely chopped	125 mL
	Sea salt and freshly ground black pepper	

1. In a large bowl, combine kidney beans, lima beans, green beans, bell pepper, green onions, carrot, oil, vinegar, dried onions and cashews. Let stand for at least 30 minutes to allow flavors to develop prior to serving. Season with salt and pepper to taste.

Warm Black-Eyed Pea Salad

Serves 4

On a cold winter day, there's nothing better than a warm salad and a cup of hot soup.

1	can (14 to 19 oz/398 to 540 mL) black-eyed peas, drained and rinsed	1
½ cup	chopped green onions	125 mL
¼ cup	chopped fresh dill	60 mL
¼ cup	extra virgin olive oil	60 mL
2 tbsp	freshly squeezed lemon juice	30 mL
¼ cup	olives, pitted and chopped	60 mL
	Sea salt and freshly ground black pepper	

1. In a saucepan over medium heat, combine black-eyed peas, green onions, dill, oil and lemon juice until slightly warm. Transfer to a serving bowl. Sprinkle with olives. Season with salt and pepper to taste.

White Bean and Jicama Salad

Serves 6

Jicama adds a nice crunch to this salad.

Tips

Jicama is a tuber from Central America with a thin tan skin and crunchy dense white flesh that can be eaten raw or cooked. I use a vegetable peeler to remove the outer skin.

If your cans of beans are larger than 14 oz (398 mL), use a total 4¹⁄₂ cups (1.125 L) drained and rinsed canned navy beans.

1¹⁄₂ cups	shredded jicama (see Tips, left)	375 mL
3	cans (each 14 oz/398 mL) navy beans, drained and rinsed (see Tips, left)	3
¹⁄₂ cup	chopped celery	125 mL
¹⁄₂ cup	French Honey Dressing (page 73) or store-bought	125 mL
3 tbsp	chopped fresh cilantro	45 mL
	Sea salt and freshly ground black pepper	

1. In a bowl, combine jicama, navy beans, celery, dressing and cilantro. Toss to evenly coat. Season with salt and pepper to taste.

White Bean Roasted Pepper Salad

Serves 6

Sweet roasted peppers round this salad off well.

2	cans (each 14 oz/398 mL) cannellini or white kidney beans, drained and rinsed	2
1	jar (7 oz/210 mL) roasted red bell peppers, drained and finely chopped	1
2	cloves garlic, minced	2
1 cup	chopped Italian flat-leaf parsley	250 mL
1 tbsp	balsamic vinegar	15 mL
	Sea salt and freshly ground black pepper	

1. In a large bowl, combine cannellini beans, roasted peppers, garlic, parsley and vinegar. Season with salt and pepper to taste.

Zucchini and Bean Salad

2 cups	sliced zucchini	500 mL
1	can (14 oz to 19 oz/398 to 540 mL) cannellini or white kidney beans, drained and rinsed	1
3 tbsp	extra virgin olive oil	45 mL
2 tsp	grated lemon zest	10 mL
2 tsp	freshly squeezed lemon juice	10 mL
	Sea salt and freshly ground black pepper	

1. In a large pot of boiling water, cook zucchini until softened, about 4 minutes. Drain and rinse with cold water. Transfer to a bowl.

2. Add beans, oil and lemon zest and juice. Season with salt and pepper to taste.

Greens and
Vegetable Salads

Greens and Vegetable Salads

The freshest ingredients make the best salads, so it's worth shopping at your local farmers' market before you start. There's a salad here for almost every imaginable vegetable, so you can use whatever you find that's at its seasonal peak.

Avocado Salad

Tip

To determine if your avocado is ripe: Hold it in the palm of your hand and press. The avocado should feel like a tomato that has a little "give."

⅓ cup	sour cream	75 mL
¼ cup	small curd cottage cheese	60 mL
1	clove garlic, minced	1
1	serrano chile pepper, seeded and finely chopped	1
2 tsp	freshly squeezed lemon juice	10 mL
1 tsp	chopped fresh dill	5 mL
2	ripe avocados, diced (see Tip, left)	2
4	butterhead lettuce leaves	4
¼ tsp	Hungarian paprika	1 mL

1. In a small bowl, combine sour cream, cottage cheese, garlic, chile pepper, lemon juice and dill. Add avocados and toss gently to coat. Arrange lettuce leaves on a serving platter. Top with sour cream mixture. Sprinkle with paprika.

Avocado and Tomato Salad with Sunflower Seeds

3	Roma (plum) tomatoes, seeded and diced	3
2	ripe avocados, diced (see Tip, page 202)	2
¼ cup	chopped red onion	60 mL
2 tbsp	extra virgin olive oil	30 mL
1 tbsp	chopped Italian flat-leaf parsley	15 mL
1 tsp	freshly squeezed lime juice	5 mL
2 tbsp	Spicy Sunflower Seeds (page 273)	30 mL

1. In a medium bowl, combine tomatoes, avocados, red onion, oil, parsley and lime juice. Transfer to a serving platter. Sprinkle with sunflower seeds.

Beet and Mint Salad

- **Roasting pan, lined with parchment paper**
- **Preheat oven to 400°F (200°C)**

2 lbs	beets, peeled and thinly sliced (about 6 medium)	1 kg
2 tsp	granulated sugar	10 mL
2 tsp	balsamic vinegar	10 mL
½ cup	chopped fresh mint	125 mL
2 tsp	freshly squeezed lime juice	10 mL

1. In prepared roasting pan, arrange beets in a single layer. Sprinkle with sugar and vinegar. Roast in preheated oven until fork-tender, 45 to 60 minutes, depending on the thickness of the beets. Let cool.

2. Toss beets with mint and lime juice. Serve on a platter.

Beet and Orange Salad

Serves 4

This bright red and orange salad will disappear from the buffet table in no time.

Tip

I like to freshly grate the nutmeg using a fine Microplane-style grater — the taste of fresh is like no other.

1½ lbs	beets, cooked, peeled and sliced (about 4 medium)	750 g
1	can (10 oz/287 mL) mandarin oranges, drained	1
1 tbsp	granulated sugar	15 mL
1 tsp	ground cinnamon	5 mL
½ tsp	freshly grated nutmeg	2 mL

1. In a large bowl, combine beets, oranges, sugar, cinnamon and nutmeg. Let marinate for 30 minutes prior to serving.

Roasted Beet and Onion Salad

Serves 6

Sweet beets and onions make this salad look good and taste even better.

- **Roasting pan, lined with parchment paper**
- **Preheat oven to 400°F (200°C)**

1½ lbs	beets, peeled and sliced (about 4 medium)	750 g
1 lb	onions, sliced	500 g
¼ cup	extra virgin olive oil	60 mL
1 cup	chopped pecans	250 mL
	Sea salt and freshly ground black pepper	

1. In prepared roasting pan, arrange beets and onions in a single layer. Top with ½ cup (125 mL) water and oil. Roast in preheated oven until beets are fork-tender and onions are browned, 45 to 60 minutes, depending on the thickness of beet slices. Let cool.

2. Transfer roasted beets and onions to a serving platter. Sprinkle with pecans. Season with salt and pepper to taste.

Asian Cucumber Salad

Serves 4

If you like, serve
this with pita or little
toasts to scoop it up.

Tip
Use a mandoline to
get perfectly even
cucumber slices.

½ cup	chopped red onion	125 mL
2 tbsp	granulated sugar	30 mL
1 tbsp	rice wine vinegar	15 mL
1 tsp	sea salt	5 mL
1	large cucumber, peeled and thinly sliced (see Tip, left)	1
2 tsp	chopped fresh dill	10 mL

1. In a small saucepan over medium heat, combine red onion, ¼ cup (60 mL) water, sugar, vinegar and salt and bring to a boil, stirring to dissolve sugar. Boil for about 4 minutes. Remove from heat. Stir in cucumber and let cool completely. Stir in dill.

Cucumber and Pine Nut Salad

Serves 4

This creamy salad
has a crunchy,
nutty taste.

Tip
To toast pine nuts: Place
nuts in a single layer
on a baking sheet in
a preheated 350°F
(180°C) oven for 6 to
8 minutes, or until
fragrant and golden,
stirring once or twice.

Variation
You can use any
toasted nuts you like.

2	large cucumbers, thinly sliced	2
2	cloves garlic, minced	2
1 cup	sour cream	250 mL
2 tbsp	chopped fresh dill	30 mL
¼ cup	pine nuts, toasted (see Tip, left)	60 mL
	Sea salt	

1. In a large bowl, combine cucumbers, garlic, sour cream and dill. Sprinkle with pine nuts and season with salt to taste.

Cucumber Dill Salad

This is a fast and easy salad that is easily doubled or tripled to feed a crowd.

Tip

You can use either peeled or unpeeled cucumbers in this salad, as you please.

2	large cucumbers, thinly sliced (see Tip, left, and page 205)	2
1 tsp	sea salt	5 mL
¼ cup	chopped fresh dill	60 mL
1 tbsp	white vinegar	15 mL
⅔ cup	sour cream	150 mL

1. In a colander over a bowl, sprinkle cucumber slices with salt. Let drain for 1 hour. Rinse and pat dry with paper towels.

2. In a large bowl, combine dill, vinegar and sour cream. Add cucumbers and toss to coat.

Cucumber Tofu Salad

Serves 4

A spicy dressing gives this salad a nice kick. The sprouts add crunch.

Tip

Salting the cucumber draws out the excess water.

1	large English cucumber, peeled and diced (see Tip, left)	1
1 tsp	sea salt	5 mL
2 tbsp	canola oil	30 mL
6 oz	tofu, drained and cut into small cubes	175 g
½ cup	bean sprouts	125 mL
½ cup	Smoked Chipotle Vinaigrette (page 50)	125 mL

1. In a colander over a bowl, sprinkle cucumber slices with salt. Let drain for 1 hour. Rinse and pat dry with paper towels.

2. In a skillet, heat oil over medium heat. Add tofu and sauté until lightly browned on all sides, about 2 minutes per side. Remove and drain on paper towels.

3. In a serving dish, combine cucumbers, tofu, sprouts and vinaigrette. Toss to coat.

Date and Carrot Salad

This warming winter salad is fragrant with spices and full of flavor.

½ cup	pitted dates, finely chopped	125 mL
3 tbsp	freshly squeezed lemon juice	45 mL
3 tbsp	freshly squeezed lime juice	45 mL
1 lb	grated carrots	500 g
1	clove garlic, minced	1
½ tsp	ground cumin	2 mL
½ tsp	ground coriander	2 mL
½ tsp	sea salt	2 mL
¼ tsp	Chinese 5-spice powder	1 mL
¼ tsp	ground cinnamon	1 mL
¼ tsp	Hungarian paprika	1 mL
2 tbsp	extra virgin olive oil	30 mL
2 tbsp	chopped fresh mint	30 mL
1 tbsp	chopped Italian flat-leaf parsley	15 mL

1. In a small bowl, combine dates and lemon and lime juices and soak for 15 minutes.

2. Drain dates, reserving juice mixture. In a large bowl, combine dates and carrots. Set aside.

3. In a bowl, whisk together reserved juice mixture, garlic, cumin, coriander, salt, Chinese 5-spice powder, cinnamon and paprika. Vigorously whisk in oil. Pour over carrots and dates and stir well to coat. Stir in mint and parsley. Let stand at room temperature for 1 hour prior to serving.

Eggplant, Lemon and Caper Salad

Serves 4

Serve this salad with cold pasta or with bread and salami as an appetizer.

¼ cup	canola oil	60 mL
3	medium eggplants, cut into cubes (see Tip, page 184)	3
2 tsp	grated lemon zest	10 mL
1 tbsp	freshly squeezed lemon juice	15 mL
2 tbsp	drained capers	30 mL
2 tbsp	chopped Italian flat-leaf parsley	30 mL
	Sea salt and freshly ground black pepper	

1. In a skillet, heat oil over medium heat. Add eggplants and sauté until golden and softened, about 8 minutes. Drain on paper towels.

2. In a bowl, toss together eggplants, lemon zest and juice, capers and parsley to coat. Season with salt and pepper to taste.

Creamy Spiced Eggplant Salad

Serves 4

The big flavor of this salad is a match for hearty meats.

¼ cup	canola oil	60 mL
3	medium eggplants, diced (see Tip, page 184)	3
2	cloves garlic, minced	2
1 tbsp	freshly squeezed lime juice	15 mL
½ tsp	ground cumin	2 mL
½ tsp	ground coriander	2 mL
4	Roma (plum) tomatoes, sliced	4
2 tbsp	sour cream	30 mL
	Sea salt and freshly ground black pepper	

1. In a skillet, heat oil over medium heat. Add eggplants and sauté until golden and softened, about 8 minutes. Drain on paper towels. Let cool.

2. In a large bowl, combine garlic, lime juice, cumin and coriander. Add eggplants, tomatoes and sour cream and toss to evenly coat. Season with salt and pepper to taste.

Spicy Eggplant Salad

Serves 4

The mellow hues of the tomatoes and the grilled eggplant makes this salad lovely to look at.

- **Preheat broiler**

2	medium eggplants, thinly sliced (see Tip, page 184)	2
2 tbsp	extra virgin olive oil	30 mL
4	Roma (plum) tomatoes, seeded and diced	4
2	cloves garlic, minced	2
1 tbsp	freshly squeezed lemon juice	15 mL
1 tsp	ground cumin	5 mL
1 tsp	curry powder	5 mL

1. Brush eggplant slices all over with oil and arrange on a baking sheet in a single layer. Broil until softened and lightly brown on each side, about 4 minutes per side. Transfer to a bowl.

2. Add tomatoes, garlic, lemon juice, cumin and curry powder. Let stand for 45 minutes. Arrange on a serving platter.

Grilled Eggplant Onion Salad

Serves 4

This salad is so versatile you can make it on the grill or under the broiler.

- **Preheat broiler or grill to medium**

3	medium eggplant, sliced (see Tip, page 184)	3
1	medium red onion, sliced	1
¼ cup	extra virgin olive oil	60 mL
¼ cup	chopped Italian flat-leaf parsley	60 mL
⅓ cup	pine nuts, toasted (see Tip, page 205)	75 mL
½ cup	Old Venice Italian Vinaigrette (page 44)	125 mL
	Sea salt and freshly ground black pepper	

1. Brush eggplant and red onion slices with oil. Broil or grill until lightly browned, 5 to 7 minutes per side.

2. Transfer to a serving platter. Sprinkle with parsley and pine nuts. Drizzle with vinaigrette. Season with salt and pepper to taste.

Endive and Blue Cheese Salad

Serves 4

Serve this salad with hot-from-the-oven crusty French bread.

Variation

Any blue cheese suits this salad. Try Roquefort from France, Stilton from England or Gorgonzola from Italy.

3 cups	chopped Belgian endive	750 mL
1 cup	chopped romaine lettuce	250 mL
1 cup	chopped celery	250 mL
1 cup	chopped walnuts, toasted (see Tips, page 211)	250 mL
2 tbsp	chopped Italian flat-leaf parsley	30 mL
1/2 cup	Parmesan Vinaigrette (page 45)	125 mL
4 oz	blue cheese, crumbled (see Tip, left)	125 g

1. In a large bowl, toss together endive, romaine, celery, walnuts, parsley and vinaigrette until coated. Sprinkle with blue cheese.

Orange and Onion Salad

Serves 4

This is simply beautiful on a holiday buffet.

Variation

Slice 4 oz (125 g) mozzarella cheese, then tuck between each pair of orange and onion slices.

Salad

3	large navel oranges, peeled and sliced	3
1	red onion, thinly sliced	1

Dressing

2 tbsp	apple cider vinegar	30 mL
1 tbsp	canola oil	15 mL
1 tsp	granulated sugar	5 mL
1/2 tsp	garlic salt	2 mL
1/4 tsp	chili powder	1 mL
	Sea salt and freshly ground black pepper	

1. *Salad:* Arrange alternating slices of orange and red onion on a serving platter.

2. *Dressing:* In a bowl, whisk together vinegar, oil, sugar, garlic salt and chili powder until sugar is dissolved. Season with salt and pepper to taste. Drizzle over orange and onion slices.

Asparagus and Citrus Salad

Tips

Grate regular oranges for the zest. The rind of blood oranges doesn't yield as much flavor.

If blood oranges are unavailable or not in season, you can use navel oranges for this salad.

To toast walnuts: Place nuts in a single layer on a baking sheet in a preheated 350°F (180°C) oven for 10 to 12 minutes for halves, 8 to 10 minutes for chopped, or until fragrant and golden, stirring once or twice.

Dressing

1 tsp	grated orange zest (see Tips, left)	5 mL
1/3 cup	freshly squeezed blood orange juice (see Tips, left)	75 mL
2 tbsp	finely chopped shallots	30 mL
1 tbsp	balsamic vinegar	15 mL
1 tbsp	sherry wine vinegar	15 mL
2 tbsp	extra virgin olive oil	30 mL
	Sea salt and freshly ground black pepper	

Salad

1 1/2 lbs	asparagus, trimmed	750 g
	Ice water	
3 to 4	blood oranges, segmented	3 to 4
1/4 cup	chopped walnuts, toasted (see Tips, left)	60 mL

1. *Dressing:* In a small bowl, whisk together orange zest and juice, shallots and balsamic and sherry wine vinegars. Let stand for at least 20 minutes or for up to 3 hours. Slowly whisk in oil. Season with salt and pepper to taste. Set aside.

2. *Salad:* Cut each asparagus spear in half or in quarters and cook in boiling salted water until tender-crisp, 4 to 5 minutes. Drain well and transfer to a bowl of ice water to set color and stop cooking. Remove with tongs or slotted spoon and toss with dressing.

3. Divide orange segments and asparagus evenly onto 4 salad plates. Season with additional salt and pepper to taste. Top each serving with walnuts.

Artichoke, Shrimp and Mandarin Orange Salad

Serves 6

This salad may be fast and easy, but its flavors are exotic.

Tip

If you can't find frozen artichokes use 2 (14 oz/398 mL) cans, drained.

Variation

For a spicy change, substitute Smoked Chipotle Vinaigrette (page 50) for the Chenin Blanc Vinaigrette.

2 lbs	cooked salad shrimp	1 kg
1	package (20 oz/600 g) frozen cooked artichoke hearts, thawed (see Tip, left)	1
1	can (10 oz/287 mL) mandarin oranges, drained	1
1	head iceberg lettuce, chopped	1
½ cup	Chenin Blanc Vinaigrette (page 39)	125 mL

1. In a large bowl, toss together shrimp, artichoke hearts, oranges, lettuce and vinaigrette to coat. Let stand for 15 minutes to allow the flavors to develop prior to serving.

Grilled Leek and Fennel Salad

Serves 4

When fresh leeks and fennel appear at the farmers' market, I know it's time to make this salad.

Tips

To wash leeks: Cut the bulb in half lengthwise, then submerge in a sink filled with cold water and swish to remove dirt.

To prepare fennel: Trim off a thin slice from the base of the bulb, as well as the tough and stringy outer layers. Trim off the darker green outer tops, leaving only the more tender and lighter inner bulb. Thinly slice the bulb lengthwise, trimming out any tough core.

- **Preheat barbecue grill to medium**

2 lbs	leeks, white and light green parts only, cleaned and cut into 2-inch (5 cm) lengths (see Tips, left)	1 kg
2	large bulbs fennel, sliced (see Tips, left)	2
¼ cup	extra virgin olive oil	60 mL
2	Roma (plum) tomatoes, sliced	2
¼ cup	chopped shallots	60 mL
2 tbsp	chopped fresh thyme	30 mL
¼ tsp	hot pepper flakes	1 mL

1. In a pot of boiling salted water, cook leeks until softened, 4 to 5 minutes. Using a slotted spoon, transfer leeks to a colander to drain, reserving water in the pot. Let water return to a boil and add fennel. Boil until slightly tender, for 5 minutes. Drain.

2. Brush leeks and fennel all over with oil. Grill until light brown grill marks show, about 3 minutes.

3. In a large bowl, combine leeks, fennel, tomatoes, shallots, thyme and hot pepper flakes.

Grilled Leek, Pepper and Cheese Salad

Serves 4

This is a pleasure to grill outdoors under the stars on warm summer nights.

- **Preheat barbecue grill to medium**

2 lbs	leeks, white and light green parts only, cleaned and cut into 2-inch (5 cm) lengths (see Tips, page 213)	1 kg
2 tbsp	extra virgin olive oil	30 mL
1	jar (7 oz/210 mL) roasted red peppers, drained	1
1 tsp	chopped fresh thyme	5 mL
4 oz	goat cheese, sliced	125 g
½ cup	Lemon Dijon Vinaigrette (page 42)	125 mL

1. In a pot of boiling salted water, cook leeks until softened, 4 to 5 minutes. Drain.

2. Brush leeks with oil. Grill until light brown grill marks show, about 3 minutes per side.

3. In a large bowl, toss together leeks, roasted peppers, thyme, cheese and vinaigrette.

Marinated Mushrooms

Serves 4

Here's a salad that makes a great side dish for a steak or beef Wellington.

½ cup	Old Venice Italian Vinaigrette (page 44)	125 mL
4	cloves garlic, minced	4
3 cups	small button mushrooms, stems removed	750 mL

1. In a large skillet over medium heat, combine vinaigrette and garlic and heat until gently boiling. Reduce heat to low. Add mushrooms and stir to coat. Loosely cover with foil and simmer until softened, about 5 minutes.

2. Let mushrooms cool completely before serving.

Mushroom Salad

12 oz	button mushrooms, stemmed and sliced	375 g
	Grated zest and juice of 2 lemons	
	Grated zest and juice of 1 lime	
3 tbsp	sour cream	45 mL
1 tsp	chopped fresh dill	5 mL
	Sea salt and freshly ground white pepper	

1. In a large bowl, toss together mushrooms, lemon zest and juice, lime zest and juice, sour cream and dill. Season with salt and white pepper to taste.

All-Summer Potato Salad

Tip

If you are taking this salad outdoors, be sure to keep it on ice in the cooler, so the mayonnaise doesn't go bad in the summer sun.

1 cup	Traditional Mayonnaise (page 100) or store-bought	250 mL
1 cup	onion, minced	250 mL
½ cup	chopped green onions	125 mL
¼ cup	Dijon Mustard (page 112) or store-bought	60 mL
3 tbsp	rice vinegar	45 mL
2 tsp	sea salt	10 mL
1 tsp	chopped fresh tarragon	5 mL
¼ tsp	freshly ground black pepper	1 mL
2	hard-boiled eggs, chopped (see Tips, page 138)	2
3 lbs	white fingerling potatoes, cooked and cut into quarters (see Tips, page 138)	1.5 kg
2 cups	diced celery	500 mL

1. In a large bowl, whisk together mayonnaise, onion, green onions, mustard, vinegar, salt, tarragon and pepper. Add eggs, potatoes and celery and toss to coat well. Cover and refrigerate for 4 hours prior to serving or for up 3 days.

Warm German Potato Salad

4 lbs	red potatoes, cut into quarters	2 kg
8 oz	bacon slices	250 g
1 tbsp	all-purpose flour	15 mL
2 tbsp	granulated sugar	30 mL
1/4 cup	white wine vinegar	60 mL
1/2 cup	chopped green onions	125 mL
1/2 tsp	sea salt	2 mL
1/2 tsp	freshly ground black pepper	2 mL
1/2 tsp	mustard seeds	2 mL

1. In a large pot of boiling salted water, cook potatoes until tender but still firm, about 15 minutes. Drain and let cool.

2. In a large deep skillet over medium-high heat, cook bacon until evenly browned and crisp. With tongs, transfer bacon to a paper towel to drain. Set aside.

3. Add flour to bacon fat remaining in skillet and cook, stirring, until lightly browned, about 2 minutes. Reduce heat to medium. Add sugar, 1/3 cup (75 mL) water and vinegar, and cook, stirring, until thickened, about 5 minutes.

4. Crumble bacon and add with potatoes and green onions to skillet, and stir until coated and heated. Stir in salt, pepper and mustard seeds. Serve warm.

Moroccan Salad

1	jar (7 oz/210 mL) roasted red peppers, drained	1
8 oz	feta cheese, crumbled	250 g
2 tbsp	extra virgin olive oil	30 mL
2 tbsp	drained capers	30 mL
2 tsp	grated lemon zest	10 mL
	Sea salt, optional (see Tip, left)	

1. In a bowl, combine roasted peppers, feta, oil, capers and lemon zest. Season with salt to taste, if needed.

Easy Roasted Pepper Salad

1 tbsp	canola oil	15 mL
1 cup	diced onion	250 mL
3	cloves garlic, minced	3
2	jars (each 7 oz/210 mL) roasted red peppers, drained and chopped	2
4	Roma (plum) tomatoes, cut into wedges	4
1 tsp	granulated sugar	5 mL
1 tsp	freshly squeezed lime juice	5 mL
	Sea salt and freshly ground black pepper	

1. In a skillet, heat oil over medium heat. Add onion and sauté until softened, about 2 minutes. Add garlic, roasted peppers and tomatoes and sauté until softened, about 6 minutes. Transfer to a large bowl. Stir in sugar and lime juice. Season with salt and pepper to taste.

Roasted Pepper and Tomato Salad

When I conducted a culinary tour of Chicago's Little Italy, we came across a deli with this wonderful salad.

1	jar (7 oz/210 mL) roasted red peppers, drained	1
6	Roma (plum) tomatoes, sliced	6
½ cup	diced red onion	125 mL
3	cloves garlic, chopped	3
¼ cup	chopped Italian flat-leaf parsley	60 mL
2 tbsp	extra virgin olive oil	30 mL
2 tsp	grated lemon zest	10 mL
½ tsp	hot pepper flakes	2 mL

1. In a large bowl, toss together roasted peppers, tomatoes, red onion, garlic, parsley, oil, lemon zest and hot pepper flakes.

Grilled Tomato and Cheese Salad

Serves 4

If your barbecue is warm from grilling, you can make this salad quickly.

Tip

To chiffonade basil: Stack the leaves with the largest on the bottom. Roll them up tightly, jelly-roll fashion, then finely slice across the roll. This prevents the basil from being bruised in the cutting, and prematurely darkening.

• **Preheat barbecue grill to medium**

6	Roma (plum) tomatoes, thickly sliced	6
2 tbsp	extra virgin olive oil	30 mL
12 oz	fresh mozzarella, cut into cubes	375 g
¼ cup	fresh basil chiffonade (see Tip, left)	60 mL
2 tbsp	pine nuts, toasted (see Tip, page 205)	30 mL
¼ cup	Parmesan Vinaigrette (page 45)	60 mL
4 cups	salad greens	1 L

1. Brush tomatoes all over with oil. Grill until charred, about 4 minutes per side. Let cool, then coarsely chop. Transfer to a large bowl.

2. Add mozzarella, basil, pine nuts and vinaigrette, and gently toss together. Arrange greens on a platter and top with tomato mixture.

Sun-Dried Tomato and Pepper Salad

Serves 4

My guests love this salad as an appetizer served with pita chips.

½ cup	oil-packed sun-dried tomatoes, drained and chopped	125 mL
2	Roma (plum) tomatoes, seeded and chopped	2
1 cup	chopped red bell pepper	250 mL
1 cup	chopped yellow bell pepper	250 mL
3	cloves garlic, minced	3
2 tbsp	extra virgin olive oil	30 mL
1 tbsp	balsamic vinegar	15 mL
2 tsp	chopped fresh tarragon	10 mL
1 tsp	granulated sugar	5 mL
1 tsp	drained capers	5 mL
	Sea salt and freshly ground black pepper	

1. In a large bowl, combine sun-dried tomatoes, Roma tomatoes, red and yellow bell peppers, garlic, oil, vinegar, tarragon, sugar and capers. Season with salt and pepper to taste.

Parisian Salad

Serves 4

The sidewalks of Paris boast so many great bistros with wonderful salads. To recreate that French feeling, I serve this continental combination with a crusty baguette.

4 cups	finely chopped romaine lettuce (about ½ head)	1 L
6	Roma (plum) tomatoes, sliced	6
½ cup	diced cucumber	125 mL
½ cup	chopped red onion	125 mL
½ cup	Champagne Vinaigrette (page 39)	125 mL

1. In a large bowl, toss together romaine, tomatoes, cucumber, red onion and vinaigrette until well coated.

Red and Green Salad

Serves 6

In my house, this salad is served every holiday season. Wedges of bright red, crescents of white and little "trees" of green make a dish fit for the festivities.

Tips

Pick the brightest red tomatoes you can find for the visual impact.

Use a mandoline to get perfectly even cucumber slices.

Variation

Add $1\frac{1}{2}$ cups (375 mL) cauliflower pieces to include all the colors of the Italian flag for your next World Cup party.

2 lbs	Roma (plum) tomatoes, seeded and quartered (about 8) (see Tips, left)	1 kg
3 cups	broccoli florets, cut into bite-size pieces	750 mL
1	cucumber, halved lengthwise, seeded and thinly sliced (see Tips, left)	1
1 cup	Creamy Roma Dressing (page 69)	250 mL

1. In a bowl, combine tomatoes, broccoli, cucumber and dressing. Let marinate for 1 hour prior to serving.

2. Transfer to a glass serving dish so you can see the salad well.

Istanbul Tomato Salad

Serves 4

Turkey is a fantastic, exotic place for traveling foodies to explore. You will find many cafés with cool summer salads made from fresh local ingredients.

4 cups	finely chopped romaine lettuce (about 1/2 head)	1 L
4	Roma (plum) tomatoes, sliced	4
1/2 cup	diced green bell pepper	125 mL
1/2 cup	diced red bell pepper	125 mL
1/2 cup	diced cucumber	125 mL
1/2 cup	chopped red onion	125 mL
1/2 cup	Lemon Dijon Vinaigrette (page 42)	125 mL
8 oz	feta cheese, crumbled	250 g
1/4 cup	kalamata olives, pitted and chopped	60 mL

1. In a large bowl, toss together romaine, tomatoes, green and red bell peppers, cucumber, red onion and vinaigrette. Transfer to a serving platter and sprinkle with feta and olives.

Tomato and Cucumber Salad

Serves 4

Made in minutes, this creamy salad lets the fresh taste of late-summer tomatoes and cukes really shine.

2	cucumbers, peeled and thinly sliced (see Tips, page 220)	2
4	Roma (plum) tomatoes, sliced	4
1/4 cup	sour cream	60 mL
2 tsp	chopped fresh tarragon	10 mL
2 tsp	white wine vinegar	10 mL
	Sea salt and freshly ground black pepper	

1. In a large bowl, toss together cucumbers, tomatoes, sour cream, tarragon and vinegar. Season with salt and pepper to taste.

Tomato Bread Salad

Serves 4

In Italy they use day-old bread for salads and soups. Fresh bread just doesn't taste as good for this.

Tip

To chiffonade basil: Stack the leaves with the largest on the bottom. Roll them up tightly, jelly-roll fashion, then finely slice across the roll. This prevents the basil from being bruised in the cutting, and prematurely darkening.

1 lb	day-old bread (preferably unsalted Italian bread)	500 g
	Cold water	
4	large heirloom tomatoes (about 1 lb/500 g), seeded and chopped	4
1 cup	chopped red onion	250 mL
¼ cup	fresh basil chiffonade (see Tip, left)	60 mL
2 tbsp	Chenin Blanc Vinaigrette (page 39)	30 mL

1. Tear bread into bite-size pieces and place in a shallow dish. Pour in enough cold water to cover and soak for 15 minutes. With palms, press water out of bread. Transfer bread to a large bowl. Add tomatoes, red onion and basil and toss to combine. Drizzle with vinaigrette.

Thai Vegetable and Fruit Salad

While walking the markets of Bangkok I noticed many vendors selling fresh fruit salads. Here's my take on those salads that you can make at home. The dressing is very light and subtle, but a little goes a long way.

Salad

2 cups	pineapple cubes	500 mL
2	small mangos, sliced	2
2	apples, such as Golden Delicious or Pippin, unpeeled and sliced	2
4	lychees, peeled, halved and pitted	4
1 cup	sliced peeled cucumber	250 mL
1 cup	bean sprouts	250 mL
1	Roma (plum) tomato, sliced	1
1/2 cup	chopped red onion	125 mL
1/4 cup	chopped shallots	60 mL
2 cups	chopped romaine lettuce	500 mL

Dressing

2 tbsp	coconut milk	30 mL
2 tbsp	granulated sugar	30 mL
1 tbsp	fish or oyster sauce	15 mL
1/4 tsp	Bold Chili Sauce (page 115) or store-bought	1 mL

1. *Salad:* In a large bowl, combine pineapple, mangos, apples, lychees, cucumber, bean sprouts, tomato, red onion and shallots. Set aside.

2. *Dressing:* In a small saucepan over medium heat, combine coconut milk, sugar, fish sauce and chili sauce and bring to a boil. If too thick, add water to thin. When it starts to bubble, pour over pineapple mixture. Add romaine and toss well.

Spicy Chile Jicama Salad

Serves 4

Also called "Mexican potato," jicama has migrated into North American cuisine, and is here to stay. Crisp and sweet, it mingles well with hot chiles.

Tip

Jicama is a tuber from Central America with a thin tan skin and crunchy dense white flesh that can be eaten raw or cooked. I use a vegetable peeler to remove the outer skin.

2 cups	diced peeled jicama (see Tip, left)	500 mL
1/2 tsp	sea salt	2 mL
1/2 cup	chopped red onion	125 mL
2	serrano chile peppers, seeded and minced	2
1 tsp	grated lime zest	5 mL
2 tsp	freshly squeezed lime juice	10 mL

1. In a large bowl, combine jicama and salt. Let stand for 20 minutes. Drain off excess liquid. Add red onion, chile peppers, and lime zest and juice. Transfer to a covered bowl and refrigerate for 45 minutes to allow the flavors to develop prior to serving.

Meat and Poultry Salads

Meat and Poultry Salads

When you add protein to a salad, it becomes a satisfying and complete main dish. That's how I like to serve these salads in the summer, so I don't have to warm up the oven, but they are delicious — on their own or on the side — any time of year. In the recipes, I've indicated the number of servings for a side salad, so double the amounts to make a hearty entrée. And check if your chosen salad can be made ahead. Most of these can — a real plus if company is coming.

Vietnamese Beef Salad

Serves 6

In Saigon markets you can find many great salads just like this one.

Tip

To toast sesame seeds: Place seeds on a baking sheet and toast in a preheated 350°F (180°C) oven for 5 to 7 minutes, or until fragrant and golden, stirring once or twice.

Salad

2 tbsp	canola oil	30 mL
1½ lbs	beef tenderloin, cut into strips	750 g
2	small red chile peppers, seeded and chopped	2
12 oz	shiitake mushrooms, stems removed, caps thinly sliced	375 g
2 cups	salad greens	500 mL
1 cup	grape tomatoes, cut in half	250 mL
½ cup	sliced cucumbers	125 mL
2 tbsp	sesame seeds, toasted	30 mL

Dressing

½ cup	chopped green onions	125 mL
3	cloves garlic, minced	3
2 tbsp	chopped Italian flat-leaf parsley	30 mL
2 tbsp	freshly squeezed lime juice	30 mL
2 tbsp	fish or oyster sauce	30 mL
1 tsp	lightly packed brown sugar	5 mL

1. *Salad:* In a skillet, heat oil over medium heat. Add beef and chile peppers and sauté to desired doneness, 2 to 4 minutes. Add mushrooms and sauté until slightly wilted, about 2 minutes. Let cool slightly.

2. Arrange greens, grape tomatoes and cucumbers on a serving platter. Top with cooled beef mixture. Sprinkle with sesame seeds.

3. *Dressing:* In a small bowl, whisk together green onions, garlic, parsley, lime juice, fish sauce and brown sugar until sugar is dissolved. Drizzle over salad.

Taco Salad

Serves 8

My mom makes this great salad with minimal effort. You can make a huge batch and serve it on a platter for a crowd.

Tip

To make guacamole: In a bowl, combine 2 halved and mashed avocados, 2 tsp (10 mL) lime juice, ½ cup (125 mL) finely minced shallots, 2 seeded and diced Roma (plum) tomatoes, 1 chopped jalapeño pepper, 2 minced cloves garlic and 2 tbsp (30 mL) chopped fresh cilantro. Use within a few hours as the guacamole will darken. Makes 2 cups (500 mL).

2 tbsp	olive oil	30 mL
1	onion, sliced	1
2	cloves garlic, minced	2
2 lbs	ground beef or ground turkey	1 kg
2 tsp	taco seasoning	10 mL
12 oz	corn chips	375 g
8 cups	salad greens	2 L
8 oz	Cheddar cheese, shredded	250 g
8 oz	Monterey Jack cheese, shredded	250 g
2	Roma (plum) tomatoes, diced	2
½ cup	sour cream	125 mL
½ cup	Guacamole (see Tip, left) or store-bought	125 mL
1 cup	Ranch Dressing (page 79) or store-bought	250 mL

1. In a large skillet, heat oil over medium heat. Add onion and sauté until translucent, about 4 minutes. Add garlic and sauté for 2 minutes. Add ground beef and cook, breaking up with a spoon, until lightly browned, about 8 minutes. Add taco seasoning and ½ cup (125 mL) water and cook, stirring, until liquid has evaporated, about 5 minutes. Set aside.

2. Divide corn chips, greens, Cheddar and Monterey Jack cheeses and tomatoes evenly onto 8 plates. Top with beef mixture, then top with 1 tbsp (15 mL) each of the sour cream and guacamole. Drizzle with dressing.

Thai Beef and Mango Salad

2 tbsp	canola oil	30 mL
2	cloves garlic, minced	2
1 lb	beef tenderloin, cut into strips	500 g
3 tbsp	reduced-sodium soy sauce	45 mL
2	mangos, cut into slivers	2
	Sea salt and freshly ground black pepper	

1. In a skillet, heat oil over medium heat. Add garlic and sauté until softened, about 2 minutes. Add beef and soy sauce and sauté to desired doneness, 2 to 4 minutes.

2. Divide mangos and beef mixture evenly onto 4 plates. Season with salt and pepper to taste.

Curried Pork Tenderloin Salad

8 oz	pork tenderloin, thinly sliced	250 g
3	cloves garlic, minced	3
3 tbsp	freshly grated gingerroot	45 mL
3 tbsp	rice wine vinegar	45 mL
3 tbsp	canola oil	45 mL
2 tsp	minced lemongrass (see Tip, left)	10 mL
2 tsp	mild curry powder	10 mL
8 oz	bean sprouts	250 g
8 oz	vermicelli pasta, cooked, drained and cooled	250 g
2 cups	salad greens	500 mL

1. In a large resealable plastic bag, combine pork, garlic, ginger, vinegar, oil, lemongrass and curry powder. Seal bag and marinate for 1 hour in the refrigerator. Drain pork, discarding marinade.

2. In a skillet over medium heat, sauté pork until just a hint of pink remains inside, 8 to 10 minutes. Set aside and let cool.

3. In a bowl, toss together bean sprouts, pasta and pork.

4. Arrange greens on a serving platter. Top with pasta and pork mixture.

Bacon and Apple with Blue Cheese Salad

Serves 4

I love using applewood smoked bacon for a rich taste.

8 oz	smoked bacon slices, preferably applewood, crumbled	250 g
1 cup	diced apple, such as Pippin, Granny Smith or Rome	250 mL
2 cups	torn romaine lettuce	500 mL
3 tbsp	Buffalo Blue Cheese Dressing (page 63) or store-bought	45 mL
	Sea salt and freshly ground black pepper	

1. In a bowl, combine bacon, apple and romaine. Toss with dressing to coat. Season with salt and pepper to taste.

Avocado and Prosciutto Salad

Serves 4

I enjoyed this salad in a small trattoria in Tuscany.

2 cups	salad greens	500 mL
3	ripe avocados, diced (see Tip, left)	3
6 oz	prosciutto, chopped	175 g
1/3 cup	chopped Italian olives	75 mL
1/4 cup	Italian Herb Vinaigrette (page 42)	60 mL

1. Divide greens evenly onto 4 plates. Set aside.
2. In a large bowl, gently toss together avocados, prosciutto, olives and vinaigrette. Arrange on salad greens.

Tip

To determine if your avocado is ripe: Hold it in the palm of your hand and press. The avocado should feel like a tomato that has a little "give."

Waldorf Rice Salad

The Waldorf Astoria hotel in New York City has an amazing history of legendary guests and events. More than 100 years after they were first created, many of the salads served there in the late 1800s, are still classics today. Here is my rendition of the hotel's famous rice salad.

Tip

To toast walnuts: Place nuts in a single layer on a baking sheet in a preheated 350°F (180°C) oven for 10 to 12 minutes for halves, 8 to 10 minutes for chopped, or until fragrant and golden, stirring once or twice.

2 cups	cooked rice, any variety	500 mL
1	red apple, chopped (unpeeled)	1
1	green apple, chopped (unpeeled)	1
½ cup	chopped celery	125 mL
½ cup	diced cooked ham	125 mL
⅓ cup	Traditional Mayonnaise (page 100) or store-bought	75 mL
2 tbsp	sour cream	30 mL
¼ cup	chopped fresh basil	60 mL
	Sea salt and freshly ground black pepper	
4	large iceberg lettuce leaves	4
½ cup	chopped walnuts, toasted (see Tip, left)	125 mL

1. In a bowl, combine rice, red and green apples, celery, ham, mayonnaise, sour cream and basil. Season with salt and pepper to taste.

2. Place one lettuce leaf on each plate. Divide rice mixture evenly onto 4 leaves. Sprinkle with walnuts.

Potato Sausage Salad

Tip

To cook potatoes: Place whole potatoes in a pot of cold salted water, bring to a simmer over medium heat and cook until fork-tender. Do not allow to boil or the skins will burst and allow potato flesh to absorb water. If desired, peel slightly cooled potatoes, then cut into bite-size pieces.

1 lb	small fingerling potatoes, cooked and cut into bite-size pieces (see Tip, left)	500 g
8 oz	cooked spicy sausage, chopped	250 g
½ cup	chopped shallots	125 mL
2 tbsp	chopped Italian flat-leaf parsley	30 mL
1 tbsp	chopped fresh tarragon	15 mL
3 tbsp	Italian Herb Vinaigrette (page 42) or store-bought	45 mL
	Sea salt and freshly ground black pepper	

1. In a bowl, gently combine potatoes, sausage, shallots, parsley, tarragon and vinaigrette. Season with salt and pepper to taste.

Asian Chicken Salad

Serves 6

When I was a chef for the Walt Disney Company, the kitchen staff would share monthly potlucks. One of the cake decorators would bring this tasty salad with its light dressing.

Tip

If you have any leftover greens from this salad, use it as a topping for a hamburger.

1 lb	boneless skinless cooked chicken, shredded (about 3 cups/750 mL)	500 g
3 cups	shredded napa cabbage	750 mL
1/2 cup	grated carrots	125 mL
1/4 cup	chopped fresh mint	60 mL
1/4 cup	chopped Italian flat-leaf parsley	60 mL
2 tbsp	Japanese Dressing (page 57)	30 mL
	Sea salt and freshly ground black pepper	

1. In a bowl, combine chicken, cabbage, carrots, mint, parsley and dressing. Toss to coat. Season with salt and pepper to taste.

Chinese Chicken Salad

Serves 4

This is my version of takeout Chinese salad. Try it for lunch or dinner.

Tips

Make the dressing 2 to 3 days ahead to allow the flavors to develop prior to serving, then cover and refrigerate it.

So the almonds don't get soggy, add them just before serving.

You can also use this dressing for an easy marinade for pork or chicken.

Variation

Try using fresh spinach leaves, instead of salad greens, for a heartier meal.

Salad

4 cups	salad greens	1 L
1 lb	boneless skinless cooked chicken, cut into bite-size pieces	500 g

Dressing

¼ cup	apple cider vinegar	60 mL
2 tbsp	freshly squeezed orange juice	30 mL
2 tbsp	granulated sugar	30 mL
1 tsp	Dijon Mustard (page 112) or store-bought	5 mL
1 tsp	sea salt	5 mL
½ cup	canola oil	125 mL
2 tbsp	poppy seeds	30 mL
2 tbsp	sliced almonds, toasted (see Tip, page 130)	30 mL

1. *Salad:* Divide greens evenly onto 4 plates. Top with chicken. Set aside.

2. *Dressing:* In a bowl, whisk together vinegar, orange juice, sugar, mustard and salt. While whisking, pour in oil in a thin steady stream and whisk until emulsified. Stir in poppy seeds and almonds. Drizzle over salad.

Broccoli Chicken Salad

Variation

Substitute cooked cauliflower for the broccoli.

2 cups	cooked broccoli florets, cooled	500 mL
2 cups	farfalle (bow tie) pasta, cooked, drained and cooled	500 mL
2 cups	shredded cooked chicken	500 mL
2 tbsp	Creamy Two-Cheese Italian Dressing (page 70)	30 mL
	Sea salt and freshly ground black pepper	

1. In a large bowl, combine broccoli, pasta, chicken and dressing. Season with salt and pepper to taste.

Chicken and Roasted Corn Salad

Salad

8 oz	large shell pasta, cooked, drained and cooled	250 g
2 cups	shredded cooked chicken	500 mL
1 cup	Roasted Corn (page 271)	250 mL
1/2 cup	chopped fresh basil	125 mL
1/4 cup	chopped roasted red bell pepper	60 mL

Dressing

3 tbsp	canola oil	45 mL
1 tbsp	balsamic vinegar	15 mL
1 tsp	red wine vinegar	5 mL
1 tsp	Dijon Mustard (page 112) or store-bought	5 mL
	Sea salt and freshly ground black pepper	

1. *Salad:* In a bowl, combine pasta, chicken, corn, basil and roasted pepper. Set aside.

2. *Dressing:* In a bowl, whisk together oil, balsamic and red wine vinegars and mustard. Toss with pasta mixture. Season with salt and pepper to taste.

Chicken and Pear Salad with Pecans

Tip

To toast pecans: Place nuts in a single layer on a baking sheet in a preheated 350°F (180°C) oven for 10 to 12 minutes for halves, 8 to 10 minutes for chopped, or until fragrant and golden, stirring once or twice.

3 cups	chopped butterhead lettuce	750 mL
2 cups	shredded cooked chicken	500 mL
2 cups	chopped pears	500 mL
1 cup	chopped radicchio	250 mL
1 cup	chopped baby spinach leaves	250 mL
¾ cup	chopped pecans, toasted (see Tip, left)	175 mL
3 tbsp	Blue Cheese Dressing (page 62) or store-bought	45 mL
1 tbsp	crumbled blue cheese	15 mL
	Sea salt and freshly ground black pepper	

1. In a bowl, combine lettuce, chicken, pears, radicchio, spinach and pecans. Drizzle with dressing and toss to coat. Top with blue cheese. Season with salt and pepper to taste.

Citrus Chicken Salad

1 tbsp	Traditional Mayonnaise (page 100) or store-bought	15 mL
1 tbsp	liquid honey	15 mL
1 tsp	Dijon Mustard (page 112) or store-bought	5 mL
2 cups	orange segments	500 mL
3 cups	shredded napa cabbage	750 mL
1 cup	grated carrots	250 mL
½ cup	chopped celery	125 mL
¼ cup	chopped green onions	60 mL
2 tbsp	chopped fresh tarragon	30 mL
1 lb	boneless skinless cooked chicken, shredded (about 3 cups/750 mL)	500 g

1. In a large bowl, combine mayonnaise, honey and mustard. Add orange segments, cabbage, carrots, celery, green onions, tarragon and chicken. Toss to coat.

Chicken Salad

I created this recipe using an entire deli-roasted chicken. If you have part of a chicken, you can adjust the recipe accordingly.

Tip

If you process the chicken mixture for too long, you will get a creamy consistency. Avoid this by pulsing the mixture as described.

Variation

If you have a fresh herb — such as tarragon, dill or rosemary — on hand, chop and add 2 tbsp (30 mL) to the mixture.

- **Food processor**

½ cup	sliced red onion	125 mL
3	cloves garlic	3
3 oz	cream cheese, softened	90 g
⅓ cup	Traditional Mayonnaise (page 100) or store-bought	75 mL
¼ tsp	sea salt	1 mL
¼ tsp	freshly ground black pepper	1 mL
1	3-lb (1.5 kg) deli-roasted chicken, skin and bones removed	1
1	large head Boston lettuce	1

1. In a food processor fitted with a metal blade, process red onion until finely chopped, about 20 seconds. In the last 5 seconds, add garlic through the feed tube. Add cream cheese, mayonnaise, salt and pepper and pulse about 3 times. Add chicken and pulse 6 times or until coarsely chopped (see Tip, left).

2. Divide lettuce leaves evenly onto 6 plates. Top with chicken mixture.

Curried Chicken Pasta Salad

Serves 6

This delicate curry salad has just the right amount of zip.

Tip
Depending on the brand, you may need to drain the yogurt to avoid a watery dressing.

Salad

2 cups	penne pasta, cooked, drained and cooled	500 mL
2 cups	shredded cooked chicken	500 mL
4	Roma (plum) tomatoes, seeded and cut into strips	4
1 cup	cooked baby green peas, cooled	250 mL

Dressing

½ cup	plain yogurt (see Tip, left)	125 mL
1 tsp	mild curry powder	5 mL
2	cloves garlic, minced	2
1	serrano chile pepper, seeded and chopped	1
2 tbsp	chopped fresh cilantro	30 mL
	Sea salt and freshly ground black pepper	

1. *Salad:* In a bowl, combine pasta, chicken, tomatoes and peas.

2. *Dressing:* In a bowl, blend together yogurt, curry powder, garlic, chile pepper and cilantro. Drizzle over chicken mixture. Season with salt and pepper to taste.

Dijon Chicken Salad

Serves 4

I like to serve this salad with garlic bread to complete the meal.

4 cups	diced cooked chicken	1 L
½ cup	chopped green onions	125 mL
½ cup	chopped red bell pepper	125 mL
2 tbsp	chopped fresh dill	30 mL
2	cloves garlic, minced	2
¼ cup	Traditional Mayonnaise (page 100) or store-bought	60 mL
2 tbsp	Dijon Mustard (page 112) or store-bought	30 mL
	Sea salt and freshly ground black pepper	
2 cups	salad greens	500 mL

1. In a large bowl, combine chicken, green onions, bell pepper, dill, garlic, mayonnaise and mustard. Stir to coat. Season with salt and pepper to taste. Arrange greens on serving platter. Top with chicken mixture.

Orange Lemon Chicken Rice Salad

Serves 4

With the zing of citrus and an almond crunch, this chicken mix offers lively taste, color and texture. And it's the perfect choice for a light summer lunch.

1 lb	boneless skinless cooked chicken, diced (about 3 cups/750 mL)	500 g
2 cups	cooked rice, any variety, cooled	500 mL
1 cup	orange segments	250 mL
1/2 cup	lemon segments, optional	125 mL
2 tbsp	Lemon Dijon Vinaigrette (page 42)	30 mL
2 tsp	Dijon Mustard (page 112) or store-bought	10 mL
1/2 tsp	granulated sugar	2 mL
3 tbsp	chopped fresh chives	45 mL
1/2 cup	sliced almonds, toasted (see Tip, page 130)	125 mL

1. In a large bowl, combine chicken, rice, orange segments, lemon segments, if using, vinaigrette, mustard, sugar and chives. Stir to coat. Sprinkle with almonds.

Tarragon Chicken Salad

Serves 4

I think tarragon was invented to make chicken taste better, and combining the two is so French.

Tip
Serve this salad on a toasted bagel or on a bed of greens that have been tossed with an herb vinaigrette.

1 lb	boneless skinless cooked chicken, shredded (about 3 cups/750 mL)	500 g
1/2 cup	Traditional Mayonnaise (page 100) or store-bought	125 mL
1/4 cup	chopped fresh tarragon	60 mL
2 tbsp	chopped green olives	30 mL
2 tsp	Tarragon Pickle Relish (page 118) or store-bought relish	10 mL
1 tsp	grated lemon zest	5 mL
1 tsp	freshly squeezed lemon juice	5 mL
1 tsp	sea salt	5 mL
1 tsp	freshly ground white pepper	5 mL
2 tbsp	chopped cashews	30 mL

1. In a bowl, using a fork, combine chicken, mayonnaise, tarragon, olives, relish, lemon zest and juice, salt and white pepper. Sprinkle with cashews.

Hot-and-Sour Peanut Chicken Salad

The peanut marinade on the chicken is sure to please everyone, and so are the spicy Asian flavors.

Marinade

¼ cup	canola oil	60 mL
2 tbsp	smooth peanut butter	30 mL
2 tbsp	chopped fresh cilantro	30 mL
1 tbsp	white wine vinegar	15 mL
2	red chile peppers, seeded and chopped	2
2 tsp	freshly grated gingerroot	10 mL
2 tsp	lightly packed brown sugar	10 mL
2 tsp	fish or oyster sauce	10 mL
2	cloves garlic, minced	2
½ tsp	sea salt	2 mL

Salad

2 tbsp	canola oil	30 mL
1 lb	boneless skinless chicken, cut into bite-size pieces	500 g
2 cups	shredded napa cabbage	500 mL
½ cup	grated carrots	125 mL
½ cup	bean sprouts	125 mL

1. *Marinade:* In a bowl, whisk together oil, peanut butter, cilantro, vinegar, chile peppers, ginger, brown sugar, fish sauce, garlic and salt. Place in a large resealable plastic bag. Add chicken, shaking to coat. Seal bag and marinate chicken mixture for 1 hour in the refrigerator.

2. *Salad:* In a large skillet, heat oil over medium heat. Add chicken, reserving marinade, and brown on both sides, 8 to 10 minutes total. Add reserved marinade and bring to a simmer. Cover and simmer, stirring, until chicken is no longer pink inside, 10 to 15 minutes.

3. Arrange cabbage, carrots and bean sprouts on a serving platter. Top with chicken.

Pacific Rim Chicken Salad in Lettuce Cups

Serves 4

If you like, you can cook the marinated chicken on a grill instead of in a skillet.

Marinade

¼ cup	sesame oil	60 mL
¼ cup	chopped green onions	60 mL
4 tsp	hot chili paste	20 mL
3 tbsp	rice vinegar	45 mL
1 tbsp	reduced-sodium soy sauce	15 mL
1 tbsp	freshly grated gingerroot	15 mL
1 tsp	grated lemon zest	5 mL
1 tbsp	freshly squeezed lemon juice	15 mL
5	cloves garlic, minced	5
2 tsp	freshly ground black pepper	10 mL

Salad

3 tbsp	canola oil	45 mL
2 lbs	boneless skinless chicken, cut into bite-size pieces	1 kg
8 to 10	large butterhead lettuce leaves	8 to 10
8 oz	bean sprouts	250 g
½ cup	julienned carrots	125 mL

1. *Marinade:* In a bowl, whisk together oil, green onions, chili paste, vinegar, soy sauce, ginger, lemon zest and juice, garlic and pepper. Place in a large resealable plastic bag. Add chicken, shaking to coat. Seal bag and marinate chicken mixture for at least 30 minutes in the refrigerator but no longer than 12 hours. Drain chicken and discard marinade.

2. *Salad:* In a large skillet, heat oil over medium heat. Add chicken and brown for about 2 minutes per side. Reduce heat to low. Cover and cook, stirring, until chicken is no longer pink inside, 15 to 20 minutes.

3. Place lettuce leaves on a serving platter. Divide chicken evenly onto lettuce leaves. Top with bean sprouts and carrots.

Tangy Chicken Salad

Variations

Substitute pork or
turkey for the chicken.

Marinade

3	cloves garlic, minced	3
4 tbsp	canola oil, divided	60 mL
2 tbsp	reduced-sodium soy sauce	30 mL
2 tsp	granulated sugar	10 mL
2 tsp	freshly squeezed lime juice	10 mL
1 tsp	fish or oyster sauce	5 mL
1	small red chile pepper, seeded and chopped	1
1 lb	boneless skinless chicken breasts, thinly sliced	500 g

Salad

1	can (8 oz/227 mL) water chestnuts, drained and chopped	1
½ cup	chopped cashews	125 mL
¼ cup	chopped shallots	60 mL
2 cups	salad greens	500 mL

1. *Marinade:* In a large resealable plastic bag, combine garlic, 2 tbsp (30 mL) of the oil, soy sauce, sugar, lime juice, fish sauce, chile pepper and chicken. Seal bag and marinate chicken mixture for 30 minutes in the refrigerator. Drain chicken, reserving marinade.

2. In a skillet, heat remaining 2 tbsp (30 mL) of the oil over medium heat. Add chicken and cook until no longer pink inside, 8 to 10 minutes total. Remove chicken and set aside.

3. *Salad:* Add reserved marinade to skillet and cook, stirring, until thickened, 10 to 15 minutes. Add water chestnuts, cashews and shallots. Return chicken to skillet and stir to coat. Arrange greens on a serving platter. Top with chicken mixture.

Warm Chicken Hazelnut Salad

Tip

To toast hazelnuts: Place nuts in a single layer on a baking sheet in a preheated 350°F (180°C) oven until lightly browned, 8 to 12 minutes. Transfer them onto a damp tea towel, then fold over the towel corners and rub the nuts until most of their skins come off.

Dressing

2 tbsp	canola oil	30 mL
2 tbsp	hazelnut oil	30 mL
1 tbsp	white wine vinegar	15 mL
2	cloves garlic, minced	2
1 tbsp	chopped fresh tarragon	15 mL

Salad

3 cups	baby spinach leaves	750 mL
1 cup	grape tomatoes, cut in half	250 mL
½ cup	chopped green onions	125 mL
2	boneless skinless chicken breasts, cut into strips	2
	Sea salt and freshly ground black pepper	
2 tbsp	canola oil	30 mL
1 cup	hazelnuts, toasted, skinned and chopped (see Tip, left)	250 mL

1. *Dressing:* In a bowl, whisk together canola and hazelnut oils, vinegar, garlic and tarragon.

2. *Salad:* Arrange spinach on a serving platter, then scatter with grape tomatoes and green onions.

3. Season chicken with salt and pepper to taste. In a skillet, heat oil over high heat. Add chicken strips and sauté until lightly browned and no longer pink inside, 5 to 7 minutes. Arrange chicken over spinach mixture. Drizzle dressing on top. Sprinkle with hazelnuts.

Turkey Mango Rice Salad

Tip

Depending on the brand, you may need to drain the yogurt to avoid a watery dressing.

Variation

Substitute chicken for the turkey.

2 tbsp	canola oil	30 mL
1 cup	chopped onion	250 mL
1	clove garlic, chopped	1
2 tbsp	red curry paste	30 mL
2 tsp	apricot or peach jam	10 mL
2 tbsp	vegetable broth	30 mL
3 cups	diced cooked turkey	750 mL
2 cups	salad greens	500 mL
½ cup	plain yogurt (see Tip left)	125 mL
3 tbsp	Traditional Mayonnaise (page 100) or store-bought	45 mL
2 cups	diced mango	500 mL
2 cups	cooked rice, any variety, cooled	500 mL
2 tbsp	Fresh Spicy Ginger Dressing (page 55)	30 mL
	Freshly ground black pepper	

1. In a large skillet, heat oil over medium heat. Add onion and sauté until softened, about 3 minutes. Add garlic and curry paste and sauté for 2 minutes. Stir in jam and broth and mix well. Add turkey and stir until coated. Transfer to a bowl and let cool.

2. Arrange greens on serving platter. In a large bowl, stir together yogurt, mayonnaise, mango and rice. Add turkey mixture and toss to coat. Spoon over greens. Drizzle with dressing. Season with black pepper to taste.

Turkey Salad

Serves 4

I cook a huge turkey for the holidays so I can use the leftovers to make this salad for the days after.

Tip

Serve this turkey salad on a bagel or on a bed of greens with vinaigrette.

1 lb	boneless skinless cooked turkey, shredded	500 g
½ cup	Traditional Mayonnaise (page 100) or store-bought	125 mL
¼ cup	chopped fresh dill	60 mL
2 tbsp	chopped green olives	30 mL
2 tsp	Tarragon Pickle Relish (page 118) or store-bought relish	10 mL
1 tsp	freshly squeezed lime juice	5 mL
1 tsp	sea salt	5 mL
1 tsp	ground white pepper	5 mL
½ tsp	Hungarian paprika	2 mL

1. In a bowl, using a fork, combine turkey, mayonnaise, dill, olives, relish, lime juice, salt, white pepper and paprika. Mix just to combine.

Fish and Seafood Salads

Fish and Seafood Salads

When you want to treat your family and friends to something special, nothing says "I love you!" like fish and seafood — and serving it is a heart-healthy choice, as well. To cater to particular preferences, you can substitute favorite fish or seafood in any of these salads.

Salmon Ginger Salad

Serves 4

The ginger tickles your taste buds.

12 oz	skinless salmon fillet, cooked and flaked	375 g
2 cups	arugula leaves	500 mL
½ cup	chopped red bell pepper	125 mL
½ cup	chopped fresh cilantro	125 mL
¼ cup	Creamy Ginger Spice Dressing (page 68)	60 mL
	Sea salt and freshly ground black pepper	

1. In a bowl, combine salmon, arugula, bell pepper, cilantro and dressing. Season with salt and pepper to taste.

Salmon Rice Salad

Serves 4

Wild rice adds texture and color to this salad.

2 cups	cooked wild rice, cooled	500 mL
1 lb	skinless salmon fillet, cooked and flaked	500 g
1 cup	crumbled feta cheese	250 mL
½ cup	diced cucumber	125 mL
½ cup	grape tomatoes, cut in half	125 mL
2 tbsp	Traditional Mayonnaise (page 100) or store-bought	30 mL
2 tsp	freshly squeezed lemon juice	10 mL
	Sea salt and freshly ground black pepper	

1. In a bowl, combine rice, salmon, feta, cucumber, grape tomatoes, mayonnaise and lemon juice. Season with salt and pepper to taste.

Salmon with Avocado Salad

Serves 4

Creamy ripe avocados and smoked salmon pair up in a perfect lunch salad.

Tip
To determine if your avocado is ripe: Hold it in the palm of your hand and press. The avocado should feel like a tomato that has a little "give."

12 oz	hot-smoked salmon, chopped	375 g
2	ripe avocados, diced (see Tip, left)	2
½ cup	chopped green onions	125 mL
½ cup	sliced almonds, toasted (see Tip, page 130)	125 mL
2 tbsp	Parmesan Vinaigrette (page 45)	30 mL
2 cups	salad greens	500 mL
	Sea salt and freshly ground black pepper	

1. In a bowl, combine salmon, avocados, green onions, almonds and vinaigrette. Toss with greens. Season with salt and pepper to taste.

Smoked Salmon Noodle Salad

Serves 4

I like the contrast of the crunchy rice noodles with the silky salmon and tomatoes.

1 cup	crispy chow mein noodles	250 mL
8 oz	smoked salmon, chopped	250 g
½ cup	chopped drained canned bamboo shoots	125 mL
¼ cup	chopped fresh cilantro	60 mL
1	Roma (plum) tomato, diced	1
¼ cup	Cilantro and Lime Vinaigrette (page 40)	60 mL
2 cups	romaine lettuce	500 mL
	Sea salt and freshly ground black pepper	

1. In a bowl, combine noodles, salmon, bamboo shoots, cilantro, tomatoes and vinaigrette.

2. Arrange romaine on a serving platter. Top with salmon mixture. Season with salt and pepper to taste.

Smoked Salmon Salad with Dill

6 oz	smoked salmon, chopped	175 g
1 cup	thinly sliced fresh fennel	250 mL
½ cup	thinly sliced cucumber	125 mL
2 tbsp	chopped fresh dill	30 mL
¼ cup	extra virgin olive oil	60 mL
2 tbsp	freshly squeezed lime juice	30 mL
	Sea salt and freshly ground black pepper	

1. In a bowl, combine salmon, fennel, cucumber, dill, oil and lime juice. Season with salt and pepper to taste.

Tarragon Tuna Salad

4	cans (each 6 oz/170 g) solid white tuna, packed in water, drained and flaked	4
½ cup	Traditional Mayonnaise (page 100) or store-bought	125 mL
¼ cup	chopped fresh tarragon	60 mL
1	dill pickle, diced	1
2 tsp	freshly squeezed lemon juice	10 mL
1 tsp	sea salt	5 mL
1 tsp	ground white pepper	5 mL
½ tsp	Hungarian paprika	2 mL

1. In a bowl, using a fork, combine tuna, mayonnaise, tarragon, pickle, lemon juice, salt, white pepper and paprika. Mix just to combine.

Tip
Serve this tuna salad on the side with toasted bread and cheese or on a bed of greens drizzled with a vinaigrette.

Whitefish Herb Salad

2 cups	flaked smoked whitefish, skinned	500 mL
½ cup	chopped celery	125 mL
½ cup	chopped green onions	125 mL
¼ cup	Traditional Mayonnaise (page 100) or store-bought	60 mL
¼ cup	plain yogurt (see Tip, page 243)	60 mL
2 tsp	chopped fresh tarragon	10 mL
2 tsp	grated lemon zest	10 mL
1 tbsp	freshly squeezed lemon juice	15 mL
	Sea salt and freshly ground black pepper	

1. In a bowl, combine whitefish, celery, green onions, mayonnaise, yogurt, tarragon and lemon zest and juice. Season with salt and pepper to taste.

Seafood Apricot Salad

12 oz	skinless whitefish fillets, cooked and flaked	375 g
6 oz	cooked jumbo shrimp, chopped	175 g
½ cup	dried apricots, finely chopped	125 mL
2 tbsp	Shallot Dressing (page 97)	30 mL
2 cups	salad greens	500 mL
	Sea salt and freshly ground black pepper	

1. In a bowl, combine whitefish, shrimp, apricots and dressing.

2. Arrange greens on a serving platter. Top with whitefish mixture. Season with salt and pepper to taste.

Shrimp and Artichoke Basil Salad

Tip

For the freshest taste, rinse the drained artichoke hearts, then pat dry on paper towels.

1 lb	cooked medium shrimp	500 g
1	jar (13.75 oz/390 mL) marinated artichoke hearts (see Tip, left), drained	1
½ cup	chopped red onion	125 mL
3 tbsp	chopped fresh basil	45 mL
2 tbsp	Parmesan Vinaigrette (page 45)	30 mL
2 cups	salad greens	500 mL
	Sea salt and freshly ground black pepper	

1. In a large bowl, combine shrimp, artichoke hearts, red onion, basil and vinaigrette.

2. Arrange greens on a serving platter. Top with shrimp mixture. Season with salt and pepper to taste.

Shrimp and Melon Salad

2 cups	cooked white rice, cooled	500 mL
10 to 12 oz	cooked medium shrimp	300 to 375 g
2 cups	cubed fresh melon, such as casaba, honeydew or cantaloupe	500 mL
2	ripe avocados, diced (see Tip, page 247)	2
½ cup	chopped green onions	125 mL
2	cloves garlic, minced	2
¼ cup	Lemon Dijon Vinaigrette (page 42)	60 mL

1. In a bowl, combine rice, shrimp, melon, avocados, green onions, garlic and vinaigrette.

Shrimp and Avocado Citrus Salad

Tip

To toast pine nuts: Place nuts in a single layer on a baking sheet in a preheated 350°F (180°C) oven for 6 to 8 minutes, or until fragrant and golden, stirring once or twice.

Salad

2 cups	salad greens	500 mL
1 lb	cooked medium shrimp	500 g
2	ripe avocados, diced (see Tip, page 247)	2
1 cup	pink grapefruit segments	250 mL
1 cup	orange segments	250 mL
2 tbsp	pine nuts, toasted (see Tip, left)	30 mL
	Sea salt and freshly ground black pepper	

Dressing

1 tbsp	freshly squeezed lemon juice	15 mL
1 tbsp	freshly squeezed lime juice	15 mL
1 tbsp	freshly squeezed orange juice	15 mL
1 tbsp	liquid honey	15 mL
1/3 cup	canola oil	75 mL
1 tbsp	chopped fresh dill	15 mL

1. *Salad:* Arrange greens on a serving platter. Scatter with shrimp, avocados, grapefruit and orange segments, and pine nuts. Season with salt and pepper to taste.

2. *Dressing:* In a small bowl, whisk together lemon juice, lime juice, orange juice and honey. While whisking, pour in oil in a thin steady stream. Add chopped dill. Drizzle over salad.

Shrimp and Scallop Salad

Serves 4

Combine two shellfish favorites for this luxurious dish.

8 oz	cooked large shrimp, chopped	250 g
8 oz	cooked scallops, chopped	250 g
2	Roma (plum) tomatoes, diced	2
1	ripe avocado, diced (see Tip, page 247)	1
1/2 cup	sour cream	125 mL
2 tsp	chopped fresh dill	10 mL
2 cups	salad greens	500 mL

1. In a bowl, combine shrimp, scallops, tomatoes, avocado, sour cream and dill.

2. Arrange salad greens on a serving platter. Top with shrimp mixture.

Shrimp and Tomato Salad

Serves 6

I love the bite of tart blue cheese in this dish.

1/3 cup	canola oil	75 mL
1 cup	chopped onion	250 mL
1/2 cup	chopped red bell pepper	125 mL
4	Roma (plum) tomatoes, quartered	4
1 lb	medium cooked shrimp	500 g
1/2 tsp	dried oregano	2 mL
2 tbsp	chopped Italian flat-leaf parsley	30 mL
4 oz	blue cheese, crumbled	125 g
	Sea salt and freshly ground black pepper	

1. In a skillet, heat oil over medium heat. Add onion and sauté until lightly browned, about 3 minutes. Add bell pepper and sauté until softened, about 3 minutes. Add tomatoes, shrimp and oregano. Sauté until shrimp is heated through, about 3 minutes.

2. Arrange shrimp mixture on a serving platter. Garnish with parsley and blue cheese. Season with salt and pepper to taste.

South-of-the-Border Seafood Salad

Serves 4

Chipotle peppers heat up this simple seafood salad for summer.

Tips

Check the crabmeat and remove any little pieces of shell prior to use.

I also like to serve this as an appetizer. Use tortilla chips in place of the salad greens.

1 lb	cooked salad shrimp	500 g
4 oz	canned crabmeat (see Tips, left)	125 g
½ cup	grated carrots	125 mL
½ cup	chopped green onions	125 mL
¼ cup	Creamy Zesty Chipotle Dressing (page 70)	60 mL
2 cups	salad greens	500 mL
	Sea salt and freshly ground black pepper	

1. In a bowl, combine shrimp, crabmeat, carrots, green onions and dressing. Refrigerate for 20 minutes to allow the flavors to develop prior to serving.

2. Arrange greens on a serving platter. Top with shrimp mixture. Season with salt and pepper to taste.

Prawn and Mushroom Salad

To serve this flavorful mix on giant crostini, I slice a baguette in half lengthwise, then toast it and top with the salad.

Tips

Depending on their location, some fishmongers, stores and restaurants may label larger shrimp as prawns. I suppose "large shrimp" is an oxymoron.

It's easier to slice the toasted baguette into 4 servings after the salad is spread on top. You can also cut the bread diagonally into 1-inch (2.5 cm) thick slices, and toast until light brown, then let your guests spread the salad on top.

1 lb	cooked prawns, finely chopped (see Tips, left)	500 g
3	cloves garlic, minced	3
¼ cup	extra virgin olive oil	60 mL
6 oz	small button mushrooms, finely chopped	175 g
2	Roma (plum) tomatoes, diced	2
¼ cup	chopped Italian flat-leaf parsley	60 mL
	Sea salt and freshly ground black pepper	
2	baguettes, optional (see Tips, left)	2

1. In a large bowl, combine prawns, garlic, oil, mushrooms, tomatoes and parsley. Season with salt and pepper to taste.

2. Slice baguettes in half, if using, and top with salad mixture, or serve in individual bowls.

Prawn Salad with Roasted Eggplants

Tip

To cook hard-boiled eggs: Arrange a single layer of eggs in a saucepan and add enough cold water to cover by 1 inch (2.5 cm). Bring to a boil over high heat. Remove from heat and, without draining the water, cover and let stand for 10 minutes. With a slotted spoon, carefully transfer each egg into a large bowl of ice water. Let cool completely for at least 5 minutes. Remove eggshells under cool running water.

- Roasting pan, lined with parchment paper
- Preheat oven to 400°F (200°C)

Salad

2	medium eggplants, thinly sliced (see Tip, page 135)	2
	Sea salt	
1 lb	cooked large prawns (see Tips, page 254)	500 g
3	cloves garlic, minced	3
1	hard-boiled egg, finely chopped (see Tip, left)	1
¼ cup	chopped shallots	60 mL
¼ cup	chopped fresh cilantro	60 mL
2	red chile peppers, seeded and finely chopped	2

Dressing

2 tbsp	sesame oil	30 mL
2 tbsp	fish or oyster sauce	30 mL
1 tbsp	freshly squeezed lime juice	15 mL
1 tbsp	freshly squeezed lemon juice	15 mL
1 tsp	lightly packed brown sugar	5 mL
	Sea salt and freshly ground black pepper	

1. *Salad:* Place eggplants in roasting pan. Sprinkle with salt on both sides and arrange in a single layer. Roast in preheated oven until lightly browned, about 30 minutes. Let cool.

2. Arrange eggplants on a serving platter. Top with prawns, garlic, egg, shallots, cilantro and chile peppers.

3. *Dressing:* In a large bowl, whisk together oil, fish sauce, lime and lemon juices, and brown sugar until sugar is dissolved. Drizzle over salad. Season with salt and pepper to taste.

Ceviche Salad

1 lb	cooked salad shrimp	500 g
12 oz	salmon fillet, skinned and chopped	375 g
8 oz	sea scallops, cut into small pieces	250 g
2	Roma (plum) tomatoes, diced	2
1	mango, diced	1
1 cup	chopped red onion	250 mL
1	red chile pepper, seeded and diced	1
1 cup	freshly squeezed lime juice	250 mL
2 tbsp	granulated sugar	30 mL
2 cups	grapefruit segments	500 mL
2 cups	orange segments	500 mL
	Sea salt and freshly ground black pepper	
	Extra virgin olive oil	

1. In a large bowl, combine shrimp, salmon, scallops, tomatoes, mango, red onion and chile pepper. Cover with lime juice and sugar. Cover and refrigerate for at least 30 minutes or until fish and seafood are opaque.

2. Drain shrimp mixture, discarding marinade, and toss with grapefruit and orange segments. Season with salt and pepper to taste. Drizzle with oil.

Scallop and Green Bean Salad

Tip

If fresh tarragon is not available, use 1½ tsp (7 mL) dried instead.

Salad

8 oz	green beans, trimmed	250 g
	Ice water	
1 lb	sea scallops	500 g
1 tbsp	canola oil	15 mL
2 cups	salad greens	500 mL
½ cup	chopped green onions	125 mL
	Sea salt and freshly ground black pepper	

Dressing

2 tbsp	red wine vinegar	30 mL
2 tbsp	hazelnut oil	30 mL
1 tbsp	chopped fresh tarragon (see Tip, left)	15 mL

1. *Salad:* In a large pot of boiling salted water, cook green beans for 5 minutes. Drain and place in a bowl of ice water to set color and stop cooking.

2. Pat scallops dry with paper towels. In a skillet, heat oil over high heat. Add scallops, in batches as necessary, and cook until browned on both sides, 2 to 4 minutes per side. Let cool.

3. Thoroughly drain beans. In a large bowl, combine beans, greens and green onions. Divide evenly onto 4 plates. Top with scallops. Season with salt and pepper to taste.

4. *Dressing:* In a bowl, whisk together vinegar, oil and tarragon. Drizzle over salad.

Avocado Crab Potato Salad

Creamy avocado, buttery lettuce and crab come together in a rich salad that you can serve as a complete lunch.

Tip
Check the crabmeat and remove any little pieces of shell prior to use.

2 cups	torn butterhead lettuce	500 mL
1 lb	white fingerling potatoes, cooked and cooled (see Tips, page 260)	500 g
½ cup	chopped Italian flat-leaf parsley	125 mL
1	can (10 to 12 oz/300 to 375 g) crabmeat, drained (see Tip, left)	1
2	large ripe avocados, sliced (see Tip, page 247)	2
1 cup	grape tomatoes, cut in half	250 mL
	Sea salt and freshly ground black pepper	
¼ cup	Old Venice Italian Vinaigrette (page 44) or store-bought	60 mL

1. Divide lettuce, potatoes, parsley, crabmeat, avocados and grape tomatoes evenly onto 4 salad plates. Season with salt and pepper to taste. Drizzle with vinaigrette.

Crab and Arugula Salad

If you can find Dungeness crab for this salad, it's even more delectable.

1	can (10 to 12 oz/300 to 375 g) crabmeat, drained (see Tip, above)	1
½ cup	finely chopped red bell pepper	125 mL
½ cup	chopped red onion	125 mL
¼ cup	Traditional Mayonnaise (page 100) or store-bought	60 mL
2 tbsp	drained capers	30 mL
2 tbsp	chopped Italian flat-leaf parsley	30 mL
1 tbsp	grated lemon zest	15 mL
2 tbsp	freshly squeezed lemon juice	30 mL
3	drops hot pepper sauce	3
	Sea salt and freshly ground black pepper	
2 cups	arugula	500 mL

1. In a large bowl, combine crabmeat, bell pepper, red onion, mayonnaise, capers, parsley, lemon zest and juice and hot pepper sauce. Season with salt and pepper to taste. Arrange arugula on a serving platter. Top with crab mixture.

California Sushi Salad

Serves 4

*Manashita Ichiro,
a sushi chef in Los
Angeles, invented
the California roll,
which has become
an all-time favorite
of North American
sushi fans. Now
I have created a
salad with the same
popular ingredients.*

Tip

Nori comes in many
different colors from
dark green to black.
I like the dark green
for this salad. Make
sure to taste the salad
prior to seasoning with
salt, as the nori tends
to add flavor.

Salad

2	sheets sushi nori (seaweed), cut into small pieces (see Tip, left)	2
2 cups	cooked white rice, cooled	500 mL
1 cup	diced peeled cucumber	250 mL
1 cup	flaked cooked crabmeat	250 mL
2	ripe avocados, diced (see Tip, page 247)	2
2 tsp	freshly squeezed lemon juice	10 mL

Dressing

2 tbsp	reduced-sodium soy sauce	30 mL
1 tsp	prepared wasabi	5 mL
½ tsp	minced drained pickled ginger	2 mL

1. *Salad:* In a bowl, combine nori, rice, cucumber, crabmeat, avocados and lemon juice. Set aside.

2. *Dressing:* In a bowl, whisk together soy sauce, wasabi and ginger. Drizzle over salad and toss to coat. Arrange on a serving platter.

Rich Lobster Salad

This luxurious salad is delicious and decadent, and designed for true lobster lovers.

Tip

To cook potatoes: Place whole potatoes in a pot of cold salted water; bring to a simmer over medium heat and cook until fork-tender Do not allow to boil or the skins will burst and allow potato flesh to absorb water. If desired, peel slightly cooled potatoes, then cut into bite-size pieces.

Salad

2 cups	salad greens	500 mL
½ cup	chopped Italian flat-leaf parsley	125 mL
1	jar (7 oz/210 mL) artichoke hearts, drained (see Tip, page 250)	1
1	can (10 oz/287) mandarin oranges, drained	1
¼ cup	chopped green onions	60 mL
2	Roma (plum) tomatoes, diced	2
1 lb	white fingerling potatoes, cooked and cooled (see Tip, left)	500 g
2 cups	flaked cooked lobster meat	500 mL

Dressing

3 tbsp	frozen orange juice concentrate	45 mL
¼ cup	unsalted butter	60 mL
	Sea salt	
Pinch	cayenne pepper	Pinch

1. *Salad:* In a large bowl, combine greens, parsley, artichoke hearts, oranges, green onions, tomatoes and potatoes. Divide evenly onto 4 plates. Top with lobster.

2. *Dressing:* In a microwavable dish, combine orange juice concentrate, butter, salt and cayenne. Microwave on low for 30 seconds or until butter is melted. Whisk to combine. Drizzle over salad.

Fruit-Based Salads

Fruit-Based Salads

Luscious and colorful, fresh fruit provides the inspiration for these fast, fabulous salads. And it only takes a few ingredients to assemble most of these uncomplicated combinations.

Ambrosia Salad

Serves 6 to 8

This typical ambrosia salad is my sister Pattie's favorite. It's a must at every holiday dinner.

1 cup	sour cream	250 mL
1 cup	mini marshmallows	250 mL
1 cup	drained mandarin oranges	250 mL
1 cup	drained crushed pineapple	250 mL
1 cup	sweetened flaked coconut	250 mL

1. In a bowl, combine sour cream, marshmallows, oranges, pineapple and coconut. Tightly cover and refrigerate for 8 hours to allow the flavors to develop prior to serving or for up to 6 days.

Watergate Salad

Serves 8

This yummy salad has nothing to do with Nixon and Watergate. The origin of the name is unknown, but the salad made its debut in the 1970s after the development of pistachio pudding, a key ingredient in the salad.

1	can (20 oz/575 mL) crushed pineapple with juice	1
1	box (4-serving size) instant dry pistachio pudding	1
9 oz	nondairy whipped topping	280 g
1 cup	miniature marshmallows	250 mL
½ cup	chopped pecans, toasted (see Tip, page 235)	125 mL

1. In a large bowl, combine pineapple and pudding. Fold in whipped topping, marshmallows and pecans. Tightly cover and refrigerate for 2 hours to allow the flavors to develop prior to serving or for up to 2 days.

Blake Family Salad

Serves 6

Jan and Sabrina Blake, two of my students, attend many of my classes and always sit in the front row. They wanted me to share their family's favorite salad in this book — and here it is.

Salad

8 cups	salad greens	2 L
2 cups	chopped celery	500 mL
2 cups	green grapes, sliced in half	500 mL
1 cup	fresh raspberries	250 mL
3	kiwifruits, peeled and chopped	3
½ cup	Glazed Hot Pecans (page 270)	125 mL

Dressing

¼ cup	canola oil	60 mL
2 tbsp	red wine vinegar	30 mL
2 tbsp	granulated sugar	30 mL
½ tsp	sea salt	2 mL

1. *Salad:* In a large bowl, combine greens, celery, grapes, raspberries, kiwis and pecans. Set aside.

2. *Dressing:* In a small bowl, whisk together oil, vinegar, sugar and salt until sugar is dissolved. Drizzle over greens mixture and toss to coat.

Grapefruit and Avocado Salad

Serves 4

Pink grapefruit makes a colorful splash in this dish.

2 cups	salad greens	500 mL
2 cups	grapefruit segments	500 mL
2	ripe avocados, diced (see Tip, page 247)	2
¼ cup	chopped red onions	60 mL
¼ cup	chopped green onions	60 mL
¼ cup	Chenin Blanc Vinaigrette (page 39)	60 mL
	Sea salt and freshly ground black pepper	

1. In a bowl, combine greens, grapefruit segments, avocados, red onions, green onions and vinaigrette. Season with salt and pepper to taste.

Minted Melon and Citrus Salad

Salad

2 cups	honeydew melon chunks	500 mL
1	tangerine, segmented	1
1	orange, segmented	1

Dressing

2 tbsp	extra virgin olive oil	30 mL
1 tbsp	chopped fresh mint	15 mL
1 tsp	Dijon Mustard (page 112) or store-bought	5 mL
1 tsp	red wine vinegar	5 mL
1 tsp	liquid honey	5 mL

1. *Salad:* In a bowl, combine melon and tangerine and orange segments.

2. *Dressing:* In another bowl, whisk together oil, mint, mustard, vinegar and honey. Drizzle over melon mixture and toss to coat.

Melon, Raspberry and Parma Salad

3 cups	cantaloupe chunks	750 mL
2 cups	fresh raspberries, chopped	500 mL
8 oz	Parma ham, chopped	250 g
1 tsp	grated orange zest	5 mL
1 tbsp	freshly squeezed orange juice	15 mL
½ tsp	freshly grated gingerroot	2 mL

1. In a large bowl, combine cantaloupe, raspberries, ham, orange zest and juice and ginger. Let stand for 30 minutes to allow the flavors to develop prior to serving.

Apple and Blue Cheese Salad

Serves 4

Apple and cheese make a perfect marriage — the added ingredients keep the relationship interesting.

2 tbsp	freshly squeezed lemon juice	30 mL
3	apples, such as Pippin, Granny Smith or Rome, cut into cubes	3
4 oz	blue cheese, crumbled	125 g
1/4 cup	chopped red onion	60 mL
1 tbsp	chopped Italian flat-leaf parsley	15 mL
2 tbsp	Traditional Mayonnaise (page 100) or store-bought	30 mL
1 tsp	Dijon Mustard (page 112) or store-bought	5 mL
1 tsp	granulated sugar	5 mL

1. Stir lemon juice into a bowl of water and add apples.

2. In another bowl, combine blue cheese, red onion, parsley, mayonnaise, mustard and sugar. Drain apples, add to cheese mixture and toss to coat.

Watermelon and Feta Salad

Serves 4

Watermelons with seeds seem to have more flavor, so that's the type I choose. The watermelon makes this salad so juicy and delicious it doesn't need any dressing.

2 cups	cubed watermelon	500 mL
1 cup	crumbled feta cheese	250 mL
1/4 cup	sliced black olives	60 mL
2 tbsp	sunflower seeds, toasted	30 mL

1. In a bowl, combine watermelon, feta, olives and sunflower seeds. Let stand for 30 minutes.

Variation

Be creative and experiment with different toasted seeds or nuts such as pumpkin seeds or chopped pecans.

Fig and Goat Cheese Salad

Serves 4		
Sweet fresh figs make this a delightful springtime salad.		

2 cups	spring mix salad greens	500 mL
4	ripe figs, trimmed and cut into wedges	4
1 cup	crumbled goat cheese	250 mL
½ cup	chopped pecans, toasted	125 mL
¼ cup	canola oil	60 mL
2	hard-boiled eggs, sliced (see Tips, page 138)	2
	Sea salt and freshly ground black pepper	

1. In a bowl, combine salad greens, figs, goat cheese and pecans. Drizzle with oil and toss to coat. Arrange egg slices on top. Season with salt and pepper to taste.

Grapes and Gorgonzola Salad

Serves 4		
Sweet grapes and tart Gorgonzola balance this fruity summer salad.		

1 lb	green or red seedless grapes, cut in half	500 g
8 oz	Gorgonzola cheese, crumbled	250 g
3 tbsp	chopped fresh basil	45 mL
2 tbsp	extra virgin olive oil	30 mL
2 tsp	balsamic vinegar	10 mL
	Freshly ground black pepper	

1. Arrange grapes on a serving platter. Crumble Gorgonzola over top and sprinkle with basil. Drizzle with oil and vinegar. Season with pepper to taste.

Pear, Shrimp and Mango Salad

Serves 4		
On a hot day, stay cool with crisp pears, pink shrimp and orange mango.		

4	ripe pears, sliced	4
8 oz	cooked small salad shrimp	250 g
1	mango, sliced	1
3 tbsp	Radda Vinaigrette (page 47)	45 mL
	Sea salt and freshly ground black pepper	

1. Arrange rows of pears, shrimp and mango on a serving platter. Drizzle with dressing. Season with salt and pepper to taste.

Accompaniments
for Salads

Accompaniments for Salads

Crisp toppings and spiced nuts are all the rage on salads. The extra texture and flavor provide a lively contrast to the softer greens and vegetables. In the past few years I have seen an explosion of different "salad toppers" in the produce section. Here, I've created a few to mix and match for truly unique salads. Keep these on hand — you can also use them to sprinkle on soup.

Cheese Tuiles

Serves 6

Keep your eye on the baking tuiles as they can burn very quickly — in less than 30 seconds. I like to stand up the tuiles in a salad to create height.

Tips

Make the tuiles in the morning of the day they will be served.

Store in a cool, dry place. Do not refrigerate them, or they will become soggy.

Variation

You can add 1 tsp (5 mL) dried herbs to the cheese before baking. Choose herbs that complement the salad you'll be serving.

- **Preheat oven to 350°F (180°C)**
- **2 baking sheets, lined with parchment paper**

5 oz	Parmesan cheese, grated (about 1¼ cups/300 mL)	150 g

1. Place 6 equal mounds of Parmesan on each baking sheet. Bake, one sheet at a time, in preheated oven until golden brown and melted, 5 to 6 minutes. Let cool completely on baking sheet prior to removing to a cooling rack.

Cheese Puffs

Tip

You can store these puffs in a dry container at room temperature just as you do bread. Do not refrigerate them or they will become soggy.

- Preheat oven to 425°F (220°C)
- 2 baking sheets, lined with parchment paper

1	package (18 oz/540 g) puff pastry, thawed	1
1	egg, beaten	1
1 cup	freshly grated Parmesan cheese, divided	250 mL

1. On a lightly floured surface, roll out thawed pastry into two 14- by 10-inch (35 cm by 25 cm) sheets. Brush top of both with beaten egg.

2. Sprinkle each sheet of pastry with $\frac{1}{2}$ cup (125 mL) of the Parmesan. Press cheese into dough. Starting at one short side, fold in half. Cut crosswise into $\frac{1}{4}$-inch (0.5 cm) strips. Working with one strip at a time, hold each end in your hands and twist in opposite directions. Place on prepared baking sheet, at least $\frac{1}{2}$ inch (1 cm) apart. Repeat with second sheet of puff pastry. Bake in preheated oven until golden brown and puffed up, 18 to 24 minutes.

Fried Capers

Tip

For best results, fry the capers in small batches so you don't overcook them.

$\frac{1}{2}$ cup	canola oil	125 mL
$\frac{1}{4}$ cup	drained capers	60 mL

1. In a skillet, heat oil over medium heat. Add capers in small batches, frying until light brown and crunchy, about 2 minutes. Drain on paper towels.

Garlic Croutons

Makes 4 cups (1 L)

I always seem to have extra bread left over. Homemade croutons are the perfect way to use every crumb.

Tip

Store croutons in an airtight container in a cool, dry place. Do not refrigerate them, or they will become soggy.

- Preheat oven to 350°F (180°C)
- Baking sheet, lined with parchment paper

⅔ cup	olive oil	150 mL
3	cloves garlic, minced	3
1 tsp	dried parsley	5 mL
½ tsp	dried onion flakes	2 mL
¼ tsp	sea salt	1 mL
¼ tsp	freshly ground black pepper	1 mL
4 cups	cubed day-old bread	1 L

1. In a large bowl, combine oil, garlic, parsley, onion flakes, salt and pepper. Add bread cubes and mix to coat evenly.

2. Spread on prepared baking sheet in a single layer. Bake in preheated oven, turning occasionally, until golden brown, 12 to 16 minutes.

Glazed Hot Pecans

Makes 1½ cups (375 mL)

These pecans add sweetness and crunch on a salad dressed with a light vinaigrette.

Tip

Store glazed pecans in an airtight container in a cool, dry place. Do not refrigerate them, or they will become soggy.

- Preheat oven to 350°F (180°C)
- Baking sheet, lined with parchment paper

1½ cups	pecan halves	375 mL
1	egg white, beaten	1
½ cup	granulated sugar	125 mL
¼ tsp	cayenne pepper	1 mL

1. In a bowl, combine pecan halves, egg white, sugar and cayenne.

2. Spread on prepared baking sheet in a single layer. Bake in preheated oven, turning occasionally, until caramelized, 20 to 22 minutes. Let cool completely before removing from baking sheet. They will dry and harden when cooling.

Fresh Herbed Croutons

**Makes 4 cups
(1 L)**

When teaching in France, my rule was "fresh bread daily," so we could make croutons with any leftover day-old bread.

Tip

Store croutons in an airtight container in a cool, dry place. Do not refrigerate them, or they will become soggy.

- **Preheat oven to 350°F (180°C)**
- **Baking sheet, lined with parchment paper**

⅔ cup	herbed olive oil	150 mL
2 tsp	chopped fresh tarragon	10 mL
1 tsp	chopped fresh dill	5 mL
½ tsp	chopped fresh rosemary	2 mL
½ tsp	dried parsley	2 mL
½ tsp	dried onion flakes	2 mL
¼ tsp	sea salt	1 mL
¼ tsp	freshly ground black pepper	1 mL
4 cups	cubed day-old bread	1 L

1. In a large bowl, combine oil, tarragon, dill, rosemary, parsley, onion flakes, salt and pepper. Add bread cubes and mix to coat evenly.

2. Spread on prepared baking sheet in a single layer. Bake in preheated oven, turning occasionally, until golden brown, 12 to 16 minutes.

Roasted Corn

**Makes 2 cups
(500 mL)**

I enjoy roasted corn kernels shaved from the cob and sprinkled on top of a spicy salad with a peppery dressing.

Tip

You can roast and use 2 cups (500 mL) frozen corn kernels if fresh corn is out of season.

2 tbsp	olive oil	30 mL
3	ears corn, kernels removed (about 2 cups/500 mL) (see Tip, left)	3
½ tsp	sea salt	2 mL
¼ tsp	cayenne pepper	1 mL

1. In a skillet, heat oil over medium heat. Add corn, stirring until completely roasted, about 10 minutes. Sprinkle with salt and cayenne. Let cool. Transfer to a covered dish and refrigerate until ready to use for up to 4 days.

Peppered Walnuts

**Makes 2 cups
(500 mL)**

*Hot and spicy, these
walnuts are great on
Asian salads.*

Tip

Store peppered
walnuts in an airtight
container, in a cool,
dry place. Do not
refrigerate them,
or they will
become soggy.

- **Preheat oven to 350°F (180°C)**
- **2 baking sheets, lined with parchment paper**

¾ cup	granulated sugar	175 mL
2 tbsp	unsalted butter	30 mL
2 cups	walnut halves	500 mL
1 tsp	sea salt	5 mL
1 tsp	freshly ground black pepper	5 mL
½ tsp	ground cumin	2 mL
¼ tsp	cayenne pepper	1 mL

1. In a small heavy-bottomed saucepan over high heat, cook sugar, stirring, until it turns light caramel color, 4 to 5 minutes. Remove from heat and carefully add butter and stir until melted. Add nuts and stir to coat evenly.

2. Transfer nuts to one of the prepared baking sheets in a single layer. Bake in preheated oven, tossing every 5 minutes, until nuts are toasted, about 15 minutes.

3. Remove from oven and place in a large bowl. Add salt, black pepper, cumin and cayenne and quickly toss to coat evenly. Transfer nuts to other prepared baking sheet and separate nuts with a fork. Let cool completely before using.

Spicy Sunflower Seeds

Makes 2 cups (500 mL)

When I was a kid, sunflower seeds were the rage. I never knew how good they could be on salads until I tried this recipe.

Tip

Store spicy sunflower seeds in an airtight container, in a cool, dry place. Do not refrigerate them, or they will become soggy.

- **Preheat oven 350°F (180°C)**
- **Baking sheet, lined with parchment paper**

2 cups	raw unsalted sunflower seeds	500 mL
2 tbsp	granulated sugar	30 mL
¾ tsp	sea salt	3 mL
½ tsp	ground cinnamon	2 mL
⅛ tsp	ground allspice	0.5 mL
⅛ tsp	curry powder	0.5 mL
⅛ tsp	cayenne pepper	0.5 mL
1 tbsp	water	15 mL
1 tbsp	canola oil	15 mL
2 tsp	vanilla extract	10 mL
1 tsp	lightly packed brown sugar	5 mL

1. Spread sunflower seeds on prepared baking sheet. Toast in preheated oven, stirring occasionally to make sure they brown evenly, for 6 minutes. Leave oven on.

2. In a small bowl, stir together granulated sugar, salt, cinnamon, allspice, curry powder and cayenne. Set aside.

3. In a medium saucepan over medium heat, combine water, oil, vanilla and brown sugar. Bring to a boil, whisking constantly. Stir in toasted seeds and continue stirring until shiny and liquid has evaporated, 1 to 2 minutes.

4. Transfer seeds to a bowl. Sprinkle with spice mixture and toss well to coat. Spread coated nuts on same prepared baking sheet and return to preheated oven for another 4 minutes. Let cool on pan.

Sources

Equipment and Services

Calico Cake Shop
7321 Orangethorpe Avenue
Buena Park, California 90621
714-521-2761
www.calicocakeshop.com
Small tools for cooking and baking.

George Geary, CCP
www.georgegeary.com
Author's website, full of recipes, tips, culinary tour information and teaching locations. Baking pans and tools also sold here.

Golda's Kitchen
866-465-3299
905-816-9995
www.goldaskitchen.com
Online shopping site. Offers a large range of baking, cooking and measuring equipment; chocolate and confectionery supplies; and a wide assortment of kitchen tools, knives and appliances. Ships worldwide.

Ingredients

Oils, Extracts, Spices and Dried Herbs

O&Co.
Mediterranean Food Merchants
877-828-6620
www.oliviersandco.com
Olive oils from the Mediterranean and other food items. Boutiques in more than 14 countries from France to Canada to the U.S.

Penzeys Spices
262-785-7676
800-741-7787 (U.S. Only)
www.penzeys.com
Family-owned company. Many stores throughout the U.S., and growing.

The Spice House
847-328-3711
www.thespicehouse.com
Fresh spices. Many hard-to-find items such as more than 12 different salts and peppers, dried tomato powder, and more. Ships worldwide.

Index

Library and Archives Canada Cataloguing in Publication

Geary, George
    350 best salads & dressings / George Geary.

Includes index.
ISBN 978-0-7788-0240-2

1. Salads. 2. Salad dressing.
I. Title. II. Title: 350 best salads and dressings. III. Title: Three hundred fifty best salads & dressings.

TX740.G42 2010   641.8'3   C2009-906692-0

More Great Books
from Robert Rose

Appliance Cooking

- 200 Best Pressure Cooker Recipes
  by Cinda Chavich
- 200 Best Panini Recipes
  by Tiffany Collins
- The Juicing Bible, Second Edition
  by Pat Crocker
- The Mixer Bible, Second Edition
  by Meredith Deeds and Carla Snyder
- The 150 Best Slow Cooker Recipes
  by Judith Finlayson
- Delicious & Dependable Slow Cooker Recipes
  by Judith Finlayson
- 125 Best Vegetarian Slow Cooker Recipes
  by Judith Finlayson
- The Healthy Slow Cooker
  by Judith Finlayson
- Slow Cooker Comfort Food
  by Judith Finlayson
- The Dehydrator Bible
  by Jennifer MacKenzie, Jay Nutt & Don Mercer
- 300 Slow Cooker Favorites
  by Donna-Marie Pye
- 250 Best American Bread Machine Baking Recipes
  by Donna Washburn and Heather Butt
- 250 Best Canadian Bread Machine Baking Recipes
  by Donna Washburn and Heather Butt

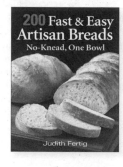

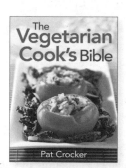

Baking

- 1500 Best Bars, Cookies, Muffins, Cakes & More
  by Esther Brody
- 200 Fast & Easy Artisan Breads
  by Judith Fertig
- The Complete Book of Pies
  by Julie Hasson
- 125 Best Chocolate Recipes
  by Julie Hasson
- 125 Best Cupcake Recipes
  by Julie Hasson
- Bars & Squares
  by Jill Snider
- Cookies
  by Jill Snider
- Complete Cake Mix Magic
  by Jill Snider

Healthy Cooking

- 125 Best Vegetarian Recipes
  by Byron Ayanoglu with contributions from Algis Kemezys
- 125 Best Vegan Recipes
  by Maxine Effenson Chuck and Beth Gurney
- The Vegetarian Cook's Bible
  by Pat Crocker
- The Vegan Cook's Bible
  by Pat Crocker
- The Smoothies Bible
  by Pat Crocker

- Diabetes Meals for Good Health
  by Karen Graham, RD
- Canada's Diabetes Meals for Good Health
  by Karen Graham, RD
- 200 Best Lactose-Free Recipes
  by Jan Main
- 500 Best Healthy Recipes
  Edited by Lynn Roblin, RD
- Complete Gluten-Free Cookbook
  by Donna Washburn and Heather Butt

- 250 Gluten-Free Favorites
  by Donna Washburn and Heather Butt
- The Best Gluten-Free Family Cookbook
  by Donna Washburn and Heather Butt
- America's Complete Diabetes Cookbook
  Edited by Katherine E. Younker, MBA, RD
- Canada's Complete Diabetes Cookbook
  Edited by Katherine E. Younker, MBA, RD

Recent Bestsellers

- The Complete Book of Pickling
  by Jennifer MacKenzie
- 12,167 Kitchen and Cooking Secrets
  by Susan Sampson
- Baby Blender Food
  by Nicole Young

- 200 Easy Homemade Cheese Recipes
  by Debra Amrein-Boyes
- The Convenience Cook
  by Judith Finlayson
- Easy Indian Cooking
  by Suneeta Vaswani

Health

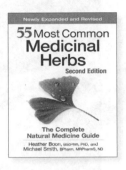

- 55 Most Common Medicinal Herbs Second Edition
  by Dr. Heather Boon, B.Sc.Phm., Ph.D. and Michael Smith, B.Pharm, M.R.Pharm.S., ND
- Canada's Baby Care Book
  by Dr. Jeremy Friedman MBChB, FRCP(C), FAAP, and Dr. Norman Saunders MD, FRCP(C)
- The Baby Care Book
  by Dr. Jeremy Friedman MBChB, FRCP(C), FAAP, and Dr. Norman Saunders MD, FRCP(C)

- Better Baby Food Second Edition
  by Daina Kalnins, MSc, RD, and Joanne Saab, RD
- Better Food for Pregnancy
  by Daina Kalnins, MSc, RD, and Joanne Saab, RD
- Crohn's & Colitis
  by Dr. A. Hillary Steinhart, MD, MSc, FRCP(C)
- Crohn's & Colitis Diet Guide
  by Dr. A. Hillary Steinhart, MD, MSc, FRCP(C), and Julie Cepo, BSc, BASc, RD